SPIRITWALKING

Living and Working with the Unseen

A Psychic Handbook

Written and Illustrated

by

Poppy Palin

Winchester, UK
Washington, USA

First published by O Books, 2007
O Books is an imprint of John Hunt Publishing Ltd.,
The Bothy, Deershot Lodge, Park Lane, Ropley, Hants, SO24 0BE, UK
office1@o-books.net
www.o-books.net

Distribution in:

UK and Europe
Orca Book Services
orders@orcabookservices.co.uk
Tel: 01202 665432 Fax: 01202 666219 Int. code (44)

USA and Canada
NBN
custserv@nbnbooks.com
Tel: 1 800 462 6420 Fax: 1 800 338 4550

Australia and New Zealand
Brumby Books
sales@brumbybooks.com.au
Tel: 61 3 9761 5535 Fax: 61 3 9761 7095

Far East (offices in Singapore, Thailand, Hong Kong, Taiwan)
Pansing Distribution Pte Ltd
kemal@pansing.com
Tel: 65 6319 9939 Fax: 65 6462 5761

South Africa
Alternative Books
altbook@peterhyde.co.za
Tel: 021 447 5300 Fax: 021 447 1430

Text copyright Poppy Palin 2007

Design: Stuart Davies

ISBN: 978 1 84694 031 6

A CIP catalogue record for this book is available from the British Library.

Printed by CPI Antony Rowe, Chippenham, UK

SPIRITWALKING

Living and Working with the Unseen

A Psychic Handbook

Written and Illustrated

by

Poppy Palin

BOOKS

Winchester, UK
Washington, USA

DEDICATION

This book is for Matt Jackson and Paula (Bodhi) Brightwell with thanks for all they have done for me and for all they endeavour to do for others. Matt and Bodhi are living proof that there are generous, compassionate souls who walk with spirit in the modern age. For similar reasons I would also like to dedicate it to the beautiful Kate Fowler-Reeves and her courageous husband Shaun for all they do for our creature-kin.

It is also for my companions in spirit and for Glen McHale and Becky Haynes –'til you meet again, for there are more worlds than this.

But perhaps most of all this book is for all the beautiful trees whose selfless giving has once again made it possible for me to share my thoughts and experiences with you.

Give them honour.

By the Same Author

Season of Sorcery, Capall Bann, *1998*

Wildwitch, Capall Bann, *1999*

Walking with Spirit, Capall Bann, *2000*

Soul Resurgence, Capall Bann, *2000*

The Waking the Wild Spirit, Tarot Deck and Book Set,
Llewellyn, *2002*

Green Spirituality (written as Rosa Romani) Green Magic, *2004*

Craft of the Wild Witch, Llewellyn, *2004*

Spellcaster (one chapter as part of a collective work),
Llewellyn, *2005*

The Greening, Wild Spirit, *2005*

And do I really have a hand in my forgetting?
Nico, *The Fairest of the Seasons*

God is everywhere. God is here: we have to recognise the divinity of everything and live accordingly
Kalindi, speaking to Satish Kumar in *You Are, Therefore I Am* (Green Books 2002)

The Magic is in me, the Magic is making me strong! I can feel it, I can feel it!
Francis Hodgson - Burnett, *The Secret Garden* (MDS, 2003)

CONTENTS

ACKNOWLEDGMENTS

I would like to thank the following people for their inspiration and support while I was engaged in this book's painful birthing process. Although my writing is a very solitary affair there are always those behind the scenes who motivate me to carry on…even if they don't know it! This goes especially to those kind souls who send me encouraging e-mails and letters. Your support has meant all the difference to me between carrying on and giving up. Thank you for giving me faith that my words are reaching people and helping them. Bless you for your generosity of spirit.

For inspiration there's Maggie, Shaun and Nathan who are tireless animal rights activists, along with Rachel Nelson. There is also the wonderful Alice Pink who selflessly saves our feathered friends from harm and Anne McCreanor, Jenny Gehlhar, Annabelle Walter and Nicole whose unstinting work on behalf of non-human beings rouses me to speak my truth and walk my talk. Proceeds from this book will go to animal welfare charities within the South West of England.

For personal support during the hardest time I have known I would like to thank Germaine Knight and Andy Mac Lellan for their being on hand even when they themselves are suffering. Likewise to Tim Hyde and Dr. Ramana without whom I could never have completed this book. Thanks to the gorgeous Helen Read for coming to the rescue even when times were tough for her and to Pretenders Too for making a musical dream come true, however briefly. My gratitude also goes to Susan Mears, Julian Robbins and John Hunt for their support of my work – may it reach those who need it!

Finally (and last but definitely not least) immense thanks to my generous parents and to my kind, loyal, brave hero, Gary Howe, who has really showed me the meaning of 'in sickness and in health'. *I love you.*

AUTHOR'S NOTE

It seems fitting that this book should feature many of my own snippets of spiritual guidance gained over the years, given to me by my trusted *unseen* mentors via what is known as channelled writing – a technique I will give instruction on in Chapter Nine. I have approached these spirit mentors with care, using the safety procedures given in Chapter Four on psychic protection, thus ensuring that the spirits are genuine and that they always speak from the highest good.

I share my spiritual guidance with a hope that it will inspire others to really get involved with their own *unseen* mentors and to walk with spirit more fully. The words I have been given deserve inclusion as they show the depth and breadth of wisdom, humour, insight and incisive comment that we can glean if we are prepared to go within, as well as without, to talk to spirit. I have therefore chosen to include a sample of such guidance at the start of each new chapter, both to set the tone and offer food for thought.

I am not able to quote a named being as 'author' of each piece as my guidance comes from many sources, including my own eternal spirit-self, and so instead I will state *'from guidance'*. By the absence of an 'author' I am not wishing to claim these words as solely my own, nor do I wish to negate anyone whose words I use, but it is impossible to give each quote a named source. In its stead I would like to thank all of my guiding companion spirits for their loving care over the years...spirits who have always informed me wryly that it is the guidance itself that matters, not the nature of the guide.

Bless you all!

INTRODUCTION

The Re-membering

'We are God. How can that which is dreamed not be in the dreamer and the dreamer not present as the witness of the dream? Is not the artist present in each of their creations even as the art resides within them? You are the Creator!'
From Guidance

Let us begin with an analogy, the first of many in this book. Let us say that we, as human beings, are like batteries. *Rechargeable* batteries.

Within a household battery there are hidden elements such as cadmium (which we could observe with the naked eye if the cell were broken open) and mysterious forces such as electrons (which we could not see). These internal elements help to store the essential power that we need to run our gadgets – we cannot readily observe them but we know that they must be in there for the battery to work. Within our own physical body there are hidden aspects such as internal organs (which we could see with the naked eye if our body were opened surgically) and cells (which we could not see). These internal elements all serve to run our physical aspect, even though we cannot readily observe them on the surface.

A battery stores and releases animating energy so that when they are placed within our gadgets they may perform for us. With batteries this energy is electrical in nature and is something that can be classed as invisible to the naked eye. Yet for all its invisibility it is undoubtedly powerful and has the ability to transform an inanimate appliance into a functioning one. Our bodies too are reliant on an animating energy that allows them to work well and this vital animating aspect is *spiritual*. Like electrical energy it too is (generally) invisible yet powerful and transfomative. We are as batteries that depend on a working relationship of outer casing, inner workings and an animating source to function. By this we can witness that there is an essential and inescapable connection between what we consider to be visible and what we consider to be invisible, an interdependent relationship between the *seen* aspect of existence and the mysterious *unseen* workings that give it life and purpose.

This relationship of seen and unseen, as well as their individual relevance, is something we understand inherently when we incarnate into this physical dimension. As babies we accept ourselves as both physical/corporeal and ethereal/spiritual beings and know not to dismiss either aspect of ourselves. We have a deep awareness of our inner nature and its power as well as a fascination with our new bodies and the miraculous world around us. We remember who and what we are and what we need. Indeed, we know we have a maxim to live by and it is this: *as within, so without.*

Because of this awareness we know that, just like rechargeable batteries, our own power supplies need to be replenished. We need to top up our unseen, spiritual energy just as a battery needs to be plugged into the mains source to build up its reserves of electrical power. As newborns and young children we know that we have to connect up back to the eternal Source to ensure that we are full of that essential spark, that life-force, that gives us our own personal glow. As our bodies are fed, stimulated and rested so do we naturally spend time acknowledging and replenishing our spirit. As infants without responsibilities we are allowed this time for inner work.

The problem for us humans is that as soon as we grow up a little and are engaged with the all-consuming business of manifest living, with all that tricky life-stuff that seems like the only reality, we seem to get distracted from the numinous unseen core of our nature. We forget to relate to ourselves spiritually, thinking we are somehow purely corporeal and, if we look after our bodies, totally self-sustaining and durable. All the while we run around convincing ourselves that everything's fine, that we are physically independent, and mentally indestructible, when in reality we are simply running on half-power, or even scraping by on empty. In such a state of unbalance between the seen and unseen aspects of ourselves life quickly becomes meaningless and we lose our innate sense of purpose. This then leads us to focus even more on our material selves as we seek obvious manifest solutions to our malaise. We are desperate for a reunion with the invisible aspect of our being and the rejuvenating, uplifting life-force energy of the Source even though we have now forgotten how, or even why, we may do this.

This separation we may clearly term as the *forgetting*, a process that occurs both individually and collectively.

Sometimes we just need a gentle reminder, not only of our need to recharge those unseen batteries but also of just how to plug ourselves back in to the spiritual power supply. This book serves as such a reminder. It offers us a way to understand this process and encourages us, as tangible physical beings, to safely explore the world of unseen energy. Moreover, it stands as a guide for us to recall how to touch base with our energetic Source and to re-connect – to *re-member* ourselves. We express this as the *re-membering*, and not the more usual remembering, as it reminds us that we are indeed re-building something out of its constituent member parts – we are actively putting what we are back together again; re-uniting body and soul, external, internal and eternal, seen and unseen.

This book will also draw our attention back to the realisation that by recharging ourselves, becoming re-energised with spirit, we become the very empowering Source we seek. How can this be? Well, to explain let us return to our battery analogy.

When we plug the battery charger back into the mains source of electricity then we actively form a connection that includes the original supplier of power, our local electricity generator and our recharging device. Neither battery nor power source can remain uninvolved for as soon as one is connected to the other by pins, wires, sockets, etc then *they become one*, an indivisible stream of pure power. It is only by deliberately pulling a plug or flicking a switch that we can stop this flow; while the energy is moving we cannot divide it. So, we can observe that recharging is a deep relationship that unites both the *creator* of the energy and its *receiver*.

When we talk of our own spiritual recharging and re-connecting we are clearly not talking about the power stations and generators that originate electrical energy but rather about linking up with the spiritual Source that is the originator of unseen spirit energy – the Creator. This we do not with cables and sockets but through specific directed means, such as by *entering the silence* or by prayer, both of which we shall discuss later in this book. By this we retain our individual essence but by connecting to the Creator we also become greater than ourselves, experiencing enlivening union even as we maintain our own personal energy. In this we are one – *alone* but essentially *all one* simultaneously.

We can, of course, never be entirely cut off from our Source but we can struggle by in a state of unawareness of connection, functioning in seeming isolation with a weak, blocked link. The strengthening of this link, via a conscious act of connection, brings us strength and joy – *empowerment* – and this, along with the understanding of the unseen energies we have been discussing, lies at the heart of this book. This is what we call *spiritwalking*.

And at last we come to mention spiritwalking! We may have been wondering why so far in a book on spirituality we have been instead discussing batteries, not spirits? Well, the basic analogy of the re-chargeable battery is central to all that follows here, not only because it gives us a readily identifiable centre from which to begin – the relationship between our seen body (the battery), unseen energy (the power accessed/stored) and the Creator (the energy generator) – but because it allows us to understand that spirit energy is very much like electrical energy and so deserves the same respectful awareness from the outset. By this we mean that it is, to all intents and purposes, invisible and it can bring beneficial revitalisation and illumination...*or profound harm*. Just as when we work with electricity, we need tried and tested methods and protection when we walk with spirit.

Spiritwalking is simply a guide that will enable us to recharge our energies safely and enjoyably, enabling us to walk more effectively and meaningfully in both the material, and the unseen, worlds. This we may do for the benefit of all Creation, or, as well shall express it from here on in, *for the good of the All*.

What, after all, could be more important than that?

Come with me and walk with spirit!

CHAPTER ONE

SPIRITED SOULS

'Spirit is the quiet wave that binds the poetry, just as it is the meaning of every sonnet. Who can maintain the wonder of the whole work when words are prised apart and analysed away from the original fiery lyricism of poet's intent? Equally who would seek to contain sunlight in a jar, separating illumination from its numinous source? Spirit and creation, and consequently the Creator, are indivisible – they are perfect partners bound to dance together and the soul is ever the witness of this.

All of life's mysteries find expression in our soul's unique experience and the Creator, originator of the life-force that animates all things, can never be outside of this experience.'

From Guidance

Before we begin the fundamental and essential business of looking at our own spiritual selves, an area that provides us with the most convenient source of primary study, we should first define what we mean by spirit.

What is the Meaning of Spirit?

When we discuss spirit in this book we are referring to that which is unseen and yet perceptible, the source of *animation* that dwells deep within each created being. Here the term animation refers not just to discernible manifest movement but also to an inner enlivening force – *life-force*. We cannot usually physically see the animating force that dwells in each expression of being (for, as we have ascertained previously, it is unseen, like electricity) but we can certainly feel it for it is a tangible energy. It is the mysterious hidden essence that gives us our essential vitality, beyond mere corporeal appearances, and which can be *sensed* as a presence in all created beings from the indomitable graveyard yew tree to the most delicate violet, from the mined mineral to the mountain and from the singularly perfect spiral of a tiny shell to the molten core of a super-volcano. This essential energetic quality of enlivenment, *spirit*, makes all fellow beings that we share the planet with (up to, and including, the planet itself) equal in the dance of life. Other en-spirited beings may not be able to talk with us and have freedom of movement or a recognisable language as we do but they are similarly given their unique resonance and impetus by the same life-force as are we. Spirit energy connects us all, now matter how disparate our nature or how different our worldly physicality – it is the great unifier.

So, spirit is mystery made known in each perfect part of creation. It is that internal spark from the eternal flame of Source energy that gives each being its particular presence as it is temporarily held within their physical form. Yet spirit can also be discarnate, without a bodily form, expressing itself as pure energy unencumbered by the material world. Being able to tune into this unifying force within all created beings, as well as sensing the presence of spirit beyond the confines of our present physical dimension, is what a spiritwalker learns to do.

How May We Identify the Presence of Spirit?
Even if we are not particularly tuned in to such subtle resonances we will have most likely shared one of the following moments when we have unwittingly engaged with the spirit of another being and,

indeed, with our own innate spirit.

Have we:

* *Seen something familiar in a stranger's eyes that we recognise whilst having never seen their physical self before?* This deep, seemingly irrational, connection occurs when their spirit-essence, sensed through the soul-windows of their eyes, meets our own. Often this sense of knowing another spirit is due to a profound similarity, or an equally profound difference, between their inner resonance and our own.

* *Had goosebumps or a shiver up the spine when hearing a particularly affecting piece of music or a particular instrument played well?* Music can carrying the intent of the human spirit that created it which in turn touches our own spirit even when the maker of that music may be physically absent. Similarly if we find something particularly jarring or repellent then our spirit will ripple with distaste resulting in a bodily shudder.

* *Felt a strong tingling in the hands when placing them on a rock?* This may occur as the vital essence within reaches us, unbidden, revealing the life-force within even the most inert seeming being and can be a thrilling experience.

* *Experienced an emotional response when witnessing a natural phenomenon?* This could include, for example, a particularly glorious sunset or hearing the wing-beats of many starlings moving as one entity as they go to roost.

* *Experienced being deeply moved by a human drama?* Maybe our spirit has been profoundly affected upon being present at a birth or death, even when the person involved was not related to us in an emotional way. Yet it can also be affected

by just hearing a story of human suffering or upon watching a documentary on human triumph over intense hardship.

• *Felt ourselves connecting with our own powerful spirit when we rise above human pettiness and act with unconditional kindness?* Perhaps we may do this by witnessing the pain inside someone who has wronged us, even when we want to hate them, thus enabling ourselves to rise above our human response and forgive them. Or perhaps such a feeling has occurred when we have engaged in giving without any thought of receiving in recompense, for the sheer joy of sharing our abundance. By practicing altruism we connect ourselves directly to the ever-giving Source and consequently feel that surge of pure power that flows between our Creator and ourselves when we act with unbridled compassion and generosity.

• *Seen the pale and dazzling glow that all beings emit?* This luminosity surrounds each part of creation, from tree to slug to human to pebble. As well as seeing it this glow can also be sensed it by touch, again we may receive that strange tingling in the palms as the resonance or vital energy that we each give off can be experienced as an actual force. This is not necessarily a being's 'aura', which is more usually discerned as bands of colour, but rather a radiance which hugs the form much more closely and which simply denotes the presence of that animating spirit within.

• *Witnessed the departure of a spirit from a companion animal?* In so doing we may have been able to observe how the creature concerned seems somehow like a flat parody of their former selves, a toy almost, once their spirit has gone. The difference between the animated form of a living creature and the dead and empty 'suit of clothes' (the body that it leaves behind) is striking.

- *Been drawn by another's spirit, for instance feeling a compulsion to go and be with a particular tree as if it were reaching out to us with invisible hands?* This soul, or spirit, connecting goes far beyond any physical attraction, indeed we may have no manifest idea why we are drawn to something or someone.

With the examples above, which may be more or less familiar to us, we can perhaps accept that it is well for us to give an *en-spirited* status to all of our kin be they housed in the manifest forms of fish, fowl, flowers, ferns, fjords or whatever else. When we do this we immediately give new meaning and purpose to our existences, bringing a lost magic back to life and the vital *extra*-ordinary back to the ordinary. How foolish it has been for humanity to lose its animistic camaraderie with all of its kin in creation and how very vainglorious! Such separationalist philosophy, speciesism, or *human-centricity,* is an attitude that gets us to some very dangerous positions very quickly. Extinction of species, pollution and genocide are but three of the results of such a shortsighted hypothesis of life for impatient, human-centric modern mankind. This book will help us foster a vision of reality that reveals a living planet and, indeed, a sentient universe that is populated by our fascinating equals, not those that we may have dominion over. It helps us to behave as if the expression of the Creator energy found within each creation truly matters, living with a *relational* philosophy.

Further Ways of Defining and Discerning Spirit

Whether we are talking about the spirit of a human or any other type of created being what we are discussing, as so often with magical or esoteric themes, is a paradox : *spirit is in us but it is also beyond us at the same time.* Spirit is *in* the world but not *of* the world. It is contained within our temporary and temporal human 'suit of clothes', our body, (or that of a butterfly or bear), but it is not contained by it permanently. It will go on even when we ourselves have cast off the worn out suit/body that has housed us for this *incarnation.* It was there before we incarnated into this particular body and it will be there after we have outgrown our use for the learning vehicle we know as our physical self. Spirit cannot be cast off for *it is us,* the essential and eternal us; it is the energy that sustains us *and* it is our true and eternal nature (and that of all other aspects of creation). Energy cannot cease to be but only be transmuted. What we are dealing with in this book therefore is an eternal force, an animating power with a creative motivation, which cannot be destroyed, only transformed; it is a fluid, free-flowing energy that can be either temporarily 'housed' or unrestrained. Wherever it flows, into whatever form, it should certainly be acknowledged and respected.

At this point it may be well to ask 'are we not all made of energy anyway?' because without this question it may seem that our inner spirit is the only energy whilst we, the physical humans, trees, rocks and creatures are not made of energy but rather something much more dull and mundane. Of course this is not the case. As we know, *everything is created of energy.* It is only the frequency of the vibration of the energy – the marvellous movement of its molecules and the dance of its electrons – that allows us to witness it in its manifest form.

The universe, the physical seen universe, is clearly made of billions upon billions of tiny whizzing particles of energy which move at differing rates and have differing elemental constituents, resulting in their particular particulate density and tangible internal structure. If something is seen by us as solid and can be witnessed in three-dimensions then this generally tells us that the vibration of its particles is relatively slow and their size or make-up reasonably dense with the electrons that connect the atoms being strong and tightly packed. This description could be witnessed in a heavy metal. We can reasonably state that we perceive 'solids' on a sliding scale from the energetic slowness and density that constitutes a huge granite boulder to the less slow and dense, but still undeniably solid, appearance of a sea sponge…or even a sponge cake. In a three-dimensional; 'solid' reality it is often difficult for us to be exact about the atomic density of what we witness in relation to another solid, it is only be the contrast of, for example, a leaf (solid) falling through the air (unseen, gaseous) that we may make a clearer distinction and witness the displacement achieved by one expression of energy meeting another. Our world is defined for us, more or less, by the contrast of supposed emptiness (air, space) with form (everything else).

Liquids are again tangible in our three-dimensional reality whilst being markedly 'quicker' and less fixed and dense in energetic terms. Heat, when applied to water makes the liquid assume the more energetic form of steam. Gaseous substances like steam take this quickening/refining of energetic levels up again so that we may only discern them in our reality by smell or colour or a sensation, such as a dampness or chill. From this far end of our perceptual reality let us go one stage further to that which lies on the edge of our discernment. Spirit is at the next level of 'energetic speed' from gas. Pure spirit-energy is so fast, refined and 'high frequency, low density' that it is difficult to physically perceive in grounded human terms. We cannot readily see it in three-dimensional terms but it is there none-the-less, animating all beings with life-force energy.

So, spirit has a very fast rate of vibration especially when compared to, say, a planet like Mars, a piece of glass, a raindrop or even the steam from our kettle. Mars is a solid we can observe, glass is something we can see and feel, as is rain, and steam can be detected as a moist cloud. Spirit, rather like the wind, or breath, is something that can only be sensed as a feeling on skin or how it affects things it touches. We can acknowledge the wind, the breath and spirit, even though we cannot literally quantify them as we can with denser expressions of energy like a table, shoe or a rabbit. Yet the difference between wind, breath and spirit is that the former two are dependant on externals (the planet's atmospheric pressure or the respiration of a being) whilst spirit is independent. Spirit can indeed be discerned by the way it animates a solid, such as a lizard or a bird, yet it is also eternal and not limited to, or by, such forms.

To further illustrate this point let us return to the electrical analogy of this book's introduction. An electrical cable is made up of relatively slow, dense energy and the particles of the cable bond together to form a structure we can see with our physical eyes as well as our being able to touch it. Inside this cable is more refined electrical energy that can be felt and experienced but not readily seen. But both the cable and the electricity are by nature *energetic*. It is all a matter of vibration and of the human ability to perceive higher frequencies that allows us to discern them...or not. Spirit is like electricity, powerful yet quick and light, whilst bodies are like electrical cable, slower and denser in atomic structure. The former moves through the latter for a specific time or purpose but is not limited to it, having its own identity. Spirit and matter become working partners for a given time, as do power and cable.

Because of this sharing of an energetic universe, both the seen (apparently solid) and unseen (apparently invisible) worlds are always connected and, in fact, are inseparable. The unseen (spirit) is only unseen, as we have just discussed, because of its rapid, light energetic nature. Of course we could begin to explore other dimensions and realities at this point, as they no doubt have their part in the unseen, or counterpart, universes, yet this would be to complicate a study which has enough mystery and paradox in it already. However, an acceptance of the possibility of such other aspects of existence would serve us well and we will certainly be returning to the idea of other worlds, dimensions and 'alternative realities' as we progress.

For now we can simply state that the seen and unseen, matter and spirit, interact and cross-over all the time; there are no walls between them, rather gauzy veils that our human selves have to drawn down to prevent us from being overloaded by energetic information. Our fellow mammals, cats, have been involved in studies which show that they are more than capable of 'zoning out' signals and frequencies which they come to recognise as unimportant to the daily business of living. There is no reason to assume that we human beings, engaged as we are even in modern terms in our own version of survival have, over time, chosen to zone out that which is surplus to the requirements of physical existence. Indeed it is considered that our human senses are currently only actually able to percieve around one percent of the electromagnetic spectrum, the rest (including dark matter) being well outside of the energetic parameters in which we operate. This is a staggeringly small amount and really does show that our seen universe is only a fraction of the All.

In short we are best served to understand the energetic nature of existence without necessarily having to literally witness its truth all day, every day: it is the re-membering of the truth that is important, along with an acceptance of the presence of the unseen.

How May We Become More Aware of Spirit Again? Spiritwalking in Essence

It is for us to now re-learn the ability to pick up the signals and subtle shades, other densities and frequencies, that we have long been zoning out or assuming don't exist. Thankfully we in the modern, relatively affluent, Western world have the privilege of being able to do this for the first time in many generations, being as we are not quite so preoccupied with putting food in our bellies or providing shelter for ourselves as we once were. Yet it may be true to state that those living in more Earth-honouring, animistic tribal societies, in harmony with ancient traditions and uncluttered by the mores of modern living, have never lost this ability to witness the subtleties of spirit, the unseen being as integral to their daily lives as the seen aspects of existence. This way of being is spiritwalking in essence: *living in the material world with an active awareness of energies, frequencies and vibrations.* To walk with spirit is to hold the balance between the ethereal and corporeal, the diaphanous and the dense, for the purpose of living more fully. It is about truly being awake and no longer a sonambulist.

But before we move on to the business of spiritwalking in daily life it is appropriate to draw our attention to an important, yet subtle, difference between what we perceive of as spirit and that which we call *soul*, a word which has already cropped up. Here is the fundamental, yet fine, difference:

- Spirit is the energising life-force of the universe, it is that which flows through all creation, giving it form and enlivening it. It is life's mystical electricity, its tangible force, as we have already described.

- Soul, on the other hand, is that which makes spirit energy unique to us; it is that vital free-flowing energetic essence made into a singular expression, which is earthed and translated through our body.

Do We Have Soul? The Spirit-Soul Connection

The Greek word for 'whole being' is *holocleron*, meaning 'having all parts' and the English words 'whole' 'holistic', and indeed holy, are based on the first root of this word. If we have all our parts then we are, as we have previously discussed, fully re-membered and therefore closer to the sacred. But let us clarify what are all these parts considered to be.

Most obviously in the case of us human beings there is obviously the manifest outer, or seen, aspect of ourselves. The physical body, *soma* as the ancient Greeks referred to it, is the temporary organic shell that allows us to experience three-dimensional reality, or life as we know it in this current sphere of existence. Yet without that unseen animating energy, spirit, the body would remain a shell, or an empty suit of clothes, and there would be no life of any kind to discuss.

Spirit is a word that comes to us from the Latin *spiritus,* meaning breath (which can be witnessed today as part of the word respiration/respiratory). This breath is the unseen giver of life, the mysterious substance that is seemingly as insubstantial as air and that which allows the inhalation and exhalation, or ebb and flow, of existence. In ancient Egypt can be translated as the *ka*, the life-force that was common to all living beings; the creative power that gives sustenance. In Greek this breath or air is *pneuma* (as we can observe in the words pneumatic or pneumonia) and again it speaks of that ethereal (or etheric) essence which is beyond the physical yet which, paradoxically, animates it. Yet as well as the breath of life it is also the *awareness* of life, a consciousness that is inherent in all Creation. It is present in all things as well as *being all things*.

Although it is everywhere spirit, as pure awareness, also desires to experience itself as *somewhere*, gaining a singular viewpoint of reality as well as a collective one. In order to experience life as an individual in our physical reality, through the manifest body, this omnipresent power has to translate itself into something quite particular. Thus spirit, which is the life-force breath of all things, becomes the life-force breath of one thing, allowing itself to become individualised. It becomes a drop in the ocean as well as the ocean itself, allowing itself to detach from the impersonal One-ness of Creation to become personal and one – a singular creation.

This singular expression of spirit energy is the soul, referred to in the Greek as *psyche*. The soul effectively connects our corporeal, transient selves to our ethereal, eternal selves so that spirit may be translated into a unique shape or resonance for the purpose of eliciting a particular experience of existence. In ancient Egypt the psyche can be translated as the *ba*, the sum of immortal forces that became inherent in a human, the *person*-ality of a person. The *ba* is often depicted as a human-headed bird, imagery that binds the aerial and the grounded which is precisely the 'job description' of the soul.

Soul is a spiritual record of unique experiences gained in a phys-ical body (be that human or otherwise) that can then be translated back into the collective pool of the Greater Spirit, or the Creator Consciousness. This is something that we shall look at again and again in this work. For now we can say that the Egyptian conception of the *akh* can be seen to poetically sum up this re-unification process. Upon death the *ka* and the *ba* unite (soul taking its personal experience back to the greater collective spirit), thus becoming part of a collective comprised of the *akh*, or shining life-force, energy of all other beings – the *akh-akh*. As we are far removed from the culture that conceived of such a way of expressing things we cannot be wholly sure of this translation but certainly the basic lyricism of the process remains. This re-absorption into the akh-akh is, perhaps, the one becoming the One again, the soul brought home to that which we describe in this book as *the All*.

More About Soul

Let us return to our point about our constituent parts, the body and the spirit, and the soul that unites them. This soul-self, a kind of bridge-building middle-self, is able to store emotion and sensation. It effectively assumes the experiences and characteristics of its host body or, over many incarnations, bodies and by this is an energetic recorder of how we feel when we are in physical form. The soul's responsive, emotive aspect is why we have a genre such as 'soul music' and why we describe sensitive, passionate people as 'having soul'. If something has deep feelings present within it or if it evokes profound, perhaps almost awe-inspiring, emotion in those who encounter it then it is classified as 'soulful'. Going back to a previous point we made, it is very telling that 'the windows of the soul', the eyes, are also described in this manner. Indeed we may get a frisson of welcome familiarity, or even repulsion, when we connect eye-to-eye. Spirit, through the medium of soul, is certainly discernible.

To raise another point here that we shall certainly return to, *lost souls* are those who have identified too heavily with their temporary bodily self and who are reluctant, for one reason or another, to let go of it when it dies. This may take place when the soul makes too permanent an identification with its hosting manifest shell, thus forgetting its true spiritual nature, or when their physical life has been terminated dramatically or unexpectedly and they have no real awareness of the end of physical being. Either way, a fixed identification with the human form can cause the eternal spirit, the soul that is housed within, to suffer confusion upon the death of that form. We should remember that the body serves the soul and spirit and not the other way round – it allows the spirit, though soul, to gain new perspectives and feelings for the good of the All. In this we may respect the physical aspect of ourselves as it helps us as souls to learn and grow yet it should not be overly revered, hidden in or clung to beyond its usefulness. Sadly this is what the *forgetting* can do to us.

It may be useful for us to recall here that even the bodily expression of our being is made of spirit energy, as are the stars above us and the earthworms below us. There is nothing that exists that is not made of energy! Yet of course, as with all physical manifestations, the body is much more tangible than either spirit or soul because of its *energetic density*, or the slow frequency at which its energy vibrates. This we will return to. For now let us observe that because of this density or slow vibration the body is not able to transcend the physical Earth as is the less dense, faster soul, and so it is party to all the natural laws of being manifest – i.e. predation, starvation, disease, territorial disputes, becoming worn out and eventually, inevitably, death and decay. Perhaps it is hard for energy to remain in such a dense, slow form for too long. From the mayfly that only flies for one day to a vast unknowable planet that has spun ponderously for over a billion human years all manifest physical life seems to have a time limit on its existence in a particular shape. If we remember our true immortal, spiritual nature we can happily accept this process and know that our eternal essence, the individual soul, will move on once the host shell no longer serves us. When we come to assimilate this into our view of reality then our apparent dying is

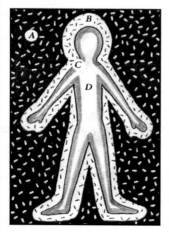

Diag.1 *Energies*

A (black with white shading) represents life-force, or spirit, energy — the essence of life that is mobile, light and of quick vibration. This is pure awareness — that which constitutes the Greater Spirit, or All, of Creation

B (white with black shading) represents our own particular life-force energy radiating out from our physical form

C (grey shading) represents life-force energy that has been made dense and slow enough to translate itself into a physical body for a particular life-time in manifest reality

D (white area) represents the life-force energy expressed as a unique eternal soul. Here it dwells within the temporary human form, giving it meaning and purpose whilst in return it gains experience and is able to develop. After the death of the host body **C** it will return to the pure awareness of the All as shown in **A**

a part of an ongoing voyage of discovery – an exciting opportunity.

It is well for us to understand and re-member the three aspects of our-current-self, acknowledging that spirit and its singular expression soul, are beyond human time even as the third physical aspect allows us to experience such boundaries, albeit for a limited period.

To reinforce this concept here is a diagram which reveals the three expressions of life-force energy involved in an 'earthed' incarnation: It matters not if we care to refer to that which dwells within us as our spirit or our soul, or whether we can see Creation in terms of many souls or of life-force energy flowing both freely and uniquely, for as long as we can grasp the unseen power involved we can learn how to work with it, however we come to label it. Yet for the purposes of this book both terms will be used where appropriate and so it is well to understand the difference as discussed here.

Now let us move on to looking at those spirited souls of ours in more detail.

CHAPTER TWO

KNOW YOURSELF INSIDE OUT

'You may only be fully 'in your power' when you sing your own song. When you imitate another's song, which you can never do successfully, you create a discord. You will experience a cacophony if you do not realise your own insistent melody in synchronisation with the rhythm of creation. All life is orchestrated! You each carry your unique rough score inside of you and within it there is always room for improvisation. Yet you may only improvise well when you know what time signature you are inherently in and which key is naturally yours.

We are here to guide you back to your internal score – a score full of glorious notes that spill across your stave, accompanied by all those equally glorious corrections you have made to it. How you now choose to interpret what is eternally written is a matter of your free will in this life. May you choose gracefully.'

From Guidance

Here begins our first real lesson. Before we can work with energies outside of our own we must learn to recognise what is ours, energetically speaking, and what is not.

How May We Perceive Ourselves Inside the 'Seen' Body?

This is one of the more challenging aspects of the work we shall be doing as spiritwalkers yet we must tackle this matter at this juncture as if we do not somehow manage to identify that which is of our own soul then we are not well equipped to be able to practice the discernment required for our journey. And why is it so testing? Well, we are all conditioned to accept, if not believe, that all that we think, feel and know comes today from either a) our mind or b) our genetic make-up. Although the much-needed 'mind, body, spirit' movement is certainly more popular than ever we will no doubt have experienced for much of our lives that the common model for understanding human behaviours and attributes is based firmly in the psychological or in physical causes and effects. We attribute the way we perceive things and react or respond to them as being inherited or conditioned and seldom, unless in a singularly religious context, do we ever come across the concept of the soul influencing our way of being. Less frequently still will we come across the notion that the soul has traits of its own.

So, here is a new way of considering the world, and specifically ourselves and our place in it, which I will gladly expound. It allows us to consider, perhaps for the first time, the difference between those things we have been taught in this life (learned/trained traits) the things we have clearly been given genetically (inherited/genetic traits) and those that we have brought with us into this incarnation as inherent parts of our spiritual make-up (soul traits). How may we do this? Well, we take a good look at what we know about ourselves as a whole today and may begin by asking ourselves the following questions.

Defining the Human Aspects – Revealing the Soul

- *What can I identify in myself as a response or reaction to something I have been told/taught as a truth or have experienced directly?* This includes beliefs, conditioned behaviours, inner knowledge (that which we have been told by others is true about ourselves) and outer knowledge (academic learning and instruction, social conditioning, drilling of any kind, tradition, superstition). It includes phobias that we can trace back to a specific life-event, learned prejudices/preferences we have observed around us or had taught to us, trained or copied skills and specific ways of behaving expected of our age/class/gender/creed/culture or society at large. It also encompasses things we can attribute to our physical surroundings or situation, the way we have learned to cope with our environs and adapt accordingly as well as ways of being we have adopted as a result of traumatic/pleasing life events. Basically this covers any learned behaviours, be they physical, mental or emotional.

• *What can I identify in myself as a family flaw or virtue, be this a physical attribute or type of thought or behaviour?* This includes inherent talents observable though the clan, inherited disabilities, family predispositions to certain ways of being be they physical, mental or emotional, ways of relating which have been (unconsciously or consciously) passed on, appearance and mannerisms specific to our kin.

• *What is there about me that seems to have no basis in the learning or familial inheritance of this life?* What remains unexplained in us by those things covered in the two previous clauses?

This unexplained remainder would include inexplicable pulls towards certain culture/land/way of being outside of our current experience or learning. Or natural talents that develop without any tutoring, encouragement or inherited skill, skills that may have had us labelled as exceptionally, if inexplicably, gifted. Perhaps there are even deficiencies in us that seem bizarre or unaccounted for by this life. Or profound beliefs in areas outside our family's, or our own, present sphere of interest/knowledge. Or memories and dreams which occur frequently and affect us greatly which are irrelevant to the current physical persona but which have a meaning which touches some other aspect of us as yet unexpressed in this life. Anything that defies the usual pigeon-holing of 'you got that from your mother's side' or 'in our family we always do it this way' or 'people of our class were taught to do things like this' etc. is of our eternal soul aspect. Similarly anything that we cannot honestly trace back to something we have read, seen, been taught or trained to do etc. is (probably) a soul trait. Indeed, if we *feel* its presence powerfully within is then it almost certainly is.

It is this latter point that may set us off on a quest as yet unembarked upon by many. Such anomalies in our make up are usually explained away as 'you probably picked that up from a film' or 'there must have been a pianist on your dad's side generations ago that we don't know about' or even perhaps just shrugged off as just a meaningless bit of 'randomness' in life. Perhaps these supposed soul traits could indeed be relegated to any of these categories if we continue with the received logic of the 'sensible' hard reality that we have become accustomed to. Yet once we begin to follow the threads that really bind us together as a whole person we will get a *sense* of the strands that are of the eternal, not the corporeal…that is to say a deep feeling. Such feelings are not necessarily emotional, they can be beyond human emotion, but they are not strictly rational either. They are intense, like a nameless yearning, born of a profound familiarity with no apparent root. We will begin to understand which are those inexplicable but certainly meaningful threads are that have no beginning or end in this life but rather have come with us, from other lives and other selves, and will go on with us after death. We will *feel* the things that are inherently ours by soul right, beyond anything that could be imposed on us in this lifetime. They are immutable soul truths, personal yet universal in their existence.

Soul Truths, Soul Traits

Let us now suggest that some of these soul traits have perhaps been formed by the experiences of other lives. For instance, we may indeed have a compelling fear of ice with no conceivable origin in this incarnation, or a feeling of great compassion for the sick that transcends any current experience. We may have an overwhelming affinity with horses although we were born in an inner city or perhaps conversely we have a terror of horses that cannot be assuaged although we have never, in this existence, been close to one. I myself suffered from a fear of fire for many years, even needing to sleep with water close to hand to dowse any flames, yet I had never even been close to a real blaze in this current life. I discovered, after much unhappiness, that this was due to another existence when I met my death in the flames.

Perhaps, more benignly, our infant skill at needlepoint is prodigious although we grew up with only a father who would not sew. Or maybe as a beginner we have an unprecedented aptitude for, or knowledge of, the German language although we hail from a monolingual English household. Such attributes and predilections can defy the cast-iron explanations so beloved of the modern Western society. Such things have been brought in with us, carried deep within our eternal energy matrix of the soul, and would exist within us no matter what physical shell, or, as I prefer, 'suit of clothes', we currently inhabit.

It is possible that profoundly affecting events in our other lives – be they 'past' lives or concurrent existences in parallel, or alternative, universes – have a lasting effect on the essence of our souls. If we think of the then we can appreciate that it will be shaped by strong emotions in a lifetime. Another metaphor for this may be to witness the soul as a sponge that becomes soaked and heavy, not with water but with *experience*. Such things as violent death, betrayal, overwhelming love, jealousy, fear and exceptional courage can scar the soul or make it more receptive and resilient, thus affecting it's inherent structure, just as water will make a sponge expand and grow more weighty or flaccid. Likewise our previous passions and aptitudes can become immeshed in the fabric of our eternal being, especially if we desired to continue what we were doing forever.

Imagine a drop of dye in a pool of water and how the dye will quickly spread through the pool turning it a different shade whilst in turn becoming diluted from its original form. The water will assimilate the dye and be coloured slightly in the process depending on the dye's initial strength. Similarly a drop of fruit cordial in a glass of water will become dilute to taste, the two fluids mingling to create new liquid that is mostly water but no longer purely so. On the other hand a drop of oil will sit in a puddle without being a natural part of its molecular structure. If the water is agitated then the oil will disperse to smaller and smaller droplets until gradually, eventually, it will be almost indiscernible within the greater fluid. Such is the action of experience, especially emotional experience, being incorporated into a soul. Some experiences are like dye or cordial and colour or flavour us a little whilst some are like oil and we cannot readily assimilate them. The energy of our experiences can, and do, affect our soul beyond the current body.

Certainly the whole of the unseen regions – energetic dimensions and levels of existence which we will discuss and work with throughout this book – have this same ability to be shaped and stretched and affected by will and wish, intense love and unbridled hate. Energy, no matter how permanent or solid it may temporarily appear to our human eyes, can always be transformed by the action of other energies. We need only look at the cliffs along a coastline to witness the action of the seemingly less dense energies of water and air upon the apparently immutable earth. Energetic action can be cumulative as well as instant and dramatic.

Sometimes a trigger in this life will allow our soul traits, be they perceived as skills or handicaps, to come to the fore more readily. Other times our limitless desire, ability or aversion – be that to play music/work with clay/help others/train dogs/avoid enclosed spaces etc. – will simply be there with us, nagging like a 'soul itch', as soon as we turn up in another incarnation. Either way the soul has the ability to exist beyond human attributes whilst being an effective carrier and transmitter of those very same attributes beyond time and place. It is, of course, a paradox.

Here it is vital to remind ourselves that the soul is not strictly human, of course, rather it just fits well into a human shaped role in a lifetime, just as the soul of a cat may fit into a panther, lynx or a domestic cat or any variation on 'cat-ness' that suits its soul-theme. Therefore soul traits are not strictly things like 'good at the piano', indeed a soul trait may be more general than that, such as 'an ability to work with sound' or 'an interest in melody and harmony'. Even these latter two descriptions are still quite human-orientated and it seems unlikely that the spirit, expressing itself as soul, would be quite so rooted in the manifest world as these two suggest. Perhaps it is that the soul starts off as having a resonance which is particularly creative, a vibration that is pre-disposed to expressing itself through sound, and so pursuing this innate disposition via various physical lives, or incarnations, either on this planet or elsewhere. Being drawn to such aspects of life and developing those themes the soul then adds new, more human attributes to its repetoire.

We could, therefore, make a sample list of such basic, root traits.

Core Traits

A pre-disposition towards colour or light

A resonance suggestive of caring/nurturing

A vibration suited to movement

A innate aura of inquisitiveness

An inclination towards sound

An inherent air of calm organisation

An energy of lyrical expressiveness

An affinity with shape and space

An instinctive feel for communication

A quality suggestive of dynamism and verve

A general feeling of gentle introspection

An essence of dependable solidity

And so on. This list is by no means exhaustive; there are many others we can, no doubt, think of. We can then give these larger traits their possible sub-traits.

Sub-Traits, Descriptive Terms

1. *Creative*: visionary, imaginative, experimental, perceptive
2. *Sensitive*: warm, compassionate, empathic, altruistic, feeling
3. *Expressive*: graceful, fluid, dynamic, aware, spontaneous
4. *Inventive*: discerning, curious, experimental, insightful, questing
5. *Communicative*: eloquent, fluent, cooperative, receptive, descriptive
6. *Effective*: methodical, ordered, pragmatic, disciplined, stabilising
7. *Responsive*: observant, visionary, aware, accommodating, giving
8. *Expansive*: romantic, demonstrative, open, idealistic, poetic
9. *Cooperative*: responsive, balanced, amenable, clear, aware, involved
10. *Aggressive*: courageous, daring, gregarious, active, challenging
11. *Reflective*: visionary, contemplative, sensitive, receptive, calming
12. *Protective*: grounded, reliable, constant, sturdy, nurturing

And any mixture of these and more.

By now should be getting a feel for this concept and can go on to look at the how the traits apply to human incarnation. Respectively the traits above could be translated as though the following examples.

Practical Earthly Applications

1. Painter, designer, decorator, art therapist, florist, jeweller,

chef

2. Nurse/doctor, parent, counsellor/therapist, healer, vet, gardener, cook

3. Dancer, explorer, athlete, performer, courier, jockey, model

4. Scientist, journalist, astronomer, explorer, archaeologist, philosopher

5. Musician/singer, sound engineer, voice coach, composer, producer

6. Teacher, team leader, manager, editor, organiser, warden, courier

7. Actor, poet, orator, writer/dramatist, sales person, workshop leader

8. Architect, designer, sculptor, graphic artist, furniture maker, stone mason

9. Teacher, fundraiser, therapist, team leader, aid worker, interviewer

10. Fire-fighter, stunt man/woman, acrobat, pilot, protester, police person

11. Nun/monk, visionary, poet, writer, artist, theologian, spiritual teacher

12. Teacher, doctor, police person, counsellor, parent, working with animals or children

From these lists and their practical, earthy implications we may, perhaps for the first time, be able to get a broader idea of what our soul type is, based on this sample of exampled traits. Remember, these are just ways of understanding, and indeed giving credence to, our eternal essence and are certainly not hewn in stone! And remember also that our earthy labels such as 'carpenter' or 'air hostess' do not sum us up in totality, rather they direct us back, if they are professions that have been chosen with love or care, to what we are at a far deeper level than our human self. We can now have fun with these concepts and even broaden our understanding of ourselves by using the examples we have just discussed. We can also go one stage further and translate our findings into symbols.

Symbols are representatives of a meaningful concept, a sign which refers to other layers of meaning or experience, and if chosen well can be tokens of empowerment. As spiritwalkers we shall be working with symbols a great deal. We can now ask the following questions of ourselves to build up a more descriptive, multi-layered symbolic representation of our true selves.

Which Symbols Suit Our Soul?

- What colour, or blend of colours, would my soul be?
- What shape?
- How big?
- What scent would my soul have?
- What element would it be most reminiscent of?
- What is its texture?
- How would it move?
- And what are my soul's key words?

From this we may come up with an animated pictogram, something like:

'Sunny orange fuzzy sphere, rolling smoothly, citrus scented, warm and glowing, sometimes bouncing happily, never stopping, seeking others, curious, resilient and positive.'

Remember here that we are not determining how we behave, as humans, or even our displayed personality, but how we feel inside which is quite apart from how our body may behave. It is valuable to note that physical ailments and life-situations can affect this core self and override or warp its essence. For instance, you may feel that you are this fuzzy orange positive circle inside but your body's hormone/chemical imbalance makes you feel depressed against your soul's will. It is usual to experience a feeling as if we are trapped inside a shell if our body is behaving contrary to our soul's nature, as if we are somehow inside a crazy car that simply won't steer straight. However hard this may seem to us it is also important to consider that such a discrepancy between our soul nature and our current bodily condition, or circumstance, may be a part of what we are learning about in this life. Nothing we come across in this work, however trivial or unrelated it may seem, is without meaning. It is all worth noting and goes towards our inner, and outer, *knowing* – that is, our ability to respond from a position of balanced understanding of energies and events.

Which brings us on to another valuable point. There is something vital we may like to note about ourselves here which is important to our development and progression through this work.

How Do We Experience the Things We Imagine?
When we ask ourselves these soul-searching questions do we:

- Primarily employ visual imagery in our imaginings, *seeing* colours, shapes and forms very easily in our mind's eye?
- Do we predominantly *hear* our imaginings in terms of sound or language? Do we witness a dialogue that describes our

imaginings?

- Do we neither use many visual nor audible cues but rather *feel* what we are imagining, perceiving it as *sensation*?
- Do we find it hard to do any of the above as we consider ourselves wholly unimaginative anyway?

These questions help us to discern if we have a certain way of imagining or perceiving things that is dominant as this will also reveal something useful about our nature to us. Or, indeed, it may reveal that we consider that we have little or no ability to imagine or perceive at all. If this latter is the case it may be well to remind ourselves that we employ imaginings of this sort every single day unconsciously and spontaneously. For example, when someone mentions a famous person to us there will be an immediate visual, linguistic or sensate experience that we will present ourselves with to cue into who they are talking about. This also applies if someone talks to us about a rosy apple, or a pair of men's formal shoes, or, especially, something we care about such as a companion animal or family member.

So, we are all very used to employing this skill in very ordinary ways and yet when we are asked to use our imaginations specifically many of us shy away, convinced we are as imaginative as a lump of lead. Not so! Witness this immediate and natural way we cue ourselves in to conversations each day and we will soon grow in faith of our own ability to imagine. It is sad to think that such a joyous and creative pursuit as imagining, in whatever way we do it, has often been drummed out of us at home or school at an early age for being a waste of time. Or something that we simply weren't good at, being more practical or physical. As if we can't be both! Now is the time to banish this limiting idea and open ourselves to our Creator-given ability to see, hear or feel things just as effectively inside ourselves as we can outside of ourselves.

If we are ever ill-convinced of the point or purpose of imagining then let us spend a few minutes looking around the room we are in. It isn't just 'pointless' art that comes from the imagination – indeed, no useful window, chair, cupboard, table or floor covering would exist if someone, somewhere, had not imagined them into being first. All that we experience daily as mundane has been dreamed up through the envisioning of another human being before its physical manifestation. We would hear no aeroplanes pass overhead, nor any cars drive by, nor any clocks ticking away if it weren't for someone's imaginings. Certainly the imagination has conjured up some pretty dreadful things over the millennia but it has also filled our daily existences with life-saving and life-enhancing items too. It would be a very empty existence if indulging the imagination were always considered a waste of time! Certainly this book would not exist if it weren't for the imaginings of humanity for paper had to be created as did printing and even language.

All that we know in our modern human world has been the result of a dream, an imagining, that may be considered frivolous for its initial nebulous, non-productive quality and yet is indispensable when it is turned into a reality. Our imagination is a fantastic gift to be encouraged, nurtured and truly rejoiced in...whether it bears physical fruit in the world or not.

Further Helpful Soul-Symbols, Metaphors and Analogies
1. Vessel and Contents, Body and Soul
Moving on from this exercise we can now use further symbols

imagery by describing our body as a vessel that holds the 'liquid of the spirit'. In this analogy we shall combine that which is more solid or tangible (the temporary physical aspect) with that which is more subtle, sinuous or liquid (the eternal spirit in the singular form of the soul). The latter is able to adapt itself to whichever container we pour it into, changing shape to fill it but never losing its essential nature, whilst the former holds it. And here is another paradox, for although the soul is supple, a fluid and adaptable medium, it is also constant, never losing its core aspects. If we consider this for a moment, our soul really is like a flowing liquid which can be bitter or sweet, viscous or insipid, steaming or icy, lumpy or smooth etc. And our physical self reveals to the world some of our soul's nature, itself being transformed by the type of 'fluid' that is poured within...just as a cup will become hot, or expand, if freshly brewed tea is poured in.

Example of such symbolic representations would be:

'My body is like a tall, fluted, frosted glass full of an icy emerald green julep with a sprig of cooling mint.'
Or
'My eternal soul feels like a warming home-made tomato soup which is poured into the small earthenware mug of my body.'

This task reveals to us our own innate inventiveness as well as our ability to know ourselves intimately as souls, just as we know ourselves, albeit temporarily, as physical human beings with a mole on our left knee, a crooked little finger on our right hand or a scar on our lower abdomen.

2. My Planet, Myself

Another question along these lines may be *'what sort of planet would I be?'*. This enters us into a new game that we can play as creators, experimenting with notions of size, shape, speed, colour etc.

Such a description of this soul-planet may read something like the following:

'My soul is a small blue-green planet which is ninety percent water and which is inhabited only by the most beautiful fish and exotic birds which roost on lush islands in these calm deep oceans'.

Or

'Inside I am a formidable giant of a planet, hot and red, smouldering and spitting, surrounded by impenetrable gas and inhabited by colossal unnameable beasts.'

Such questions and answers may seem frivolous but they can be enlightening, especially in a society or community that places little or no store in non-religious, deeply personal, matters of the spirit. How many of us have ever given that mysterious animating force, that unique energy, inside us this much scrutiny before? From such play can come many insights which give us a much more holistic view of our selves.

3. As Within, So Without

We can still push the boundaries of our inner knowledge to new depths by asking questions that can give us further symbols to work with which are highly personal, yet of the natural world around us.

Here are some examples of such further questions based around our indefatigable connection to the natural world:

- What mammal/s would my soul be?
- Which bird/s? Or fish? Or insect/s?
- What place or land?
- What tree? Or flower? Or herb?
- Which fruit?
- What kind of water? (River, rock-pool, waterfall etc.)
- Which sort of landscape? (Mountain, desert, heath etc.)

Please note, here we are not asking what our *favourite* creature or plant may be but rather *what we are*, inside. We may adore foxes but not have an 'earthy', or remotely foxy, spirit, or admire dolphins but have a distinctly airy soul, reminiscent of a Greylag goose in flight. This aligning with natural symbols is not about preference, which is so often based on physical beauty or manifest attributes, but rather a deep inner resonance that goes beyond skin to our nature…and to the soul of nature.

Once we have honestly investigated ourselves, putting aside all visual bias, and allowing our fellow beings and Creation to act as our tools for growth, we may choose to collect items that link us in with these powerful symbols. We could perhaps have a place in our homes where we make a collection of images such as postcards or magazine clippings or we may choose to carry representative models or jewellery of the appropriate creature/tree etc. with us. For succour and strength for it can indeed be comforting and empowering to have such a strong inner knowing of who we are as we move through the world.

4. I Am Who I Am

Moving on yet another stage in this inner exploration, from these answers we may be able to come up with an image or even name for our soul-selves, something such as *Little Mouse of the Big Hollow Oak, Blue Butterfly of the Sweet Waving Grass* or *Bright Salmon Leaping in the Cold North.* We may prefer something simpler such as *Tall Pine, Windswept Moor* or *Dancing Deer.*

Meaningful, or magical, names have long since been considered statements of our innate power, based as they are in deep knowledge of our true 'hidden' (unseen) self. Traditionally it was said that if someone knew your inner, or magical, name they could render you powerless or control you. Think of Rumpelstiltskin! So it may be well for us to guard our name as we would treasure of immense personal worth. This is not an act which is rooted in superstition but rather acknowledges that we value our inner knowing and have earned the right, by our quest for eternal truth, to keep such wisdoms within us. They may offer us comfort in times off hardship when it seems difficult to hold onto the notion of eternal selves at all. When the world presents us with painful challenges and all seems to be chaos it is remarkable how this one simple secret name can give us strength and a calm inner centre whilst (paradoxically again) being synonymous with the Earth that gives us our physical experience. Our name acts as a bridge that holds that vital balance between seen and unseen and it is for our knowing only. Each soul will have their own bridge, even if they are not consciously aware of it at this present time.

5. Traditional Routes to the Centre

It is well to add at this juncture that we can use traditional methods such as the divinatory disciplines of astrology, both Chinese and European, as well as the structure of the tarot to help us understand what lies at our own numinous core. I feel that it is important to say here that, just as with all the previously discussed questions and answers, astrology and the tarot offer us a *symbolic* way of understanding the world and ourselves, not a *literal* one. They are but man-made systems, not infallible absolutes, but when taken as symbolic guides they can be invaluable at giving us insights into the eternal energies present in Creation, and therefore in each being.

In astrology, both the planets and the ancient European mythic figures that give them their names are very valuable as tools for unlocking the mystery of our unseen selves. For instance, we could ascribe certain quick, bright Mercurial attributes to our soul, or be very drawn, at a deep soul level, to the courageous energies of Mars or the romantic pull of Venus. Similarly the tarot offers us archetypal figures such as the brave Fool, the wise Hierophant or the mature, compassionate Empress that may mean something profound to our spirit-selves. All these tools are helpful but what we can really glean from astrology and the tarot at this time is their use of *elemental* correspondences.

The Elements of the Soul

To discuss each element individually, using a traditional Western model which works well in practice, we can say that the element of Earth is of the Northerly direction, and represents qualities like grounded-ness, stability, practicality etc. We find Earth expressed in the traditional tarot as the suit of Pentacles and in Western astrology as Taurus, Virgo and Capricorn. To the East is we may find Air, that element of intellect, philosophy, lofty ideals and thoughts. We find the element of Air ascribed in traditional tarot as the suit of Swords and as Aquarius, Gemini and Libra in astrology. In the South we have passionate Fire, that courageous, tempestuous and transformative element. In tarot this is the suit of Wands and in astrology Aries, Leo and Sagittarius. Finally Water, aligned to the West, is the place of emotion, dream, romance and creativity. In the tarot we find Water as the suit of Cups and as the Astrological signs of Pisces, Cancer and Scorpio.

We may find that we feel equally influenced, at a soul level, by each element or we may find that we are primarily linked to one element with the other three only having subtle peripheral influences. Again this may seem fanciful to quantify an 'unearthly' unseen aspect of ourselves using manifest attributes like earth or fire and yet it is a valuable tool for understanding both how we are made at a soul level and also it gives us a way of re-balancing ourselves as we walk in human form. For example, if we consider ourselves to be a very watery soul type with very little earth and fire we may feel in order to ground ourselves more fully we need to live in a very landlocked region amongst earthing hills. Of course, if we are fundamentally watery then it may also be well for us to live by the sea and enjoy a great deal of compatible energy. Or if we feel intensely fiery at a soul level we may feel that a northern place that is high and windy in aspect may be ideal to cool us, in symbolic terms. The point here being that our soul type will influence our manifest existence and we can empower ourselves by understanding that type and so living more effectively, accordingly.

How may we really gauge what elemental balance we have in our souls? As we have reminded ourselves here our sun signs will afford us a basic insight into our true nature. For instance, in very fundamental terms, a Piscean, a water sign, has that highly emotive yet romantic and artistic temperament; a Taurean, born under an earth sign, has a more stubborn yet deeply dependable aspect whilst an Aquarian, ruled by the element of air, has a much more calculated and discerning approach to 'life, the universe and everything'. Of course, any astrologer could tell you that this view is very simplistic as it does not consider the bigger picture and a full birthchart would be necessary for more in depth analysis. Yet for now we can all ascribe basic astrological, elemental attributes to our core soul traits and sub-traits, no matter how much astrological knowledge we currently have, for every little helps us gain a deeper understanding of who and what we are and how we work.

At this juncture we can also consider if we have to incarnate into bodies with particular astrological signs for them to accommodate our kind of soul? For example, would a predominantly earthy soul feel happier and lead a more harmonious productive life if born into a Capricorn body as opposed to a Cancerian one? Or would a particularly experienced or advanced soul choose a body that was born under a sign that is in opposition to their elemental soul type just for the challenge it would bring? For example, would a dynamic practval, soul choose languid fey body for the life-journey to see how this would feel and to assimilate the learning it would engender? Or would they find a vigorous Leo or meticulous Virgoan body more appropriate for their learning and creativity?

The purpose for such questions, or for this exploration, is for us to learn to identify the difference between our body type and our soul type and to note any correlations or discrepancies and assess what this means to us for the purpose of pushing our boundaries of understanding. As we will discover throughout this work *there are no coincidences* and everything has meaning, therefore it would be both interesting and beneficial for us to give some time to our astrological aspects and what they tell us about the soul which chose this time and place to be born.

This is as far as we shall go with this subject here because this is not a work solely about the tarot or astrology and specialist books on both of these disciplines can be found in the suggested reading section at the end of this book. Yet here we have considered the four elemental building blocks of worldly life and we shall now add what is perhaps a new concept: a fifth element, ether, which lies at their centre.

Ether and the Etheric

Ether represents to us the unseen life-force, that which is not a manifest element yet which is, paradoxically, the very essence of all elements and conditions of existence. In this ether can be symbolically represented, as in modern, Western, magical terms, as both the cauldron and (paradoxically) its contents; the two are indivisible. If we think back to the diagram in the last chapter we will remember that the physical body (the cauldron of our current point) is affected by its contents, the soul, and vice versa. This is inescapable as when we are alive as human beings the body and soul act in tandem and are indeed indivisible. In Celtic myth the cauldron has always represented a mysterious, magical place of death and rebirth, the womb and tomb, the fertile void from which all is born and to which all things return. The cauldron is, essentially the melting pot of life *and* all life simultaneously. It is, essentially, both the source of inspiration and knowledge, two driving forces of creation, as well as being creation itself.

Celtic myths tell us of Cerridwen's cauldron from which Gwion, later to become the bard Taliesin, acquired his vast wisdom. Three drops flew from this mythical cauldron and burned Gwion's finger that he then quite naturally sucked, thus taking the *awen* (flowing spirit of pure inspiration) it contained within him and becoming transformed. We may think of our own transformation through the cauldron of the womb as we come to physical birth, a time when spirit calls us to be creative through physical means. Likewise we may observe that through the tomb of our physical death we take the knowledge gleaned in a lifetime back into the realm of spirit, known also as *the Ether*. The cauldron, or vessel of the physical body, acts as a doorway between seen and unseen, the physical world and the Ether, where etheric energy is transformed from matter to spirit and round again.

The powerful and emotive symbol of the cauldron may also be experienced as the Holy Grail, that which the courageous quest for in their lifetime, the place where true wisdom and union with the All can be found. The grail is not so much an object as *spirit held in the world* – it is both the holder and the held simultaneously, a representative of the union between seen and unseen. The grail clearly has transformational qualities as can be witnessed in the mythic tales of both Christ and King Arthur, both dying and resurrecting symbols of everlasting life. We may also witness it as the witches' place of power or the alchemist's crucible where she or he may transform matter into energy (or vice versa).

Ether is a substance that is in a constant state of motion, ebb and flow, and therefore is present in all interactions. Whichever way we symbolise it is at the centre of things, the hub of existence. Ether is the spirit we are to be walking with and as spiritwalkers incarnate in physical form we act as the living cauldron itself. Our bodies allow us to transmute and transform energy just as the cauldron does in myth and legend. Diag.2, below, expresses this.

So now we witness spirit as ether and can understand that it therefore must be composed of all other elements as well as being present in them. If ether lies at the centre of the compass, blending all four aspects or directions of creation, then the other elements flow into it, and indeed out again, whilst retaining their individuality. Each element holds its orientation yet also has blurred edges where they merge and melt into each other and into the centre, rather like the neighbouring colours in a rainbow that seem to merge into each other while when taken as a whole they become white light. This teaches us that we are always a complex blend of elemental influ-

Diag.2 *Ether*

A represents the Ether, or etheric realm - the hidden energetic All from which all things proceed, and to which all things return.

B shows etheric energy, or ether, moving from quick, pure spirit into slower form

C represents the living cauldron, or cup, of creation which is the doorway from spirit to matter, a place of transformation between worlds

D shows ether moving again from dense matter to lighter spirit

ences, nothing in spirit has defined edges and all things are interdependent. It is our quest to find just what blend we have within us that makes us shine with our own particular inner light.

Symbols and Self-Knowledge

Let us stress again, as it is very important, that the symbols we are working with are all based around very human or earthly ideas (which are, to be fair, all we have whilst we dwell in these bodies). Again they are certainly not literal and not meant to bind us to immutable beliefs. Yet using such tools gives us, at the very least, a way of identifying what is ours, *truly* ours, beyond all human affectations, experiences and influences. It may be hard to separate these aspects of being out at first (before blending them back together again) but perseverance will give us a more rounded, or holistic, vision of what it means to be truly alive. Not only is this vital in our forthcoming spiritwalking but also in our lives as this intimate knowledge of our eternal internal essence will make us much more power-full. To have self-knowledge, or a working understanding of the deep root of our inherent soul nature, is to own our power.

Although it is often quoted it is well to recall here that '*Gnothi se Auton*', which translates as '*Know Thyself*', was inscribed above the entrance to the Oracle of Delphi at the temple of Apollo in Ancient Greece. This quote is often credited to Socrates, who is considered to be one of the wisest philosophers that has ever lived, and although this accreditation may be a fallacy, as a succinct, powerful statement of the purpose of existence it is certainly worthy of a great seeker of truth. In *knowing ourselves* we begin to establish the sense that such inner knowledge connects us, inexorably, to that which is external also. To reiterate, the *as within, so without* maxim is very valuable to us as spiritwalkers and those who quest, unfailingly, for wisdom.

The Beauty of Inner Knowing and its Outer Applications

In our spiritwalking this self-knowledge allows us to have a clearer idea of what is ours...and what is not. This means that when dealing with the *without* aspect of existence, with (seen or unseen) events and energies outside of us, we will be able to successfully differentiate between our own innate resonance and that which is truly external, independent of us and possibly extraneous. As the book progresses we will really understand the worth of such profound inner knowing gathered at this stage.

Furthermore, the above discourse simply gives us another way, a healthier and more holistic way, of understanding who and what we are, our place in the world and that of others. It moves us away from the limited world that consists of only mind and body into the unlimited and lively realm of spirit – that which gives all life meaning and purpose as well as its innate life-spark and source. It is not a cut and dried science or rationale rather a free–flowing way of expanding what we know and feel using symbology. Once we begin to engage with this process our awareness will begin to shift away from the 'bricks and mortar' of existence and will move into the sublime and subtle realms of spirit before bringing us back again, allowing us to witness the material world with fresh wonder as well as returning our personal spiritual autonomy. All our discoveries will, we will find, take us in circles and spirals, never in straight lines to dead ends!

We can also congratulate ourselves for being one of the growing numbers of intrepid souls who are prepared to *look beyond* and remember. It is the soul that is eternal, and therefore the most vital aspect of the self, yet in the forgetting we may overlook it all together. It is for us now, as discerning and questing individuals, to re-address the balance of the ethereal and the corporeal, giving the influence of our eternal souls, and that of all other created beings, their credence.

However, before we engage in the otherworldly/worldly work proper we must ask ourselves another question. If we can answer it we will be much better equipped to deal realistically with what lies ahead.

It is this. What is our current level of 'psychic' ability?

CHAPTER THREE

RECEIVERS AND TRANSMITTERS

'We all have the ability to translate the language of the unseen
for although we have 'bought into' the illusion of physicality
our deep inner being naturally understands the subtler signals
beyond mortal speech and deed. The native tongue of our soul
is beyond an exchange of words and is instead part of the universal spirit-song, the transcendent sound of the stars and the
seas and all things between. For what is the uni-verse but *the
one song?* All we need to do is alter our perception and open
ourselves to the sibilant hiss of Creation for as part of creation
we must surely understand its cadence. To accept this process is
to embrace a miracle for we all have that latent ability to translate, and truly understand, that which was previously considered mysterious and unknowable – the incessant broadcast of
the 'invisible' world, the cosmos and beyond.'

From Guidance

Before we answer the question as regards the current level of our
psychic ability we must look at the definition of the word 'psychic'
to clarify what we mean.

Reclaiming Words and Meanings

Perhaps psychic (*psyche*-ic) is not a word that has much credibility
to us at present but the whole subject area of spirituality is currently
riddled with inadequate, emotive words and we have to use
something! From the word spiritual itself, which carries all of those

connotations of religion, (and therefore perhaps, guilt, control, alienation, disbelief or confusion) to the words that describe our way of relating to spirit, we are limited to our present vocabulary. But let us be clear, here psychic means *of the psyche*, or soul, and not something that is over-the-top or questionable in its authenticity.

To be psychic is to *be in tune with the soul*, both of others and ourselves. It means that we are willing and able to tune in to energies outside our own and give credence and acknowledgement to the unseen in an intelligent, sensitive and measured way. The key word here is *sensitive* as this is often preferred as a title for a psychic person. A sensitive would certainly choose to sit quietly on a hilltop to sense the unseen presences around them rather than conducting an ill-advised séance in search of dramatic effects to impress people. Real psychism or sensitivity is nothing to do with showmanship or cheap horror movie-style thrills. This is not to say there can't be genuinely disturbing things about spirit connection and we shall, in the course of this book, discuss these aspects. However, the notion of spirit-awareness we are discussing here has little to do with melodrama and everything to do with subtle, often wonderful, energies. This is why we need to employ our own innate sensitivity when dealing with such understated presences and feelings.

What Does It mean to be Psychic Today?
We can assume that just as we all have some degree of musical aptitude, manual dexterity or mental agility, all of us have some level of psychism or sensitivity. As we have already established, we are all born with this awareness and our current level of perception only depends on to what degree we have buried or forgotten this inherent skill. Yet no one can completely switch off their inner wisdom and

so it would be acceptable to suggest, even to the most disbelieving of individuals, that we all have the ability to be intuitive and to act wisely on that intuition. This could also be described as our having, to whatever degree, a reliably profound insight into the unseen along with the inner knowing that proceeds from this.

In this work we will come to refer to this as *seeing* and *knowing* – a combination of inner vision and deep discernment. The innate gift of seeing and knowing that we have witnessed within ourselves or others, however great or small this may be, may enable us to concur now with the premise that we are all psychically sensitive. Yet this doesn't mean we are in a position to call ourselves a psychic, any more than a halting ability to pick up a tune with one finger on a keyboard means we are a musician or the skill to add up a few figures in mentally at a supermarket check-out makes us a mathematician. It just means we all have that inbuilt faculty to psychically *see* and *know* and can uncover it and use it, just as we use our ability to add up in our heads, when we need to. It also means that we can develop what we already have.

So, as we all possess some innate psychism we can all benefit from reading this book to get fundamental knowledge and practical experience of how to use our skills more effectively. We may, if we discover our gifts to be quite pronounced, decide that we do wish to become an active psychic or spiritwalker – a person who lives and works with unseen energies for the good of the All. Yet even if we do decide to become an active spiritwalker this need not be our sole role as we can, for example, be a chef and a spiritwalker, or a mother/nurse/spiritwalker or a mechanic/father/spiritwalker. We can enhance our current role in life with our spiritwalking or we can devote all of our time to it and make a living from helping others in this way. How far we take it is up to us. This is a manual that will help us to enhance our own strengths and identify any weaknesses for the purposes of both personal empowerment and altruistic fulfilment.

We all have the capacity to re-member and to broaden our perceptions to include the unseen worlds and spirit. Indeed, in a perfect society we would all have such learning and exploration as our birth-rite; it would be encouraged from childhood as a tool for living fully. Yet at present we live in a world that has no intention of teaching its youth about their true spiritual nature, a world with terrible divisions between things that are seen let alone unseen. Some us are more inclined to challenge this bias towards the physical aspects of being than others and indeed some of us are better equipped to do so than others, naturally. If we have reached this point in the book then we can surely assume our willingness to tackle these matters and so we can proceed with confidence, as potential spiritwalkers, trusting that our inherent abilities can be developed from here on in.

How Can We Assess Our Current Psychic Aptitude?

Let us begin by discerning our current level of receptivity or sensitivity. We may have already ascertained a certain amount of inner information about this when we analysed our soul type/traits. Here let us expand our knowledge by asking ourselves some more simple questions.

Clearly we need to see how many questions we can answer in the affirmative, and how strong our response is to them. It would also be well to note from the outset if the answers to these questions come easily to us or if we have to really delve deeply inside of ourselves for them. There is no rule on how many affirmative responses make us truly psychic, nor is there a perfect score to attain – the aim is only self-knowledge and an acknowledgement of the skills and experiences we have to build on. We certainly should not give up just because we only have five moderately positive responses! Just those five responses can tell us that we have a natural level of sensitivity in some areas that can be strengthened and added to. Everyone has something to develop and it is our willingness to engage with this self-development that holds the key to our success as spiritwalkers.

Before we continue, it is inevitable that some of the points that are raised in the following questions will be new to us and as such may cause us confusion at this stage. This is nothing to be concerned about. Such points will undoubtedly crop up at some further juncture in this book so that we may really begin to understand their relevance and purpose within spiritwalking and the unseen.

Twenty Questions Which Reveal Our Innate/Current Soul Sensitivity Levels

1. *Yearning*: Do we sometimes/often 'want to go home' but don't really know what this means? Do we have a sense of apartness or not belonging and a longing to be with others who understand us? Have we felt that we belong to another race other than humanity or are from another place than Earth (or at least from a different kind of Earth)?

2. *Seeking*: Do we sometimes/often have a compulsion to learn about 'the unknown' and have a moderate/high interest in 'the unexplained'? Have we been involved in sects or religious groups as we try to find answers to the many questions we have surrounding the meaning of life and death?

3. *Soul-searching*: Do we strongly relate to people, and indeed other beings, through contact with their eyes and sometimes feel acutely attracted or repelled without really knowing why?

4. *Knowing*: Do we sometimes/often have prophetic/pre-cognitive dreams dealing with personal, local or global events? Or do we have accurate waking feelings and intuitions that something will happen to us or to someone else in the near future? Conversely do we ever perceive unknown things that have previously occurred? And do we ever know what someone will say next or who is on the telephone/at the door before we answer it? Do we find that we regularly have access to the correct answers for quiz questions that we should have no knowledge of and do we easily come by the winning numbers for competitions?

5. *Sensing*: Can we sometimes/often pick up atmospheres that others seem unaware of, including feelings of deep foreboding, danger, great joy, sadness or tension in the place that we are in? Are we aware of presences that make the area around us turn unnaturally cold or our skin prickle/hairs raise up/spine tingle etc.? Do we regularly become positively or negatively affected by atmospheric pressure and weather changes?

6. *Scenting*: Do we sometimes/often smell unseen things that others seem unaware of including strong perfumes, faeces, damp, electrical burning, flowers? Do these smells then vanish without trace?

7. *Hearing*: Do we sometimes/often hear things that others appear unaware of including, knocking, ringing, banging, voices, crying, instruments or the sounds of invisible creatures? Can we regularly hear a very high-pitched, piercing whistle for a few sec-

onds in one ear, hear 'Morse code' type signals or inexplicable electronic/buzzing/whirring sounds?

8. *Seeing*: Can we sometimes/often see things which others appear unaware of including forms, lights, energy, shadows? Do we see glowing energy or colours around people/ creatures/trees/plants? Have we seen what we would consider to be beings of other races, for example faeries or aliens, either outside or in our own home?

9. *Remembering*: Do we sometimes/often have affecting vivid dreams waking memories which do not relate to our current life nor to any time period in history or to a place/event/race/ language/religion of which we are consciously unaware/have any knowledge of? Do we ever experience speaking in an unknown language/tongue, whether consciously or unconsciously? Do we have inexplicable attractions to certain persons/places/eras that are emotional and deep?

10. *Communing*: Do we sometimes/often have active communi-cation with beings that others are not aware of? As a child did we feel as if we were surrounded by presences and consequently felt either afraid or delighted by them? Do we feel as if we are not alone, even when we are physically solitary?

11.*Time Travelling*: Do we sometimes/often feel as if we are in several places simultaneously and find our current existence overlaid with other feelings and images we cannot readily grasp or explain, as if we were living several lives at once? Do we experience missing time or a feeling of losing conscious aware-ness of our present environs although our body had apparently continued with what it was doing? Do we sometimes/often have trouble in recalling how we got somewhere or how we came to be doing something? Do we have repeated strong feelings of *deja vu* or even *jamais vu* (feeling that familiar surroundings are strange) and high incidences of apparent coincidences or synchronicity?

12. *Receiving*: Can we sometimes/often pick up on energies that belong to other people or places and find it hard to distinguish them from our own feelings? Can we pick up images/feelings/sensations for touching someone else's property, say a piece of jewellery or key? Do we frequently feel energetically drained, or overloaded, when being with certain people?

13.*Transmitting*: Can we sometimes/often can make people feel better by putting our hands on them? Or by spending time counselling them, or even just being with them? And do we usually end up giving far more than we receive back from them both physically and emotionally?

14. *Affecting*: Can we sometimes/often become dramatically influenced by certain pieces of music, songs or instruments which can send us into another place/mood/set of feelings? Likewise can a poem, painting or environment transport us completely into other states of being, be they positive or negative?

15. *Empathising*: Do we sometimes/often know where someone has pain or discomfort? Do we feel as if the pain of another is our own? And do we feel tremendous emotional pain about the plight of other people/the planet/the creatures and try our best to help in any way we can?

16. *Generating*: Do we sometimes/often affect electrical equipment, radios, cars, watches or machinery adversely or have a high turnover of light bulbs in our home? Can we feel a strong tingling sensation in our hands/feet/face when we are in the

proximity of something powerful like a standing stone or an electricity pylon? Does being in a room with a great deal of electrical equipment make us feel strange and nervous? Do we fear, or have we ever been struck by, lightning?

17. *Astral Travelling*: Can we sometimes/often leave our physical body and travel in spirit to other places, either deliberately or without meaning to do so?

18. *Disturbing*: Have we sometimes/often witnessed 'poltergeist' activity around us including banging doors, loud inexplicable noises, disappearing personal objects such as keys or books, reappearing personal objects that turn up in bizarre places (for example, a shoe on top of a light shade or a necklace in the fridge), apports (things appearing that didn't belong to us in the first place), inappropriate smells for the location/circumstances, inexplicable temperature fluctuations, a disturbed atmosphere etc.? Are we afraid of the idea of ghosts or of their actuality in our life?

19. *Suffering*: Do we sometimes/often have chronic health problems including any of the following: multiple allergies, I.B.S, depression, panic attacks, migraine, addiction, M.E /C.F.S, sudden intolerance to substances including foods and chemicals, transient rashes/irritation, nervous tension and any other persistent condition which defies explanation or treatment? Do we feel as if we have too few 'layers' and are too sensitive and open to deal with the pain of the world, hence becoming sick ourselves?

20. *Divining*: Do we sometimes/often work with tools which allow us to accurately predict/prophesy or gain insight, tools such as a pendulum, cards, crystal ball etc or else disciplines such as palmistry, astrology etc.?

Giving Ourselves Credence

Questing for inner and outer wisdom is actively promoted in our spiritwalking and ultimately it is hoped that looking at these twenty questions will have encouraged us to look beyond what we already know about ourselves. Perhaps we would never have considered some of these questions as pre-requisite for sensitivity/psychic awareness before and are surprised to discover that what we had just considered 'odd' about ourselves actually denotes a pronounced level of sensitivity/awareness.

Of course, we may never have considered such aspects as relevant before due to how we have been brought up and lived our lives until now. Because of this it may be well to also ask ourselves these additional questions:

- Were we strongly discouraged from considering our innate gifts as being of any serious importance? Were we told they were not real or dismissed as silly?
- Was the word psychic, or the 'supernatural' in general, connected with all things absurd, peculiar, frightening or bad?
- Were we encouraged to follow only one religious path and to consider all other beliefs as frivolous, ridiculous or just plain evil?
- Did we feel our parents/guardians/peers to be supportive or derisive of things that they didn't understand?
- Did they themselves ever divulge psychic feelings or experiences and if so what was their opinion or outlook on them?

It is very interesting to consider all of these factors as they will afford us a more rounded view of our present status and what chance we have had so far to develop or, indeed, to give ourselves credence at all.

Perhaps, even if we had considered ourselves as sensitive previously we would have been very reluctant to consider ourselves as powerful. It can be daunting to acknowledge just how sensitive and aware of energies we truly are in such a cut and dried, hard and fast society but it can be even harder to accept the level of personal power (and, therefore, personal *response*-ability) that we all have. By power here we refer to the strength, courage, wisdom and compassion that comes with working with energy as an able conduit and interpreter of that energy. We do not mean control or dominion over others or the land (power *over*) or even an indominitable inner strength that is purely used for our own self-ish gain (power *within*) rather we simply mean that we have acknowledged the eternal nature within us and have the ability to let spirit flow through us effectively (power *with*). Perhaps we can now give ourselves permission to really embrace this natural, wonderful side of ourselves at last and fully take on board the fact that we are spirit-walkers – those power-full people who live and work with the unseen gladly, for the good of the All. People like us are needed in this modern world!

Our own credence and self-faith are essential if we are to progress effectively from here. We need to rely on our own inner judgement on what is 'real' or, indeed, right for us and to cease to take our cues about acceptability from mainstream society, the media, figures of authority and even our neighbours, friends or colleagues. It is strongly suggested that we take this time to really weed out what are our innate prejudices, fears and hang-ups about psychism and what are external views/feelings. Remember, we should only keep what is ours (which we now have a deeper understanding of) although even that will undoubtedly be questioned and modified as we progress on the spiritual seekers path.

So, now we really have a good idea of our psychic sensitivity, based on moderate or strong positive responses to the twenty questions, we can ask ourselves what kind of spiritwalker we are, primarily, or, indeed, what manner of blend we may be in time, with training and dedication.

How do We Perceive Spirit-Information and Discern Unseen Energies?

Here there are two categories to our questioning – how we *receive* and how we *transmit*. We may find we are strong at one and weaker at the other. The aim, in time, is to be in balance as a transmitter and a receiver of spiritual information.

1. *Seer/Clairvoyant*

Receiver: Do we primarily *observe* energies (and even spirits) with our physical eyes? Have we witnessed forms that appear real to us in the manifest level of existence although others are not aware of them? And do we readily see the energies around beings as clearly as we see the being themselves? **Transmitter:** Are we able to see, with our physical sight, anything that we choose to, for example, if we want to manifest a ball of light can we actually create this and see it clearly?

2. *Visionary*

Receiver: Do we mainly *en-vision* energy/spirits with our inner, or mind's, eye? That is, can we close our eyes and picture any being that may be present with our inner sight even though we cannot physically see them? Do spirits/external unseen sources send us bold visual imagery that we can see in our head? **Transmitter:** Is our power of visualisation so strong that we can conjure up any being or form that we choose to in our imagination? Can we easily create new inner realms by the power of creative thought?

3. Clairsentient/Sensitive

Receiver: Do we chiefly get a physical *sense* of the presence of spirits or unseen energies? When there is an external energy or spirit-presence close by does our hair stand on end or our spine, hands or face tingle? Or perhaps we get goosebumps or shivers when there is a non-physical presence in our proximity? Do we get sensations like stomach-churning, or localised pain, or warmth where there is no external heat? **Transmitter:** Can we pass on any sensation we are feeling to those around us or project it into the room? Can we give healing through laying on of hands?

4. Empathetic/Psychometrist

Receiver: Do we most commonly *feel* the nearness of spirits or energies? Do we pick up sentiments such as extreme sadness or profound joy from the ether? Can we receive emotive feelings, such as those of fear or loss, easily from places, people, objects and unseen forces? Is the information we get from unseen energies/spirits given to us in terms of emotional resonance? **Transmitter:** Can we transform such a feeling into a different one, for instance, modifying anger into forgiveness, and turbulence/disturbance into peace? And can we pass on any given feeling to another person/spirit/place/object?

5. *Clairaudient*

Receiver: Do we most often physically *hear* the spirits or energies involved? Can we pick up sounds from the ether that others are unaware of such as hissing, whistling or buzzing? Do we hear the voices of unseen presences? Can we witness music without a seen source or hear 'spirit-song'? **Transmitter:** Are we able to talk to the spirits and get a response? Can we raise the frequency that we are hearing, changing its pitch or volume? Can we put out sound into the ether for a specific purpose, for instance a resonance that would facilitate healing?

6. *Scenter*

Receiver: Do we most readily use our sense of physical smell to sense the presence of spirits or energies? Is it a particular aroma that alerts us to a resonance or being? **Transmitter:** Can we use scent to attract certain energies to us?

7. *Communicant*

Receiver: Do we for the most part pick up *words* or information in our head that alert us to the presence of spirits/energies? Is our interaction with the etheric/unseen primarily language based? Do we witness resonance/being by linguistic cues even when we cannot physically detect the source of the information? Are we able to piece together these given words to produce a coherent dialogue or factual piece? Are we able to write down these words and be guided, creating 'channelled' writing? **Transmitter:** Can we send questions into the ether and get answers? Can we write to the spirits and get written responses in return?

8. *Diviner*

Receiver: Do we predominantly gauge our psychic information through the use of tools (pendulum/cards/runestones etc) and the responses they give to us? Is our ability to witness energies best transcribed through a physical implement? **Transmitter:** Can we contact or link with spirits and energies at will through our chosen tool? Can we then communicate using our chosen method/instrument/medium?

We may well be a blend of theses types so we shouldn't worry if we are not able to pigeonhole ourselves too tightly as ever this list acts a guide. And, as we have said, if we are not particularly gifted as yet as any one of these types of spiritwalker then we can chose which type would we like to be, focussing in on how we would like to develop ourselves. If we have a broad sensitivity, as revealed by the previous twenty questions, then it is reasonable to assume that at this stage we may pick our own area for special study.

In the next chapters we will look at ways that we can begin to develop these skills and strengthen our connection to the unseen. Yet before this we must learn the most fundamental practice of a reliable and successful spiritwalker – psychic protection.

CHAPTER FOUR

THE PSYCHIC HIGHWAY CODE

'You are spiritwalker – you are sensitive. You are not wearing
all the other layers that other souls clothe themselves in. You,
my friend, are here without extra coats of varnish to make you
resilient to this world. You are vulnerable even in your
strength. The coats you can put on are not of the human world
but rather of the unseen – they are psychic protection and
spirit connection.'

From Guidance

Here is, perhaps, the most important section of the book, providing
us as it does with the very foundation of effective spiritwalking.
Without it, our practice is insecure at best and dangerous at worst.
To go back to our electrical analogy, this is the chapter that allows
us to 'wire the plug correctly' so that we are safe to act as a
conduit for energy without 'blowing a fuse' or terminating the
supply. There would be no point in our having fabulous state-of-
the-art computer equipment, set up to transmit and receive long
distance communications, without a correctly wired plug! Likewise
there is no point in walking with spirit if we cannot be sure we
are safely earthed and correctly hooked up to a pure source of
power.

Before we begin with this vital work let us just answer a few
questions as regards the meaning and purpose of psychic, or soul,
protection.

Why Protect?

We need to be protected psychically, or spiritually, every time we open up to unseen forces or extraneous energies. There are beings who dwell between worlds – in other energetic realities, or etheric levels to the one we are currently in – who have codes of conduct that are distinctly *other* to our own. This does not mean that they are necessarily better or worse but rather unbeneficial to us, just as cat hair is unbeneficial to a person with an allergy. As we all know, cat hair isn't inherently evil yet it will be a problem to some none the less. When we extend our energy beyond our own tried and tested material boundaries we will always encounter other spiritual sources and forces that are unlike our own and although we cannot say that the astral levels are full of nasty, vindictive presences we can categorically state that it is best to be protected just in case our own essence does not respond well to another it may encounter.

Protection is rather like being inoculated before going to a country unlike our own with its own ailments to which we are unaccustomed. We are physically unprepared for a virus or disease that may attack us when we engage in foreign travel so we take precautions. These precautions are not fatalistic rather they are sensible and can be undertaken with a light-heart as we will know that we are far more able to enjoy our experience abroad if we are not sick. Likewise, on returning to our own country we would not appreciate having brought a foreign virus back with us and would no doubt in retrospect wish we had taken the time to inoculate ourselves adequately before we went. So it is with psychic protection. It's just a sensible precaution that will make our travelling in the unseen realms far more enjoyable and ensure our daily life between astral journeys is untroubled and psychically healthy. Like inoculations, psychic protection certainly isn't here to frighten anyone, rather to give confidence. Although it may seem to take up time initially, in the long run such an outlay of effort is well worth it.

What Are We Protecting?

The simple answer to this question is that we are protecting our life-force energy, that which is translated into the unique soul that dwells within our equally unique human body. We are safeguarding our essential energy, that which is beyond the physical yet housed within it, the unseen aspect of us that resides in the seen aspect.

Although our bodies may seem of tantamount importance to us right now, especially as we are reading this with physical eyes and holding a solid and manifest book, it is the eternal aspect of self, the soul, which is the more valuable. Although this may be hard for us to fully accept, especially when our souls live inside something that seems so essential to us right now, it is the *spiritual* aspect of us that needs our care and attention for the body is just a vehicle by which the soul may experience. This statement may sound glib at best and at worst to be a denigration of the sacred gift of flesh but it isn't, far from it. Rather it is a statement that allows us to respect the vehicle of our learning fully whilst still being able to give priority to the eternal spirit that dwells within.

We are not our bodies; we know this from our re-membering of our own soul's traits. We say 'I have a body' and not 'I am a body', thus acknowledging that mysterious 'I nature' beyond flesh. Life is a drama of invisible and visible and tending both aspects of our being keeps us in balance. We can honour the body even as we acknowledge its temporary nature and so protect it as the climate or circumstance dictates. We know we can protect our bodies with winter woollens, medicines, good nutrition, exercise and quality shelter but our only means of protecting the soul is by psychic, or spiritual, protection.

When Should We Protect?

Clearly we should psychically protect ourselves when we wish to resist anything energetic outside of ourselves, be that a force or a spirit-being, which may interfere with our eternal soul essence or our bodily comfort. If we have engaged in the questions we have so far set ourselves, and consequently have decided we are suitable spiritwalker material, then we must surely realise that we already have a heightened sensitivity to the energies around us. This means we will need to pay particular attention to the well-being of our soul that perhaps other people do not, being as they are not as receptive or responsive as we are. Psychic protection is *essential* to sensitive spiritwalkers.

Some of us may find the following suggestions of when we need to psychically protect ourselves over cautious, even in the light of our having to take special care of our spiritual selves. Yet it is worthwhile to offer these ideas as possibilities to consider if we are feeling particularly open to unseen influences or energies at a particular time. It may also be that they can clarify for us why we have felt unbalanced or even personally drained or attacked when taking part on one of the situations I am now about to share. Do not be daunted or afraid by this list of suggestions, they are only examples of what may affect us.

Circumstances that we can consider and which may require our psychic protection include:

a) **Entering into a physical situation that is highly 'peopled'**, especially if the people involved are an unknown quantity. There may have to be a degree of sharing or opening up to others in this environment. This would include seminars and parties but basically means any event in which we have to be responsive for a sustained period to the unpredictable energies of a group.

b) **Attending an event where there may be differences of opinion, hostility or clash of interests**, especially any circumstance when passionate debate is to ensue and tempers are bound to fray. Such events may include protests or demonstrations, aggressive or highly competitive contests and discussions on contentious issues.

c) **Attending a venue where there may be a considerable use of mind-altering drugs** or being in the close presence of persistent drug or alcohol users. Spiritwalkers cannot generally dabble in drugs and only take mind-altering substances in respectful circumstances for the purpose of specific questing into other realms of consciousness. Random use of unpredictable chemical substances is not advisable for a psychically open person. When we are intoxicated then we are clearly not in control of ourselves and unscrupulous unseen forces can, and often do, take the opportunity to invade our personal space. Also addictive or excessive behaviour is destructive and degrading and so we can only expect to attract energies that operate at that low level. More on this in Chapter Seventeen on *keeping it clean*.

d) **Working with, or being in, an environment with those who have significant mental illness**. Those how are 'not in their right mind' for whatever reason may be in the grip of a psychic attack.

This is not always the case but it is a bit of a chicken and egg situation. Did the attack cause the imbalance the person is suffering or did the chemical imbalance attract the predatory spirit? In either case, being in the prolonged presence of someone whose energies are highly unbalanced is not advisable for a sensitive soul unless they are well psychically protected.

e) **Spending time in a hospital, nursing home, hospice** or anywhere where there has been significant pain, suffering or repeated death. This is clearly due to the lingering energies of sadness, distress, rage, confusion etc. as well as the possibility of there being lost souls hanging around the last place they were on Earth who may latch onto us like a beacon in their darkness.

f) **Entering into a situation where there will be exaggerated fear or anxiety.** Although we may opt to help a road traffic accident victim, or a bereaved person, or a terminally ill person, or anyone who has an inflated sense of terror about a circumstance such as someone in the grip of a phobia or panic attack, we can ensure we are psychically protected from absorbing any unnecessarily disturbing, unsettling energy ourselves.

g) **Going into an environment where people are opened up psychically** and/or actively doing psychic work. Such events may include psychic fairs, esoteric workshops or religious gatherings. Opening up psychically may be permissible in a situation where the participants have built up familiarity and trust with each other, and there is a high level of expertise, but not advisable if the situation is unknown, unpredictable or very large. Not all psychics or spiritworkers are scrupulous or even particularly adept and they may only be aiming as high as the human astral and not beyond. We shall be looking in more detail at the human, or low, astral in Chapter Six.

h) **A scenario in which there is a perceived power struggle or disagreement**, such as situations with relations or colleagues in which there is conflict or manipulation. Family relations can be one of the most tense and difficult areas we will ever have to face as it is those who know us best who may feel they can abuse our good will and sensitivity by playing on our heartstrings and using emotional blackmail. It is well to be protected from invasive or manipulative energy even if it comes from our nearest and dearest who may not even realise what they are doing. Of course, it is better to sort out such situations than to be protected from them but as an interim step it is helpful.

i) **When entering a 'sacred site',** a place that has been used for magical focus or religious ritual recently or in the past. Anywhere that has been created for people to use and worship in, somewhere where people have opened up to external forces. For example an old village church or a much visited stone circle.

j) **When entering an ancient or historic place**, such as a stately home, old house, castle or the original, un-modernised part of a town. If we are sensitive or attuned to energies, as spiritwalkers undoubtedly are, then we will act as a flame for any 'spirit moths', or trapped energies, that may still be residing in these areas or places. Although we not feel the need to be fully protected is well for us to have our guard up in such environs and to be ready to activate full protection if we feel any unseen energies or beings around us.

k) **Anywhere with a bloody or traumatic past**, the site of murders, executions, battles, gaols, abattoirs etc. Here, for obvious reasons, we will definitely need to take protective precautions before entering unless *substantial* spiritual clearing and energy raising has been deliberately applied to the area previous to our arrival. If the site has not received any healing or effective psychic cleansing then it would be wise for the spirit-walker to steer clear of it, or, at the very least, question their motivations for needing to be there at all. At this stage in our development we cannot consider being there to engage in such clearing work ourselves. As with all the pertinent points about spirit and energy that have been raised so far we will come back to them in more detail as we progress.

l) **Anytime we open up to the spirits, energies and influences that are outside of our own.** This could be in meditation, prayer, tarot reading or divination communing with the companion spirits or other helper beings or giving healing.

To sum up we need protection in:

- Any circumstance which is unknown, unpredictable or volatile
- Any crowd or gathering which is not stable
- Anywhere where we feel vulnerable or ill at ease
- Anywhere were there is an active opening up to external energy
- Anywhere designated as a place where people worship or engage in rituals
- Anywhere with a considerable human history, be that known or unknown
- Anytime we tune in to spirits, energies and outside influences

How Do We Protect?

To do this we must address, then develop, what is unquestionably to be our most valuable asset as a spiritwalker. Although we already use this inherent ability to one degree or another it can be purposefully honed into a powerful catalyst for transformation. It is a way by which we may affect the deep change that some may call magic, for the outcomes we may see from such focused working may indeed seem magical.

This most potent natural resource is our *intent*.

Although in our spiritwalking we will come to concentrate on the external allies we may work with, such as the companion spirits we may call guides, our internal ally – that of our own intent – is perhaps the strongest assistant we may call upon. We can refer to our intent as *the directed power of our soul*. It is the essential energy of our eternal being (life-force) wilfully focussed and channelled and therefore it is, quite literally, our *will power*.

Recalling how we likened spirit energy to electricity We can acknowledge that working with this will power is the equivalent of directing electricity down a wire and into the device that we wish to animate, such as a CD player or vacuum cleaner. Our directing our will power into something we intend to happen, in this case our becoming psychically protected, makes the intention become a reality.

Just as:

Electrical power + active connection = an operational appliance
so does:
Life-force energy (will power) + directed focus (intent) = a fulfilled objective

The second equation is just as simple as the first equation yet it often eludes us as it deals with unseen power. However, if we think about it we cannot see electricity any more than we can see spirit, or life-force energy, but we have just come to believe in its existence because we have experienced its presence in our lives. We believe it because we see its effect. In order for us to experience the power of unseen energy in our lives we would be well served to accept that *we will see it because we believe it*. When we can own and acknowledge both the personal and the universal power of unseen energy we can siphon a stream of power from it to animate, or charge up, a specific outcome like protection and we can do this just effortlessly as we accept that our vacuum cleaner will start up as soon as we plug in and flick a switch. This realisation, and its subsequent implementation, will truly change our lives.

Let's now go one step further into revealing how intent works in a way that is just as effective as any electrical appliance. As we have previously discussed in this book, we are all part of an energetic universe that is made manifest (or not) by differences in vibrational rate. The frequency at which energy vibrates defines its own personal existence in either the material (seen) or the immaterial (unseen) world/s. When we apply our intent, directing our own energy, we cease to witness life as only three dimensional, unyielding and fixed and instead choose to enter the flow of energy that is omnipresent and multi-dimensional – *we become part of a circuit of power*. By doing this we actively realise the nature of reality and can therefore affect change simply by tuning into the vibrational frequency that we wish to reach. This is not too far beyond our grasp as we already have an excellent analogy for it.

Let us think of one of the big old analogue radios of the recent past that allowed us to move the dial to a radio station broadcasting in places such as Luxembourg, Oslo or Prague. When we moved the dial to Luxembourg we picked up the frequency broadcasted from that transmitter and our receiving radio translated it into something that we wanted to hear. The sound waves coming from Luxembourg existed before we tuned into them, they just needed a means to be made known. In this way the soundwaves from other broadcasts also existed concurrently but we were not tuned into their particular frequency so we were not able to hear them. Like radio waves coming from Luxembourg, or mobile phone messages sent from Cardiff to Glasgow, or television pictures being sent from a station in London to a home in Norwich, etheric energy is all around us right now, waiting for us to use our directed intent to tune into its high or fast frequency and use it.

So, as spiritwalkers when we align ourselves with a specific outcome, in this case psychic protection, we will achieve what we set out to do purely because we tune in and *intend it to be so*, having faith in the presence of life-force energy all around us and in the process of directed transmission and reception. We can all act as earthers and directors of life-force energy in order to achieve a desired outcome and with practice we can do it as easily, and as deliberately, as tuning a radio.

With this in mind let us now take the next step towards using our intent to psychically protect ourselves. For this we need a system to apply our intent to.

A Working System of Psychic Protection

The techniques we are about to explore will offer us a framework which is tried and tested but which can be embellished to suit the individual.

To begin, let us state that to be effectively protected we need to be:

1. *Positioned* in a way that allows us to be *earthed* whilst being conducive to the conduction of energy
2. *Joined* by our companion spirits, the unseen beings that come for our highest good, along with any other protective forces that can help us
3. *Sealed* within a protective bubble – an energetic edifice
4. *Covered* by protective symbols
5. *Attuned* to a protective frequency
6. *Operating* within a statement of intent
7. *Connected* to the Source

These are the prerequisites of any serious protective procedure to be engaged in before opening up to any external energies. Although we will also learn a more rapid response to unexpected situations, a kind of protection-on-the-go for adhoc use, it is well for us to begin here with a comprehensive guide.

Before we start the process it is helpful to state that as with so many aspects of spiritwalking protection is a very *symbolic*, rather than a literal, act. Working with the unseen we are engaged with the subtle and the mythic rather than the nuts and bolts of daily manifest living. Symbolism is the universal language we can employ when entering into an unseen dialogue, either with ourselves or the wider astral worlds, for we will come to recognise signs, shapes, scents, colours and sounds as a language beyond our everyday idiom.

So let us begin our protective routine, applying our will

power to make our intention a living reality using evocative emblematic means.

The Full Protection Procedure

1. Positioning – *Earthing and Grounding*

When we think about positioning ourselves in order to effectively transmit and receive energy, which we will need to do to protect ourselves, the tree is the most eloquent symbol for our purposes. By aligning ourselves with the great primal tree we connect with all the strength of the Tree of Life as well as the World Tree of myth and legend. Both of these archetypes bring us the key message of 'tree as bridge', acting as a link, or pivot, between worlds: the *axis mundi*. When we align ourselves with the primal tree we too become a great bridge between the unseen and the seen – our body spans the distance between that which is manifest and that which is ethereal so that we may unite the two in a place of power within.

When we are protecting ourselves via this potent tree symbolism, we are both drawing up earth energy from below and drawing down ambient power from the wider ether, just as a tree draws in water and sunlight via roots and branches. These external energies we allow to flow with, and strengthen, our own innate spirit force, allowing a new blend of power to course through us. Thus we become enlivened as well as protected, feeling our inherent potency grow as it blends with the sustaining earth and sky. The stability of the physical realm and the sustenance of the ethereal realm are mingled in the cauldron of our selves. The trunk of the tree becomes this cauldron, the living wood by which an alchemical process takes place, giving us the magnified force of creation with which to operate more efficiently.

The first suggested posture for protection, using the tree model is below.

This shows the figure sitting with a straight supported spine. The straight spine is paramount in all our positions as it represents our main conduit, the equivalent of the tree trunk, through which the energy, or the vital sap of life, flows. Our spine is the clear pipeline through which our spirit-current will circulate unimpeded, just as a solid, straight trunk helps a tree to

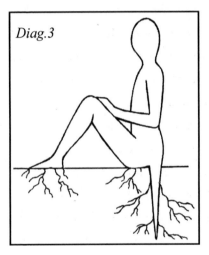

Diag.3

access the energy of the sun. Of course, life-force is strong enough to flow through any conduit but it helps if we aid that process by emulating a successful natural model. Our symbolic gesture aligns us with our purpose.

So, we can imagine the spine connecting with the ground via the buttocks which are planted squarely to provide us with a good base. Small roots may then be seen (in the mind's eye), or felt, to be pushing themselves out from our buttocks and moving down into the earth. Now the spine pushes down too, at the point of our tailbone, into a lengthening tap root. This major root then delves into the soil at our base, pushing into the ground, connecting us ever more deeply into the land below and anchoring, or earthing, us in physical reality. This great taproot is like a main wire up or down which vital energy can also flow. It is the *central interface* between the ether and the Earth/ the spiritual and the manifest/ our soul and our physical self. Subsidiary roots, or lesser wires, sprout from this taproot and spread outwards underneath us.

We may like to ask at this stage what we should do if we are not seated directly on the land and find it hard to imagine our roots pushing through the earth below us? What if we are in a modern building with a concrete floor or in a room high above the ground in a block of flats? In these scenarios I myself have seen my strong central root pushing through the concrete with little resistance, rather like a tenacious dandelion pushing through concrete paving slabs. I have also imagined my tap root snaking through the space between storeys and pushing down into the wooden floorboards beneath me, with my subsidiary roots actually growing into the wood. Thus I feel myself becoming part of the structure of the building which is itself rooted by its foundations, wires and pipes into the land. Unless we are seated directly on the earth outside then we will need to be flexible and use our imagination, and the sacred gift of our intent, to creatively get around such brainteasers posed to us by modern urban living.

So, let us return to our posture, as shown in Diag. 3. Here we can see that the legs are loosely bent and the feet planted on the ground. Not surprisingly our feet are also rooting downwards into the ground beneath us, contacting the earth and drawing up energy just as a tree does. This posture gives us the greatest input of earth energy possible as well as making sure we are fully connected to the manifest world even as we contact spirit. Of course we may not feel comfortable with bending the knees at all, rather preferring to have the legs stretched straight out in front of us with the back of the heel resting on the ground only. In this case it would be only our heels that are rooting down. This straight legged posture has the benefit of providing us with the bodily equivalent of unbent wires – straight channels by which the energy may flow easily – yet it does not give us such a stable connected feeling the bent legged posture has. It is really a matter of choice as both can offer us a symbolic reference point.

Diag. 3 also shows us the hands are resting lightly on the knees, with palms either up or down. However, if our legs are straight out then the hands will naturally rest on the thighs in the same position. Symbolically speaking, if the hands face palm up we are in a position that is receiving or open whilst if we choose to have the palms facing down onto our body then we are making a further grounding connection whilst keeping the circuit of power sealed within us. Such gestures have their own personal resonances that we will no doubt find over time and there is no right or wrong, as such. The thing to remember is that all actions should have meaning to us and not just be done because we have been told it is correct.

Although the position shown in Diag. 3 is tried and tested it should be said that it has long since been understood by Yogis and sages that sitting in meditation with the legs crossed, or in the 'lotus position', is preferable. The lotus is a flower that seeds and fruits simultaneously and its symbolism means that the traditional lotus posture is whole unto itself, the body making a complete circuit and allowing no energy to escape through stretched out limbs. However well it may work it is clearly a pose that is difficult to hold for those who are less flexible and for such efforts it requires a real resonance with the symbolism involved. As it is not assumed that those who engage in spiritwalking will be fully able bodied it is well to mention some alternatives to such a posture.

We may find it easier to hold a reclining position, rather than a seated one of whichever variety, and this is fine, again as long as the symbolism of what we are doing is taken into account. We need points by which we can root ourselves into the earth, ensuring that we are making contact with the floor squarely with our head and either our hands, feet or both. For this we can have knees bent and the feet flat on the floor, as in Diag.3, or the legs straight out with the heels down. Or we can splay our legs like a frog, bending the knees and letting the legs flop to either side, whilst placing the soles of our feet together, thus making a closed circuit. Clearly whilst we are positioning our legs we also require a way of allowing the spine to conduct energy effectively, keeping it as straight as our body will comfortably let us. We then can imagine the great tap root extending from our spine, leaving

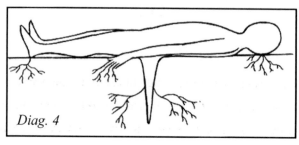

Diag. 4

our tail bone at right angles then delving down, as seen in Diag.4

Obviously if we are taking the model of the tree it might make better sense symbolically if we actually protected ourselves standing up. We can of course stand up for the protection and then sit down after to do any spirit work that follows so we do not tire ourselves. I myself only perform a protective sequence in a standing position if I am outdoors or 'on the hop' in an unexpected circumstance, which can be done discretely. It is extremely helpful to know how positioning ourselves in this way would work so let us look at this stance.

In Diag. 5 we see now that the feet and legs become an extended part of the trunk, or spine, rooting and grounding the energy but allowing it to travel straight up unimpeded. This can

Diag. 5

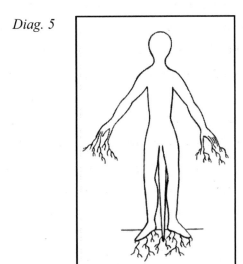

give us a great sense of strength and stability. As we can observe the arms can act as branches without our having to lift them skywards as by splaying we fingers we emulate the reaching action of twigs and shoots. Yet if we are able to do so without drawing unwanted attention to ourselves we can imagine the power moving up through our roots and trunk and into our arms, allowing them to rise. As the energy rises higher in us we can lift the arms up to shoulder, then head level, spreading the fingers and reaching up, just as a tree does, to make that connection with the spirit that dwells all around us. We hold this position for as long as it is feasible, feeling that power coursing up from the earth and simultaneously down from above, circuiting around our body as it pours in and mingles with our own spirit-energy within. This is a stature of *invocation* – a way of inviting power to come into us – as well as being a way of acknowledging and celebrating our own position as potent beings, full of natural dynamism. The arms can duly be lowered when a state of maximum power is felt to be reached.

Positioning of our bodies may seem to be secondary to the actual work of protecting our spirits yet it is complementary, a way of making a valuable statement of intent to ourselves and the energies that dwell outside of our bodies. If we get this aspect right, finding a way that is both comfortable for us physically and evocative for us spiritually, being conducive to the flow and transference of energy, then we may move onto the second stage of calling to the unseen beings who walk with us.

2. Calling the Spirits Who Love Us – *Joining Forces*

Now we have become physically well positioned – being both successfully rooted in physical reality and acting as effective conduits for energy – we need to practice a different kind of meaningful invocation. This is a respectful request for a specific outcome to occur – a kind of *prayer*. In this instance we desire for our guiding spirits, those unseen beings who come to support us for our highest possible good, to aid us in our protection. This we may do whether we know who these spirit guides are at this stage or not. We are simply asking for their strength whilst involving them in our process and acknowledging their existence. Their presence is something that we now need to have faith in, even if we are currently unable to perceive them, nor the consequences of our invoking thoughts or actions. We can be assured that if we call on our guiding spirits, or, as we refer to them here *companion* spirits, they will come.

But why call them at all, especially if we can't witness them yet? Well firstly it seems rather self-defeating to not access this additional power supply, rather like trying to run a business using a small petrol generator when there is an electrical substation at hand. It is well for us to acknowledge, and indeed utilise, the innate power of the companion spirits alongside our own even if we are relying on faith to know the veracity, and efficacy, of what we do. By trusting in the unseen reality of our unseen companions we allow their presence, and their unseen power, to be felt more strongly. It is like opening a channel, or turning on a power supply, rather than blocking it with indifference or denial.

Secondly, we are giving our companion spirits credence and an opportunity to do what they do – which is to walk with us and assist us in our growth. The spirits who have opted to work with us for an incarnation clearly want to get involved and be of service, in accordance with their chosen role of guide. The more we involve these helpful spirits the more they will be able to actively assist us as they cannot, or will not, intervene in our lives unless we ask them to directly. Their relationship with us is indeed as one of guide – one who shows the way but does not force us to follow – and therefore they will not interfere with what we do unless asked to do so. We call them our companions because they are steadfast in their company and they enjoy any interaction with us, even if as yet we are not on personal terms with them. As with any relationship the more we include them in our lives the more we will find ourselves benefiting from the link, especially in times of greater need. We will, over time, come to feel their companionship strongly (even at first it may seem as if we are talking to thin air) and, if we call on them now then by the time we come to meet them properly in Chapter Eight we will be used to their presence in our lives.

So, we are indeed well served by calling upon our (as yet) unknown spiritual mentors. The way we choose to do this is up to us – as long as we follow the basic formula with unerring courtesy we will be effective. Here is an example of how to do this:

'*Spirits who love me, those who come for my highest possible good, be with me now I pray. I ask for your strength as I protect myself. I ask that you allow no external spirit, energy or entity being breach my protection. So may it be by your will and mine.*'

We can of course substitute *spirits who love me* etc. with the actual names of the companion guides when we know them. At this stage it is assumed that we do not have the names of our guiding spirits and so we shall leave this open in our invocation for now.

We can also call on other protective powers at this stage. Many people like to call upon the four elements, and the fifth, ether, to protect and support them in what they do. I would advocate this as, like our working with the tree as a potent symbol, such interaction reminds us of our reliance on the powerful forces of existence, or functions of life, on this planet. It also re-connects us to all Creation and it the energy inherent in the All. This calling on the elements may be kept for a lengthier or deep session of spirit-communion, where utmost energy is required to keep us guarded, or it can be a part of our daily practice if we prefer. Obviously calling to the elements, or to the elemental spirit representatives of earth, air, fire and water, would be especially appropriate when we are conducting our spiritwalking outside.

So, how may we invoke the elements if we so choose? Taking into consideration their qualities, both literal and symbolic, as we have previously discussed we could say something as respectful and evocative as:

'May the power of wholesome earth, of brightening sky, of enlivening flame, of refreshing water and of the sacred essence of ether grow in strength together with me now, protecting me well.'

Or

'Spirits of the earth that nurtures me, of the breath that sustains me, of the hearth that warms me, of the blood that flows through me and of the eternal life-force that moves all things, join as one with me now for my protection, I pray.'

We will continue with our working with the elements when we move onto the next section. And indeed now we have the support and strength of the spirits, whether we have the ability to see or know them yet or not, we may proceed to this next stage.

3) **Creating and Inflating a Protective Bubble** – *Sealing Up*

The word bubble here is a bit misleading, perhaps making us think of something vulnerable that can be easily burst. Yet the bubble that we are about to create is not weak in this way, rather flexible but strong: a rubbery, translucent *membrane* between our energy and external energies that has plenty of 'give' in it. It is supple and resilient, a second skin that can be stretched but will not break.

So, firstly we need to close our eyes and imagine that our spherical protective membrane surrounds us, *before us, behind us, above us, below us, and to our left and right* – it should cover us entirely from head to foot. It does this rather as if we are standing within a large round rubber bubble or bright balloon. Perhaps, if we are happy with the balloon analogy, we may like to imagine ourselves tying a knot in one end of it, making it a totally sealed unit. We can now reach out and touch the surface of our protective creation, actually feeling its stretchy smoothness. It is real!

This rubbery surface is not opaque but rather see-through and glowing with brilliant energy. The best colours to use for this are:

- A brilliant electric blue, the gorgeous clear blue of sky, the blue of a Madonna's robe, the cold blue of a gas flame or azure flecked with gold
- The dazzling golden light of the sun with the radiance of a halo, pale and luminous, sparkling as if with a million tiny fragments of gold leaf, or the white-yellow of a candle flame
- Pure blinding white light – incandescence – or the pale

translucence of marble, shimmering with silver glitter like tiny fragments of mirror or clear and pure as quartz crystal

• Any combination of the above

In the past I have worked with a brilliant neon blue edged with a corona of gold, soft golden light full of glittering gold flake (which is suspended like dust motes in sunlight) and the dazzling blue-white of the stars, edged with the darker blue of the atmosphere that surrounds Planet Earth. All work equally effectively, and so I choose any one depending on my mood and needs. The crux of this creative exercise is to pick what feels the most strongly protective for us at that particular time.

Now we are standing within our coloured translucent bubble or balloon we can inflate it with yet more light. For this I suggest that we hold a pure intense flame in our chest area, seeing it illumine us inside as if we had a candle within. When this flame becomes stronger we can let it expand outwards, becoming more and more dazzling as it radiates from our person so that soon we cannot see our hands or feet in front of us, only brilliant light. Now the balloon of energy itself is obscured so the full blinding fire of Creation is flaring all around us, filling up the space so that the bubble around us grows bigger and more powerful. We are now in our created protective space.

We may find that if we are ever in a hurry and need instant protective coverage that we want a more uncompromising symbol of protection that can be called up immediately. For this I use a version of the bubble or balloon that is made of glass, rather like encasing myself from head to toe in a goldfish bowl, only without the hole in it. This sealed glass sphere is still translucent, obviously, and still of the same range of glowing colours that have already been suggested or it can have a mirrored outer surface, enabling it to reflect away any negative energy that we feel is being deliberately directed our way. This use of glass is an emergency measure, an instant means of keeping ourselves protected from external influences in times of crisis, but the more breathable second skin of our protective membrane is always preferable.

When we are experienced at protecting ourselves then perhaps our own companion spirits will share with us other symbolic means by which we can tackle impromptu, potentially hazardous or specialist circumstances. For now the main thing is that we cover ourselves from head to toe with light in the all-encompassing way described.

4) **Covered by Protective Symbols** – *Shielding Up*

The next part of our protective process is to place additional symbols of protection on or around us as we stand or sit within our created sphere of light.

Using symbology for our spiritual security is a creative process that reveals in a simple eloquent statement our intent to be kept safe. Without the need for lengthy invocation or explanation we are able to express our desire in a language that all can understand. Adding symbols to our bubble is rather like adding a road sign to a road – we all seem to understand what a road is for but do we know its rules, directions etc. without signs?

So, how to choose a symbol for protection? Until we have an active dialogue with our companion spirits, who can then advise us wisely, choosing a symbol that will further enhance our sense of security is a personal matter. We may base this decision either on our own spiritual lives to date – choosing to work only with those familiar emblems from the dominant religion of our culture – or we may now want to broaden our horizons, considering those symbols outside of our own experience. By this we may discover a protective form that resonates with us more deeply for not being overly commonplace, and consequently rendered ineffective, in our lives.

If we care to expand our current horizons and quest for their presence there are many ancient and beautiful symbols that come already 'charged up' with the power of previous use. Any ancient emblem has a weight of collective reinforcement over the centuries, giving it more on an instant energetic intensity. The very strangeness of foreign symbols to our present culture may imbue them with precisely the mystical potency that we seek, allowing us to experience them as powers beyond the knowing of the average modern man.

Here are some examples of symbols that we may find compelling:

- The Ancient Egyptian *Eye of Horus*, reputed to ward off evil (the 'evil eye'). Or the Egyptian cross-like symbol of eternal life, the *Ankh*
- The Northern European *Elder Futhark rune Algiz*, which has shielding properties, or the *Tiwaz* rune that can be used as a sign of our strength and victory over negative external forces
- The Eastern Om, or Aum, symbol which works as defence, raising our persona vibration so that we cannot be susceptible to any form of psychic attack
- The Oriental *Yin-Yang*, symbol of balance and wholeness within the encompassing circle of creation, would also serve in

this supportive, safeguarding capacity

- The Jewish, Christian or Islamic legends all offer us the sign of the *Seal of Solomon* that could be interpreted as a way of controlling external negative forces. The *Star of David* hexagram is one such variation on this mystical theme.
- The Native American *sun or medicine wheel* – a cross within a circle – is also a powerful ancient pagan symbol which brings together the four directions, or elements, within the enclosing circle of death and rebirth, the universal All.

There are so many potent symbols to be found through research that it is impossible to cover even a fraction of them here. It is hoped that the above will give us a taster. However, we may decide not to look outside of our experience at all and instead opt for what is tried and tested in our lives. Of course this route is equally valid as long as we are not just picking a common symbol purely because it is the easiest option. This is not a good reason to select something that should act as a powerful gatekeeper between worlds for us! However, choosing a everyday symbol because it already has a comforting, trustworthy presence in our lives is clearly acceptable as that which has given us a sense of strength in the past has a head start in our giving us faith in the procedure.

Coming from a modern Western cultural perspective, as most of us unavoidably do, we may find it more comforting in the beginning to work with a customary protective emblem such as the religious iconography of the Christian church. If we consider Christian mythology in a positive light and experience the cruciform of Christ's resurrection to be a potent symbol of eternal life then working with a bright cross, either equal armed in the Celtic fashion or with a shorter crosspiece, would be an appropriate way to embellish our protective 'structure'. It matters not if we are a practicing Christian, more that we have a sense of true vitality from its symbology – we are not being *literal* but rather *metaphorical* as ever. The cross itself has an ancient lineage pre-dating Christianity which signifies regeneration – we only need to think of the positive 'plus' sign (+). There are all manner of variations on this theme, including the pagan Chi-Ro, the symbol for the Greek *chreston*, meaning auspicious.

Alternatively perhaps we are more familiar with modern pagan practice and would prefer to work with the pentacle – a five pointed star that is the symbol of the four elements, and the fifth, ether. As we know the combined strength of these forces is very strengthening as well as strongly protective. The pentagram, the pentacle enclosed within a circle, may give us further assurance or we may opt for the circle on its own, representing the sacred round of eternal life or the Oneness of Creation.

Clearly there are other beneficial symbols that have no spiritual correlation yet which have a powerful resonance for us and these are valid also. Any positive symbol is fine as long as we know why we employ it. We may decide that we favour shapes that we feel to be strong and safe or perhaps we would prefer to use a letter or number that has come to be associated in our lives with protection or good fortune. Maybe a flower has all the symbology we need, such as the enduring symbol of a beautiful rose with its protective thorns, or maybe it is a creature such as the dog, bear, boar or dragon.

I myself have always used a shining five-pointed star as my

protective symbol. To me, this symbolises the fire of Creation, and therefore the infinite vigour of the Creator. In my mind it is a strengthening and inspirational symbol as it reminds me that we all originated from the stars and are made of the same basic material as the glorious, mysterious cosmos. It is resonant of a mystical paradox, an emblem of the unknowable made known and in that I find much poetic potency.

When I imagine my star it is inscribed in silver wire that I then charge up with my energy until it shines with incandescent white light, as if super-heated. Colour is of the essence when visualising our symbol, just as colour was vital in creating our protective bubble. I have always found highly polished silver, which has the impression of being as keen as a sword blade and reflective as a mirror, to be effective. Likewise there is a certain strength in envisioning our symbol using a cold-blue white flame, rather like a blowtorch or drawing it as we would with the fizzing fiery tip of a child's Sparkler firework. Gold that shines like the sun will also have the resonance of protection, rather like a shield. Thinking about the symbols we have already discussed, for example, a gold cross may appear to be glowing as if burnished by many strong hands whilst a Star of David may seem as if it had been created from tongues of bright blue flame.

So, when we have chosen our symbol, and its colour, where do we put them? Well, our symbols should be described on the protective sphere that we have created around us. As we stand within our bubble or balloon we may choose to 'spray' a symbol as if in silver/blue/gold/white metallic or glittery paint on the flexible surface before us, rather as a talented graffiti artist would spray a wall. Or we could 'rubber stamp' the surface, using an imaginary inkpad, complete with luminous ink. Alternatively we may choose to suspend the shining symbol from an invisible hook, like a painting. Or we could use our finger to trace the symbol on the membrane, seeing it leave a glowing after image.

Just as we ensured we were covered by our sphere in all directions – that is before, behind, above, below, to the left and right – so we may want to place our protective symbol in these areas also. It must be said that there is nothing supremely esoteric about the ordering of above, below etc. rather it is a discipline to make sure we are covered holistically. I find that such routines really are a help when working with the unseen and they serve in much the same way as checking seatbelt, mirror position and so forth when getting in a car to make a journey. If we practice this ordering routinely then it does indeed become a familiar practice and one that we do not need to waste time trying to recall.

In previous books I have suggested that we may also place our protective symbols on our personal energy portals. But what are they? This system of 'power points' or 'doorways' on the human body are rather like the places on the Earth where we experience a greater flow of energy which facilitates a heightened ability to cross into other realms. Such Earth-places would be, most notably, the locations on which our more attuned ancestors built their sacred sites, such as burial chambers, mounds, megaliths etc. These places are often sited on *ley-lines*, or *leys*, streams of energy that traverse the land and converge, creating these power spots. The dowser Albert Watkins, author of 'The Old Straight Track', brought the name ley into modern parlance. Watkins discovered that many of the sacred places in the British Isles that were sited along these invisible ancient energy paths had names ending in 'ley'. Perhaps also the word 'ley' was also associated with the 'lay of the land'.

We humans also have the detectable equivalent of ley-lines within us and places of power, or portals, sited along them. The Chinese system of acupuncture helps us to understand that these leys, known as meridians or dragon lines, are the body's energy paths and where they converge we may find a particularly potent point, or node. Just as the ancients placed 'needles of stone' into the landscape to facilitate the flow of ley-energy, so do traditional Chinese acupuncturists place needles into the human body to assist with the flow of life-force moving within us around a system of meridians.

The Hindu tradition gives the body's portals, or energy junctions where lines of flow converge, the title of *chakras*. There are many references available to us today, including my own previous books, which look into the placing, significance and symbolism of these chakra points. I will leave their explanation, and the application of this wisdom, to such specialist works as I prefer for us to think in terms of what our body may be saying to us rather than just accepting a chakra and its pre-ordained meaning. By this we continue to learn to rely on our own intuitive feelings and personal symbology.

In our learning to become self-reliant spiritwalkers we should scanning our own bodies for any place or point that feels weakened and in need of a boost. This weakness may be because we have allowed ourselves to leak power from ourselves or possibly because an external force – be that a physical source such as another human being, or a spiritual source such as an entity – is attacking us. For example, we may be having trouble expressing ourselves clearly or speaking up for what we believe to be true or we may be physically suffering with a sore/ constricted throat that has no apparent physical cause. Consequently we may feel that we are being affected by an outside source that desires to silence us and so we can psychically protect and strengthen our throat portal by placing a symbol over it.

Similarly if we are 'sick to the stomach' or have 'had a gut full' of something, or if we have unexplained pain in that area then we may need to use a protective symbol over the vulnerable abdomen or sacral portal of our body. Phrases such as these hide a wealth of information about where we feel attacked or vulnerable even if we have not yet shown a bodily manifestation of the problem. Feelings like 'I've had it up to here with it', 'I can't see clearly what to do' or 'I can't stand it' can also tell us where we may be being energetically influenced even without a physical symptom having appeared.

A protective symbol can be pinned, placed, painted or simply superimposed upon our body in our mind's eye. If we cannot visualise well we can state that we have placed the symbol there. For example:

'I have placed an incandescent crescent moon over my heart to strengthen me during this emotional turmoil. I know and feel that it is so!'

Such placing of symbols over the body's power points, which are, paradoxically, also our most vulnerable regions, is a great way to protect ourselves psychically in an unexpected situation when we feel attacked or at risk or simply in need of uplifting. Or, if we are in a hurry and need a quick all over psychic energy replenishment, then we may just place one huge symbol before us, inscribing it in the air in front of us so that it is as big as we are. This I myself do by using the tip of my finger to draw my own protective symbol, the star, in the air. I use the top of my head as the tip of the star and use my spread feet, seen through my mind's eye, as the bottom two points of the star, the other two points stretching out past my shoulders.

Symbols are shorthand for what we feel, as well as for what we desire. The more we use our favourite symbols the more of an astral reality they become and so it pays us to keep up their application so that we can all on their power, with the weight of all our previous intent behind them, in times of need.

6) **Attuned to a Protective Frequency** – *Finding our Resonance*

As we may have come to accept by now, some of us are not particularly adept at, or comfortable with, visualisation. Our soul temperament (as defined by our soul traits) as well as our physical bodies can define how much ability, or affinity, we have with the imaginative, and primarily visionary, processes described here. As spiritwalking is inclusive there is no need for any aversion or affliction to limit us when it comes to being adequately protected. Even if we can't *see* the evidence of it we can *state* that we are protected, describing the action to ourselves instead of seeing it in the mind's eye, or we can *hear* we are protected. We can think in words, and even tones, instead of images. Here we come to the use of protective sounds as well as of meaningful statements of intent.

Firstly we need to find an acceptance of our ability to 'hear in our head', using our *mind's ear*. We probably have the skill, right now, to hear a favourite song, or piece of music, in our head, complete with all its subtle nuances and vivid instrumentation. Likewise we may well be able to hear the voice of a loved one or perceive the sound of a dog barking, a cock crowing or a door slamming. Maybe we can even 'hear' a sunny day in the countryside if we put our minds to it. Here we are using our audial memory as well as our audial imagination. Once we can witness such seemingly everyday behaviour as a skill we can hone it as such.

Let us now consider the notion of pure sound. To us humans, with our receptive eardrums designed to pick up vibrations, that which we perceive as a sound is the result of a displacement of energy in the external world. As we have previously established, *everything is energy* and *everything is connected*, therefore everything has a frequency or rate of vibration as it eternally interacts with the other energies around it, displacing and being displaced. Therefore, if we were able to tune in and hear it, everything has an innate resonance or sound. It is just that some of these sounds are below or above our ear's range and we are unable to translate, or even pick up, such reverberations.

As we know, the higher or faster the rate of vibration is, the more refined, and less dense, is the expression of energy that will result. This is why, as we know, slower energies are witnessed as seen and other quicker aspects are unseen. Operating within this premise, light is obviously quicker and more refined than darkness and, as we have established, it is with pure light that we need to protect ourselves. When we attune to the brilliant white light of our protective process we need to match this brilliance with an appropriate high, fast bright and pleasing sound. By releasing this sound we instantly we double the effect of our protection as we encourage the energy around us to truly shimmer at a rapid rate.

The most effective way to release this energy of intent is to release a long single note at a pitch that seems to be resonant of intense light. The sound we make should be uplifting and joyous and it should have a particular form. It is impossible to hold a note without it having some sort of shape to it, such as *oooh* or *eeee* and in this case it is recommended that we either hold our note in the form of *ahhh* or *ummm*. This former is suggested as it is considered to be 'the name of God', turning up as it does within Ya(aa)hweh, Ja(aa)h, Jehova(aa)h, Ka(aa)li, Shiva(aa) and many others. The latter suggestion reflects what is considered to be the eternal hum of life, the sound known in Eastern traditions as the 'Om' or 'Aum'.

For myself, I have had wonderful results when articulating a sustained high pitched *ahhh* note, feeling the energy released from my body with intent and witnessing it as it travels between the seen to the unseen realms. I then repeat it, perhaps twice more, until I feel the energies have shifted up a gear. When I do this I can really hear the ringing that continues after I have expelled all of my breath and dropped the note. It is an unearthly reverberation that can almost be felt in the bones. Partaking in the resonant chant of *Nam-Myoho-Renge-Kyo* which embodies the essence of Nichiren Daishonin's Buddhism can have the same sort of bone-thrilling effect. It is as if the body becomes a tuning fork, on the same wavelength as the pure sound of the energy we expel. Just as the presence of spirit can make us shiver so can the pure intent of a beautiful protective sound make our spirit tingle and our body thrum. This exciting effect is what we are aiming for!

If we attune ourselves to the reality of an energetic universe, and accept that we live in a world of vibrations and translated frequencies, then soon enough we will be able to detect the subtle ambient sound created as the atoms of energy are displaced all around us. When we consider how each being, as well as all individual thought and speech, makes for displaced energy all the time then it is inevitable that there will be a continuous level of ambient noise even when there is nothing discernible happening around us. Existence itself, in terms of the ever-expanding nature of creation, causes an eternal displacement of energy and therefore a continuous vibration. When we are attuned, like radios, we find that our inner mind's ear, as opposed to our limited outer ear, can pick up all sorts of vibrational transmissions from the ether. The 'Aum', or hum of Creation, is composed of all of these.

To this end I have long since been able to hear radio signals, rather like Morse code, as they displace the energy in the supposed silence and stillness of the night...something that our ears are not supposed to hear! Displacement is a subtle interaction of energy but for one who can understand and appreciate the constant movement of life-force inherent in the universe it can also be discernible, to one degree or another. This opens up a whole new layer of understanding for us, allowing us to truly grasp the presence of the unseen in our lives. With such an understanding we may be able to make further leaps of perception, such as witnessing sounds as colours, shapes, textures, feelings and even scents. Any such development of our inner and outer senses should be welcomed as it will aid us in our creation of a protective space that is attuned to our highest good, as well as in our spiritwalking in general.

Yet perhaps we have found that using sound in this way is not for us. If this is the case then perhaps we would feel more comfortable in stating our intent as a truth.

6) **Statements of Intent** – *A Declaration of Reality*

Let us now consider that we often use a powerful declaration of how we mean for things to be in our daily lives without the need to back up what we say with a visualisation. For instance, we may declare 'I am never going to eat meat again!' whilst not actually seeing ourselves desisting from tucking into a plate of steak and chips. Our strength of feeling, combined with a particularly punchy declaration, is enough to make it so without us having to stop and see ourselves as, in this example, eating a meat-free diet. By this we can observe that we can make a claim based on purely on feeling or on our absolute intent and it will be, or is, so! Therefore, for example, if we were fervently focussed on our purpose we could talk ourselves through the building of our protective bubble, and the application of our protective symbols, and it would be a reality purely because we willed it so.

So, we should never feel that what we do verbally is inferior to what someone else can see with the mind's eye. I am always reminded of the wonderful animated film 'Yellow Submarine' in which a cartoon version of the Beatles defeat their enemy with words of love and peace that flow from their lips and solidify in the air – their language, imbued with intent, becoming a three-dimensional reality to be worked with. I have faith that our words can also be made into a living reality if we have that sense of conviction ourselves.

Using the potency of words we can make a protective declaration between the universe and ourselves: *a statement of intent*. This statement will clarify what is happening to us between the worlds of matter and spirit, in this case affirming that we are now psychically protected from all extraneous energies. This statement is not an invocation, or request, as we made to our companion spirits, rather it is an assertion of what we have decided is to be. It is how it is because we intend it so!

At this stage let us keep it simple, saying something like:

'By the light of truth and the power of my own eternal spirit, I am protected!'
Or
'Now I am protected from all unwanted external influence, standing in the light, filled with spiritual strength.'

7) **Connecting to the Source** – *Powering Up*

This final stage of our protective procedure concerns linking in with the power supply of the Creator and 'topping up' so that we are ready to work effectively. The next chapter covers this aspect of our 'getting connected' in more detail. For now it is enough to suggest that having established our will we now need to surrender ourselves to the highest good that is the One-ness of Creation. Now we have made our intention a reality we are best served by temporarily letting go of our individual will and joining more fully with the greater power that lies both within and beyond us.

This is not dangerous, nor is it to be feared. If we have applied ourselves to the previous six stages of protection then we are now safe to open up fully to the levels of being outside of our physical human experience. We can securely reach out, and, paradoxically, go deep inside ourselves, to experience that timeless, boundless, uplifting and sustaining quality that is the life-essence of All. We have provided ourselves with the circumstances in which to do this with ease and therefore we can now step back.

In brief what we do next is to *enter the silence*. This means we may simply be still, quiet our mind and experience being joined with the essence of All that is ever-present, behind our endless thoughts and machinations. All we need to do is stop doing, stop thinking, and *be* – entering a state of *mindful mindlessness*. The energy of creation and its endless, generous essence will do the rest. This surrendering to the silence may take practice, being unfamiliar to us, but the more secure we can feel in our protected-ness the more we will be able to relax into our role as conduits for the eternal energy of existence.

What can we expect to happen? Well, nothing…or anything! There is no one right way to feel the power. Perhaps as we engage in this process there will be a comforting, yet dazzling, darkness that enfolds us, like being wrapped in the fabric of the universe itself. Or perhaps we will sense the room around us getting brighter, even though we have our eyes closed. It is possible that we may feel as if we are blissfully moving through space, as if flying. Or perhaps, as in my case, we will feel our head being pulled gently back whilst energy courses through our body. The marvellous thing is that this energy does not discriminate and it always present and we may become a safe conduit for it at any time. The fortifying strength of connection to Source has no limits and can never be drained. In fact, as we ascertained in our Introduction, the Source, just like energy companies who supply electricity, benefits from our connecting with it as it simply gets to create even more! This is true supply and demand.

Once we have been still and open enough to invite this experience of union and connection in, then we are 'powered up'. We can simply enjoy the recharged feeling or we may then wish to proceed with any spiritwalking we may have in mind. We have now completed the essential cycle of our protective process. This may seem a daunting and long-winded cycle to us now but once it is practiced and adapted to suit our individual needs and taste then we can be sure it will become second nature, rather like the process of preparing to drive off in a car which itself seems an overwhelming task when we begin to learn to drive.

But what if we haven't always the time to go through this entire process and need a quicker version for use 'on the hop'? For instance, what if we begin to feel spiritually vulnerable when a room full of people develops a hostile energy? Or what if we find ourselves in a friend's new house that has a disturbed feeling? Well, of course we have ways of dealing with any such eventuality and what follows is an abbreviated adhoc adaptation for use in unexpected circumstances and situations that do not allow for a more in depth approach.

Emergency Protection Routine
- Immediately see ourselves standing within a sphere of light

– be that bright blue, gold or white

- Witness this sphere glowing brighter with each breath until it is dazzling
- Draw a single large protective symbol before us in shining silver
- State with passionate intent, '*I am protected from any external energy that does not come for my highest good!*' (This can be done mentally)
- Call on the companion spirits to back us up and be with us
- If we can then hear a single pure sustained 'ahhhh' note, attuning us to the highest possible energies of creation
- If there is more time then continue to breathe deeply and imagine our feet rooting into the earth where we are. Feel our connection and find our balance between earth and sky, matter and spirit.

Psychic protection may seem a little overwhelming and complicated to us right now, but once we practice protective protocol as routine, knowing what suits us as individuals, it *will* become quick, efficient and effective.

Now let us actually move on to using that protection in practice and get a little more connected.

CHAPTER FIVE

GETTING CONNECTED

'The Creator in you wants to create! Your process of creation
reflects even the most awesome natural materialisation, such
as the birth of a star, and has its own cycle of conception,
gestation and manifestation. Push out thought – move your
intent – and know, just as you know you will take your next
breath, that your directed energy *will* effect matter at the right
time. All creation breathes – internalising and then releasing –
and when you inhale an idea and exhale its pure force you are
interacting with the Universe in the same way as the Creator
does...and this is good! There is nothing that exists that
does not come out to this same sacred round, of the
endless movement in and out.'

From Guidance

We have, in the previous chapter, looked at how we may be
connected to the great cosmic All – the energy of Creation. As spiritwalkers we need to incorporate connection with Source into our
daily lives and here we will go into more detail so that we may
understand the importance of doing this regularly.

Firstly let us take a deeper look at what this means.

Aligning the Self – Coming into Harmony with the All

When we speak of aligning the self we mean bringing our unique
soul into harmony with the Greater Spirit. This we do for two
reasons:

- To ensure we are *always* topped up, or re-charged, directly from the Source so that we may live well, for the good of the All
- To ensure that the intention we have for our spiritwalking is in harmony with the munificent energy of the eternal Creator.

So, firstly how may we bring ourselves into alignment? This we can do by entering the silence as we have previously suggested, using a time of quite contemplation to allow our focus to be less human-centred (finite, limited, self-ish) and more Creator-centred (infinite, boundless, selfless). We may also describe this process as *getting into the gap* as does the best-selling author Dr Wayne W. Dyer in his work. This gap is the space between thoughts: the realm of pure awareness.

Leaving behind our temporary concerns, stilling our internal chattering and entering into a silent communion with the Greater Spirit is the best way of achieving interconnectedness. There are no short cuts, we simply have to plug in and make the circuit with Source in order to recharge. I am only re-iterating what hundreds of other teachers and books have suggested previously when I say what follows but it is an inescapable truth for those who seek such a re-union with their true selves and their Creator. It is this:

Even as little as fifteen minutes quiet time, once or twice a day, can be enough to establish a deep connection.

For something so vital and valid this is not a huge commitment, but an essential one for us as spiritwalkers. We just need to sit in a protected space, still and in silence, then open up to the energies of the All. The best approach for doing this is little and often, rather than engaging in a long session once a week. The idea is that this practice becomes as usual as any other daily act, like putting the kettle on or cleaning our teeth. It is a sustaining practice and necessary practice, like eating or washing, and as such should be treated as essential to our well-being.

Silent meditation of the kind that gets us into the gap is not a case of drifting away from ourselves as human beings but rather consciously re-membering ourselves as spirits having a human experience – that is, allowing ourselves to reconnect with our eternal essence, and its originator, beyond the corporeal. By this we actively realise that we are not just our bodies but rather we are energy and energy is *everything*! And if we are indeed everything then we really begin to understand that we are more than this life yet, paradoxically, we are also in it. We feel ourselves to be simultaneously a unique expression (a temporary body with an eternal soul) *and* a part of the whole (the life-force of Creation Itself) – an experience that is beyond all others. As spiritwalkers we actively seek to hold this balance so that we may indeed walk between the worlds of form and formlessness.

The very act of re-uniting with Source is very empowering and it will naturally give us more vitality. We become plugged into a united matrix of energy, all working in perfect harmony, rather than being like a windmill with broken sails trying to generate enough power on its own. The eternal powerhouse of the Greater Spirit, our infinite generator, generously enables us the life-force to flow through us whenever we wish. Note how we refer to *generosity* here. If we can accept that the Creator expresses pure creation, of which we are undeniably a part, then we can understand that the very act of creation is indeed generous – it is an act of unconditional giving. The more we receive and accept this energising Source-energy, forming that vital circuit, the more we will be able to emulate, as well as empathise with, that which enlivens us. This means that we will find it hard to have an intention that is less than munificent. And so the energy goes round in its natural circuit – we are in tune with the force of creation, our lives flow beautifully and we make a positive difference in the world because of it. By this we pass the force ever onwards.

So, the importance of being in harmony with the generosity of the Creator is not to be understated. It can be said here that the more we commune with the unseen – including, as we progress, having a meaningful dialogue with the companion spirits – the more we can ensure that our intent is aligned with the greater good.

So, now we really know why we do it let us look a little more at how we do it.

Entering the Silence – A Daily Practice

Before we open up to connect with energies we must always go through the protective routine. *This should be taken as the norm from hereon in.* So, let us assume that we have swiftly and easily gone through the six stages of protection and are now ready to make our connection with Source by entering the silence.

At this stage we want to alter our state of consciousness in order to move beyond the state of ordinary awareness that includes all bodily activity and the daily buzz of our thoughts. For this we will need to concentrate on our breathing. Experience of breathing techniques within yoga, or of any discipline that combines bodily relaxation with spiritual awareness, is very helpful in this matter although we can approach it now as a complete newcomer.

We may do this by simply becoming conscious of that mysterious sacred breath that moves through us like a tide, ebbing and flowing. We can hear our deep, slow breathing as the ocean being drawn in and released by the gravity of the moon, in and out. Now, we should, if possible, begin to draw the breath in for three, hold for a beat and then let go. This becomes a measured rhythm – in...*hold, two, three*...and release. We can then draw our focus into each breath as it enters us, being sucked gently but powerfully in through the nose and then expelled with a rush through the nose or mouth. Just like the sea meeting the shore and receding in an endless, hypnotic cycle.

When we feel that rhythm and are a part of that tide then we are ready to allow our slow, deep breathing to take us deeper into the silence. To do this we need to let our thoughts drift across our consciousness like dandelion seeds, watching them float by but not allowing them to take root. We are moving further from our worldly concerns and these extraneous thoughts disperse like so much thistledown into the wind. We are going into the gap between worlds, between times, letting the breath take us deeper and deeper into the mystery that lies beyond that which is daily and seen. We are entering the *beyond.*

In this space of peace, contemplation and receptivity we continue to breathe and sink deeper into the place that is not of this manifest world. Now we can witness life-force energy building at the base of the spine and moving up through our back, infusing us with vitality and joy. See the colours it brings, feel the sensations, hear its particular frequency humming. Now we can allow the spirit-energy, that essential power of creation, to flood into us, feeling it as it tingles and glows through our very being. Draw it in with each breath and allow all doubt or fear to be expelled as our breath is released, witnessing that gush of vital energy as it is drawn in and then released into the All.

We can continue to allow this drawing in and releasing cycle to continue. As we do so we may want to hold a tone, the pleasing *ahhh* sound that we make during our protective process. Breathe in and breathe out...*ahhh*. As we do this, becoming more and more absorbed in the beauty of the sound, we may want to be aware of any intent that we currently have. As we breathe out...*ahhh*...we may wish to send our thoughts into the universe, back to the Source, along with the sound. Perhaps we would like to have more energy to do all the things we enjoy. If so on the *ahhh*, the release, we can be affirming to ourselves as a statement of intent *I have boundless energy*. We could replace this affirming thought with *I am confident and fearless* or *I have a home of my own* or *I am healthy and strong* or any number of other positive statements. By doing this we are saying that something is so, acting as the expression of the Creator that we truly are and fashioning our reality through energy. The more we repeat this the more it exists or *becomes*. This is very beneficial, as any positive change will, of course, feed back into the All. How can it not when all is energetically connected?

Now we may wish to come back from the silence to the manifest world of ordinary reality and, consequently, our corporeal bodies. To do this we can continue to breathe deeply and slowly but be more aware of the breath as something unseen that flows through our physical selves. We can witness the air moving through our nasal passages, feel it inflate our lungs and hear it as it leaves us through our noses or mouths. The sacred breath once more becomes a part of our daily human experience. To become even more aware of our bodies we should then wiggle our fingers and toes, move the head slowly on the neck. The ground becomes discernible under our buttocks or back. Now we find that we are fading the sounds and smells of the manifest world back in so that they become part of our awareness once more.

Then, when we are ready, we can slowly and carefully sit or stand up and stretch.

Beginning a Record – Grounding Our Spirit-Insights

We now need to fully earth ourselves back in the physical reality in which we must currently live so that we do not feel at all disorientated. In Chapter Seven we shall look more closely at the practice grounding ourselves after we have been spiritwalking as it is a vital part of what we need to do to be safe, stable practitioners. As an introduction here I would suggest that when we return from connecting in the silence we begin to note down the experiences we have. The very act of writing, drawing, or even speaking our recollection into a tape recorder can help to put us firmly, yet gently, back into the manifest world. Noting down our findings may seem mundane at first, especially if nothing much happens to us 'out there' but over time we will build up a comprehensive record of our progress which can hold many gems of information that we overlook at the time. Every colour we see or sound we hear may be a symbol which will resonate with us at a later date.

A drink and a simple, snack, such as a rice cake and a glass of spring water, could accompany this noting activity. A preferred way of mine is to write up my observations with an accompanying cup of tea and an organic seed cake, which is nice and earthy. The very act of imbibing affirms our connection to our bodies. Likewise the act of stretching. Why else would we, and other mammals, stretch upon waking if not to feel that connection to our blood and bones again?

Here our soul has been journeying in awareness and so we need to reconnect with our physical reality – just as we do after sleep.

So, now we know how to maintain a connection to the Greater Spirit and develop our awareness of energies through entering the silence. It is hoped that we, as fledgling spiritwalkers, will regularly engage with the practice in whatever form suits us. Yet now we have the means to go about our spiritual business safely we can begin to incorporate other ways interacting with the unseen into our daily lives. Here are two more ideas to start us off on our own ongoing journey.

How Else Can We Continue to Connect and Develop?

- By prayer – *spiritually communicating an intended outcome to Source when in the silence of our deeply connected state*
- By visualisation – *actively envisioning our intended outcome into reality when in the silence of connection*

Prayer

Firstly let us consider prayer, which we have touched on briefly before. The word prayer may have negative connotations for us, as may many of the words we come across when discussing matters pertaining to spirituality. This is clearly because spirituality has long been seen as the exclusive domain of the major religions and seldom separated out into an autonomous means of expressing the eternal energetic self. As a direct result of this the notion of praying may previously have made us feel subservient, being solely the act of beseeching a distant anthropomorphised God figure into noticing us (whilst simultaneously feeling we were not worthy of notice). Also prayer may have been a means of wheedling supplication for us, a sort of bartering whereby if this omnipotent yet unknowable God did what we wanted (perhaps giving us something or stopping something from happening) we would repay by never sinning etc. Or perhaps by giving lots of money to a cause. Praying in this way allows us to think we can placate an almighty external being by grovelling and sacrificing and then walking away – until the next time we want something. This disconnected and disempowering behaviour is emphatically not what we, as spiritwalkers, mean by prayer!

Here we are approaching prayer simply as a means of expressing verbally what we desire to happen. As *co-creators* in the universe, people who have a sense of their own part in the One-ness of Being, we are as much expressing this to ourselves as we are to the Greater Spirit, or Creator. This is not supplication but rather a means of clarifying our intent and of broadcasting it energetically, using the emotive means of language to make our statement. We are saying that this is what we will to happen. When we pray we use our *will and wish*.

When this will and wish is combined with an awareness of ourselves as a valid part of Creation – as a crucial link in a vast circuit of energy – we become powerful. In our power we may then align ourselves back with the most obvious expression of omnipresent Source energy that we have in our experience, i.e. the natural physical world around us. By making comparisons and using metaphors from nature we can reinforce and amplify our innate force through prayer. For example, we may need the strength to recover from an illness that has been dragging on, leaving us feeling physically weak and ineffective, and feel that we would like to pray for a personal resurgence. By this we realise that it is valuable to witness how all things have their returns in nature, even when they have apparently waned and died back. A prayer that utilises this regenerative theme may be said something like:

> '*I stand now as part of creation, witnessing the procession and regression of the seasons, the waxing and waning of the moon, the ebb and flow of the sea. All things I know recede and return, and I am a part of all things. May the same strong, vital energy that allows the rose to bloom again from last year's cut back stem stream through me now. Let me be regenerated, rising like a neap tide once more on the ocean of One-ness, brimming with that restoring energy that allows the bare tree to become green again in spring. May my sap is rise again now, even as stars are being born in the darkness. May my eternal power rise again, like the sun on a Winter Solstice morning. By all the spirits that love me and by the Creator, so may it be.*'

We can see here that we have mentioned the spirits who love us (the companion spirits) and the Creator. Clearly when we have the names of our companion spirits we can include them and if we have a particular choice of name for the Creator then this too can be applied. By including other beings or energies in our prayers we are not beseeching them, trying to get them to act as a genie in a lamp for us, rather we are including them in the sacred round of our existence: we are acknowledging their power as well as our own, in partnership. As spiritwalkers we get stronger by seeing ourselves as part of an inclusive energetic dance. We acknowledge our allies and mentors as opposed to expecting them to save the day for us. *We are always acting and thinking as part of a circuit of power.* This is why it is beneficial to align ourselves with the natural world with our prayers as we are affirming our part in nature and therefore claiming nature's potency as our own. The metaphorical interpretation of, and alignment with, nature is a tonic for the soul, as mystics have always realised.

Perhaps when we studied our example of a regenerative prayer then some such potent imagery naturally formed within us to accompany the words. For some of us it is entirely usual to have language accompanied by colours, shapes or mental pictures and this should be encouraged, as it is the foundation of the next skill we are about to discuss. Let us now consider visualisation, either with or without the stimulating accompaniment of prayerful prose, as a way of connecting and opening up to energies for a particular purpose.

Visualisation

We have already considered the craft of visualisation when we learned how to protect ourselves. By visualisation we simply mean actively seeing with the inner, or mind's, eye just as we would with our physical sight. It is a kind of lucid dreaming – a seeing of what is unseen behind the closed lids with as much clarity, and control, as we generally do with our waking vision. Whereas prayer is a verbal statement of intent, focussed visualisation is our will and wish expressed in pictorial form, using emotive imagined scenes and symbols that are enlivened with our intent.

If we are unfamiliar with visualisation, or a just little rusty with employing it deliberately, then we can simply learn to close our eyes and switch on our inner vision in much the same way as turning on a television set or sitting down in a cinema to watch a film. We simply become aware that we are now viewing something to be broadcast, or projected, onto a screen. We can then actively conjure up the desired imagery on the blank display behind our eyes, calling it up from the vast memory store of pictorial reference in our brain. We can begin this very simply, as we have previously suggested in Chapter Two, by calling up a very mundane item from our reference library, such as a rosy apple or a pair of men's formal shoes. From there we could progress to creating a simple tableau, perhaps seeing the rosy apple sitting next to a yellow teapot and a blue and white striped mug on a scrubbed pine table in a sunny room. And from there it is only a short step to creating a moving picture in which the rosy apple could roll off the scrubbed pine table and land on a rag rug beneath, startling the ginger cat that slept there. It may seem all very elementary but is essential to practice these basics if we are to consciously re-learn how to see the unseen.

Objects may seem easy to conjure up in our inner vision but we also need to be able to witness living beings behind our closed eyelids. Part of purposefully connecting with the energy of creation through prayer and visualisation is to ask for healing and success for others. This is the altruistic part of our life and work as spiritwalkers. But how to do this effectively?

Well, I recently had a collection of recent photographs of seven friends that had expressed to me a desire for their lives to change for the better in certain ways. I used these as a way of kick-starting my visualising, or envisioning, of them and as I closed my eyes I initially recalled the still photographic image of each person. This enabled me to connect with their essence in a very real way, ensuring that what I was seeing was directly linked in to the physical reality. As I recalled photographic image I enlivened it in my mind, embellishing the still picture with the sound of their voice, their gestures, and even their scent. Then I would imagine them moving out of the scene in the photo and into the scene they wished to be in. For instance, one friend wanted to move house, so I saw her leaving her empty flat with a suitcase and posting the keys back through the letterbox before walking away for the last time. Another friend that I had a photograph of desperately needed a break with his artwork and so I saw him carrying his portfolio and stepping forward to shake the hand of a new client, then signing a contract with them.

With time and much repetition all of the things I saw in my mind's eye came to be in reality. What I had set up in the unseen, along with that person's own will and wish for it to be so, eventually became a seen fact in the physical world. We may quickly find ourselves able to do similar acts of visualisation for our own friends, family or colleagues, with their permission and suggestions (as we should only ever act for others with their consent – *to act on another's' behalf without their agreement, no matter how wise or benevolent we feel we are being, is unacceptable*). The ease of visualisation we may find with those around us may be due to our being used to observing them externally or it may be because we feel that they deserve to be helped and we feel validated and justified in doing so. The act that we may find harder is seeing our own person in our mind's eye in order to help ourselves. Yet this we also need to do as part of spiritwalking is also about empowering ourselves energetically, enabling ourselves to be the most effective we can be.

A block on visualising, and energetically working on, ourselves may be to do with the fact that we don't really know what we look like in the same way that we see other people clearly – we may know what we want to look like but not how we actually are. Indeed it may be uncomfortable for us modern Western people to truly focus on bodies that we are so often dissatisfied with. Yet we do not really need to see ourselves from the outside in order to visualise changes for ourselves. Although we may wish to see ourselves as slimmer or more muscle-bound, in which case seeing our whole physical self is necessary, we may also wish to just experience ourselves as doing new things.

I am constantly visualising myself in new circumstances but I don't do this by seeing myself as an actor in a film projected on the screen of my closed eyelids, rather by closing my eyes and then imagining that they are open again. What I see through my mind's eye is then that which I would see if my circumstances were different. For example, I visualise myself looking down at my hands and see myself holding a copy of this book, as it would be in its published form. Or feel myself sitting in a place that I would like to have the opportunity to visit, looking at the scene that unfolds before me. When we are visualising for others we cannot get inside their head to change what they see and therefore we have to see them as actors on a screen. However, we can simply change what we see around us and envision the differences without having to do this externalised viewing of our bodily selves.

It may not only be a reluctance to see ourselves from the outside that makes us hesitate about doing any praying or visualisation for ourselves. The major religions that we may have grown up with could well have discouraged us from such supposedly self-ish acts, encouraging instead an ethos of self-denial, sacrifice and suffering instead with the promise of our rewards later. Why a loving Creator would want a wretched dis-spirited creation is never quite explained! This negative prevailing message may well have become ingrained in us at a deep level whether we think we agree with it or not. As a result many of us feel that we don't deserve good things to happen, especially in a world that seems to be laden with very many bad things happening to innocents.

If this is true for us then let us stop this limiting, unhelpful attitude right now! Although it may appear self-ish to spend time on helping ourselves through creative methods it is in fact just the opposite – it is an *altruistic* act for us to practice self-development. Indeed, if we allow ourselves to go against the grain of received opinion, and instead consider what we know about the interrelatedness of all things, then we will fully accept that *what helps one benefits the All* – how can it not when we are all energetically connected?

We Are One Another

One of the central concepts of spiritwalking is this *individual interconnectedness*. Let us now use another analogy to understand this core idea. As we touched upon in our Introduction, our own bodies are made up of internal aspects that are invisible to the naked eye, these being cells. Everything we are, physically speaking, is comprised of interrelated, yet unique, cells – our hair, skin, blood and organs are all made of such interconnected cells whilst each appearing to be independent parts of us. Each cell serves a vital and unique purpose in relationship to the whole whilst being indivisible from it – it is connected and yet separate with both a collective and a personal identity.

Each part also has a relationship to the others within the whole that they make up. For instance, the cells that the kidneys comprise of are linked to those of the liver, the cells of the blood have an effect on those of the skin and bones and the cells that make up the muscles relate to those which make up the tendons. Within any whole there is also an *interdependent individuality*. When we consider our physical selves we cannot really say that our individual cells are independent of each other or, indeed, of the whole body and nor is the body able to exist independently of its cells. We can witness this in much the same way as we did when we observed that electrical energy cannot easily be divided between the generator of power and its receiver once they are connected. Likewise the drop and the ocean are one.

Now let us extend this awareness of interconnection within us outwards – *as within, so without.* As well our bodies being made up of cells, we, as living beings, are also cells within the greater body of the Creator who is All Creation. We, along with all other beings, are connected yet separate, unified into a whole body of existence but still perceptible as individuals. And, as with cells in the body, what one cell does affects all – one cell cannot remain in isolation when they are all so interconnected. From this perspective who would want to keep one cell, or a group of cells, unhealthy or at risk when it would be far better if all cells were thriving and whole? No one in their right mind would suggest that it was valid to keep some cells cancerous within a body perhaps because they didn't 'deserve' to be healthy. It would be foolish indeed to suggest that one cancerous cell wouldn't affect the others and could somehow stand in isolation. Of course anything that could be done to strengthen each and every cell would be done, for the good of the whole body.

By this we can understand that our being a vibrant recharged cell within the greater body of creation is of greater benefit to the whole than it is if we are sluggish, sick and struggling. We therefore know that our own personal recharging or self-development can make a positive difference to all the other cells in the body of Creation. What we do to empower ourselves will affect the all of which we are a unique part. We become part of a wave that moves all the drops in the ocean onwards.

Similarly when we do something self-destructive, or harmful to others, then the impact will be felt, on an energetic level, in the greater body of existence. We can turn this around and also observe that what happens in, or on, the greater body of the Earth, such as pollution or war, will affect the cells in the body, our selves. This realisation brings with it a vital shift in awareness and an increase in accountability and compassion for the spiritwalker.

So, our potential position is one of responsibility in which there is renewed power, understanding as we do that we can affect change. As spiritwalkers we aim to live in a way that holds both the individual and the collective, and the seen and the unseen, in balance. For this challenging way of being we need to be working at our full strength and so let us now firmly establish that is permissible, and indeed vital, that we take our own health and happiness as seriously as we do that of others – and that we take the well-being of others as seriously as we do our own. Without this connection to all other individual aspects of the All, and to the All itself, we are only functioning at half-power and the circuit of life-force energy is broken. It may seem hard to take this on board when society still persists in teaching us otherwise but in our role we may often need to go against what is the prevailing trend of thought and assert another way of seeing reality – one based on our walking between the worlds of matter and spirit, not solely on what is seen. In this prayers and visualisations that enable us to have this strength of purpose and courageous conviction, as well as radiant health and success, are valuable ones! We can, and should, reclaim our power in these ways.

So, visualisations, along with prayer, are the two main ways that we may come to greater effectiveness in our lives. There are many examples of those who have shrunken tumours and achieved otherwise unlikely leaps in lifestyle by such focussed spiritual, or energetic, connection. I myself have achieved amazing results when visualising things that I have needed when I could ill afford to buy them, so much so that one much needed item actually appeared on my doorstep within twenty four hours! Yet although prayer and visualisation can indeed enable us to manifest results, each of these are (usually) not enough on their own to effect change. If instant results were to always be achieved then a single prayer for a miraculous healing would routinely be answered immediately. Or every time someone vehemently proclaimed that they wished a particular person were dead there would be a lot of sudden inexplicable fatalities. Similarly we would all suddenly become famous overnight just because when we daydream we regularly see ourselves on a stage surrounded by cameras and adulation. Along with an intense, sustained focus of our topped-up energy we usually accept that we need to make physical moves towards our desired outcome before we expect to see results.

For instance, the friend I mentioned previously wouldn't have found a new place to live if she hadn't looked in the Estate Agent's window, nor would my other friend have found a new client to buy his art if he had no work to show them. It is the combination of energetic input and reinforcing actions that make for quick changes – *the unseen and the seen working in harmony.*

Similarly there may be a better chance of us to facilitate the healing we pray for if we supplement our energetic input by changing the way we live in a material sense, adopting beneficial medicinal or nutritional changes. Positive action towards our desired goal is essential as it shows that we are already moving towards that which we energetically seek. The key is to *see what we desire as if it has already happened* – and act then accordingly. The essential energy that is available to us through connection, and then directed through our intent in prayer and visualisation, is the added force that make these things possible…and even probable. Here is an equation that expresses this:

Connection to Source + directed focus + reinforcing manifest action = change.

By connecting through the silence then directing energy through prayer and visualisation we are giving our dreams, requests and creations life. When we then take steps to manifestly achieve our goals we will find ourselves surrounded by uncanny coincidences and strokes of luck as things move swiftly into alignment with our desired outcome. Whatever is given enough power and focus in the ether will come to fruition in the slower manifest soon enough and our own steps taken in the world help the process to quicken. This is a law of the universe and, as we have previously ascertained, nothing exists that it wasn't imagined, or stated as intent, first.

So, we are now able to begin to walk with spirit with assurance, renewed energy and purpose. In the next chapter we will look at where we may walk to next – getting to know the many unseen levels of existence that make up the greater All.

CHAPTER SIX

THE UNSEEN HIGHWAY

'We are travellers that walk back the way we came, knowing that in so doing we are travelling to where we have never been, without moving. Everything a spiritwalker does is with an understanding of this process of simultaneous existence, of multi-dimensional being. We know that our journey is to the far edge of the cloth of life even as our thread moves up and down in the middle and has never left the beginning. We know that we are concurrently the shining strand, the work in progress, the finished piece and the empty loom, as well as the initial dream that brings all things together. Wherever we desire to go we take with us the wisdom that we are already there, just as we have never left our destination and are making the journey right now. We are everywhere, nowhere and somewhere very specific all at the same time. This is our way.'

From Guidance.

We have already begun to understand the nature of unseen energy, expressed as spirit or soul, along with being introduced to working with this energy as potential spiritwalkers. We know how to use our own energetic intent and how to connect – moving into that which lies beyond human manifest existence, or 'ordinary' reality – and to be energetically protected as we do this. The next stage of our journey is to actually begin spiritwalking but first we need to know, and understand, where we may want to travel to. And why.

Levels of Existence – Understanding the Beyond

When we use the term the *beyond* here we are talking about any level of existence which is not the manifest one we are used to here on Earth. We use this term as such levels are simply beyond physical sight and our previous daily corporeal experience. This generalised term covers the levels closest to our own as well as those that are so far removed from our understanding that they become vague and unknowable. We are, as we may expect, much more able to have insight into the workings of the levels closest to our earthly one and so we shall begin by looking at what we will term here the lower or *human astral* which is the etheric plane that parallels our current reality.

The Human Astral

This level of being is the unseen realm that is a direct echo of our own manifest existence on Earth. Our physical presence leaves a resonant blueprint in the surrounding ether, an image of itself that is strictly energetic, not corporeal. All life has an effect on this etheric plane of existence by its very being and this level can be easily imprinted on as it is plastic or malleable, something that we can mould and manipulate whether consciously or unconsciously. The human astral is once-removed from our own level and is less dense, more mutable. We may influence its energetic make up by thought, feeling, intent, and daydream…or just by being. Our very existence causes an astral *displacement*, allowing the energy to form itself to our psychic contours rather as if we were pressing a hand into a flexible substance like latex.

An analogy for the human astral may be the environment of a fish tank. Inside the tank the fish (and their attendant accoutrements of existence such as rocks and weeds) displace the water. The water is a clear, and, to all intents and purposes, unseen aspect of this mini-world; its presence can only be discerned by the movement of the fish, including the bubbles they make as they respirate etc. It is only the old food, excrement and break down of any miscellaneous matter that makes the water cloudy and 'visible' as the fish imprint themselves upon the apparently unseen element of water as they come and go. We know that if we remove the fish and their trappings that the water would flow and fill the space they had occupied and when we add them back in the water would once again alter its flow accordingly. So it is with energy, or the ether, as it flows around us, taking on our attributes and being 'coloured' by all that we leave behind as we live. The human astral is the water that flows around us 'fish' as we swim in the 'tank of manifest life', displacing it as we go. We may be aware of our equivalent of rocks and weeds in the 'tank of life' but we are more or less unaware of the 'water', or ether, that surrounds us. Outside the tank there are other worlds that we, as captive 'fish', cannot readily see; all we know directly is the environment we currently inhabit, the world we have been placed in. We may witness this in Diag.6, next page.

The human astral, this impressionable energetic realm, has the potential to be as positive or negative just as any single human being can be. Etheric energy, as we know, is neutral by nature and it is only the way we direct it or affect it that makes it apparently positive or negative. We humans are directing and imprinting energy all the time, even if we are unaware of it. Our focussed intention, as well as the individual thoughts, desires and feelings that, all have a direct influence on the ether that flows around us. If we think about it as spiritwalkers, with sensitivity to the unseen nature of existence and

Diag. 6 the Tank of Life

A (black with white shading) signifies the wider ether, the life-force energy, as it moves around outside the 'tank of life' or the realm of physical human existence

B (white with black shading) shows us the ether as it is inside the tank . This ether makes up the human astral layer of existence

C (grey shading) signifies the displacement of the ether as the occupants move through the tank, 'colouring' the etheric, or astral, energy around them by their presence

the interconnectedness of all life then how can it not?

If we do stop to consider that the human astral reflects human life as it currently lived then we can only conclude that our nearest etheric region must be a pretty strange and daunting place right now, given the sheer amount of aggression, intolerance, pain and plain dissatisfaction that is released, albeit unwittingly, each day by the many. I say unwittingly as to be fair the vast percentage of unseen negative influence that is released is generally done with a complete lack of awareness of energies and the unseen aspect of being, let alone an understanding of the energetic impact we all have as individuals on the All. Yet we really do need to take responsibility here and now for the fact that we do cloud the 'water' of the impressionable ether of the human astral on a daily basis with the effluvia of our existences, making it into a place which can be as unpleasant as a neglected fish tank. Once we become conscious of this we become accountable as never before, realising, as we must, that every hateful thought or dream of vengeance goes into the ether to linger there just as fish excrement will build up in an uncleaned tank.

We can obviously make sure that the ether around us is clean and sweet by keeping our thoughts positive, and loving as possible. This attention to our input into the energies that constantly flow around us is just as vital to a spiritwalker as how we physically act. If we dwell on negative thoughts, giving them our time and energy, then this etheric effluvia then builds up, creating more permanent forms. These forms dwell unchecked in our nearest astral neighbourhood and so we begin to create real problems of a more tangible variety.

Let us reinforce this concept with another analogy involving our fish tank. Waste matter will build up in an untended tank and eventually will begin to attach itself to things, forming itself into new shapes and getting stuck together in corners. It will collect and gather, growing into an independent mass that cannot be filtered out in the usual way. The nature of the human astral is just like this analogous tank where, instead of fish detritus, it is our emotional and thought-energy, our *etheric* detritus, that may become coagulated and stuck. Negative human energy can mutate into new shapes, growing unwieldy and more unpleasant as it expands, and our 'tank of life' can easily become polluted with this kind of energetic build-up which then causes all manner of other difficulties. It is well for us to have the awareness to keep our energetic emissions in check before this has chance to happen.

There will be much more on the idea of such coalescent energetic shapes later, specifically in Chapter Thirteen when we come to look at thought-forms. For now let us observe the effect of the emitting of energy in Diag.7, below. Here we see four figures within the 'tank of

Diag.7 *Displacement/ Colouring*

A (black with white shading) signifies the ether, or etheric energy, of the human astral level

B (white with black shading) shows the displacement or 'colouring' of this energy as caused by an average human being

C shows the 'colouring' caused by a person feeling depression

D shows the 'colouring' of a person feeling frustration and

E the 'colouring' of a person feeling joy

Note how the energy 'coloured' by one figure reaches those around it. No one figure stands in isolation, energetically speaking, even though their physical bodies do not touch each other.

life', all contributing something to the unseen atmosphere of the human astral.

The human astral is our local etheric neighbourhood and consequently is where most casual, lazy or undisciplined psychic contact, such as a Ouija board, will take us. This will no doubt seem obvious to us now as this level is so close to our current physical one, and echoes our own physical level so succinctly that we will undoubtedly receive a response when we reach out to it. Just from who this response may be we will discuss in the subsequent chapters when we will look at the presences we can encounter. For now it is only common sense to see that any uncontrolled or half-hearted act of reaching out to contact (so-called) spirits will only take us as far as the first unseen level, the human astral. It is very easy, especially if we are impatient, or even desperate, to reach out to this level and it is not so easy to reach past it...*unless we are willing to train ourselves as spiritwalkers to do so.*

It is true to say that because our manifest realm holds goodness as well as corruption and contains cute dormice and beautiful roses as well as annoying mosquitoes and vicious alligators. So it is with the unseen equivalent of the human astral. In this we may indeed be lucky when we reach out to the human astral level – or we may be crushingly unlucky. When we have no psychic code of practice then what we receive when we tune in to the human etheric level is potluck. Our aim, as spiritwalkers, is to know where we are going, astrally speaking, and why. In this we aim to understand the nature of the human astral level, and to accept it, but not to seek guidance or clarity from it. Unless our physical world has a massive and rapid shift in its nature, from predominantly negative to overwhelmingly positive (which we can contribute towards with our own energetic awareness) then we are always guaranteed an unpredictable response if we do. There are much better places to aim for, as we will soon discover.

The outer layers of our human astral realm could be likened to those peripheral regions just outside the of the 'tank of life' that we have previously discussed. The captive beings within this tank can just about discern through the edges of the tank – or the metaphorical 'glass of human reality' – that there is something else out there. However, what it is usually remains unclear as it is so far removed from our manifest daily experience within the tank that it seems to difficult, or too risky, for most of us to understand. As questing spiritwalkers we can intentionally witness what lies in these regions outside of the restrictive tank of the human astral, our safe practice allowing us to explore these outer astral levels where humanity has not made such a strong etheric imprint. The further we travel outside of the 'tank of life' the less influence human energy has. These outer layers we may call the *local astral*: the wider etheric river that has not yet reached the greater sea.

The Local Astral

This realm or etheric region can still be influenced by our will but is not so cluttered or contaminated by the energetic detritus of our human lives. Indeed, when we visit this level we could say it is more akin to being a free salmon in a clean river than a goldfish in a tank. As a salmon we will still displace and 'colour' the water in the wilder river of life, the wider etheric, as we move through. However, just as a river is able to filter itself more effectively than a tank, so is the local astral more able to keep itself fresh and free of pollution than the human version. The wider etheric of this level is not a man-made construct like the human astral but a free-flowing natural feature and so it has its own attributes as well as those we can impose upon it by our will.

The flow of this etheric river that is closest to our 'tank of life' is the place where we may meet those who can give us concise, reliable spiritual guidance – these being our companion spirits who we will meet fully in Chapter Eight. This is clearly their dwelling place as they are not so far removed from our earthly lives as to be indecipherable and remote yet are far enough removed from the detritus of the human astral for there to be clarity and compassion. Those companions that we meet with in the local astral realms are going to be twice removed – once from our dense bodily existences and once from the 'coloured' human etheric levels that surround those bodies – and therefore we can be more certain of getting objective and genuinely spiritual input in this astral region. However, let us stress at this juncture that we will *not* meet the spirits of the dead here for it is not the place where our souls go between lives, rather it is a bridging ground where those who act as unseen guides, mentors or companions can relay messages to us from the departed and beyond.

The local astral is also the place where we can meet with avatars of earthly principles that are simultaneously close enough to our lives to have empathy and respect yet far enough away to be dispassionate and succinct. We will hear more about these generous unseen beings that give that input in Chapter Eleven.

As we will discover in the next chapter, which is concerned with our actively building with energies, the local astral can also be moulded and influenced. It is still an energetic realm that is close to our own and, as such, can still be affected by our intent. Yet the effort it takes to affect such change will be far greater than our casually or unwittingly 'colouring' the human astral as we are working with wilder energy, not the tame man-made etheric inside of the 'tank of life'. Whereas the human astral exists in tandem with dense physical life on this planet, the local astral has no such restrictions and, like a river, can flow fast or slow depending on other prevailing conditions...*and its own will*. This will does not denote that it has a personality as such but, to return to our water analogy, that it is more akin to trying to hold something still in a rushing brook than it is to holding something in a washing up bowl – there is a wild force that exists there that has nothing to do with human influence.

As well as its own essential quick, lively energy and the presence of the companion spirits, the local astral is full of other beings that have their own vivid non-human influences. Indeed, the further from the human astral, and therefore from humanity's etheric influences, we are able to travel the more we will experience this untamed natural resonance and the effects of other 'alien', or unfamiliar non-human, energies. The type of 'fish' who have chosen to swim in the wider etheric river will of course affect it and we will look at some of these beings in more detail in subsequent chapters. For now let us just accept this progression away from the 'tank of life', through the local astral and out towards its limits.

As we do this, let us imagine that there are stepping stones in the local astral river that will take us from the region closest to 'the tank of life' right across to the very far edge of it so that we may peer into, if not venture into, the wild waters beyond. We will observe that the stepping stones cannot allow us to leave the river but instead enable us to get a glimpse of the sea that the river flows into and, indeed, becomes. We may stand on the last metaphorical stepping stone, on the very shores of human understanding, and consider what lies beyond our knowing while not necessarily being able to go any further in this life. There is a good reason for this. In the case of the next level of existence it is due to the fact that the next astral level on from the local astral it is in fact the Land of the Dead – *The Summerlands*

Land of Permanent Summer

I have used the Celtic term The Summerlands for the realm of the dead. Whatever we choose to call this level of existence lies outside of our local astral and is part of the *greater astral*, or cosmic sea. This is the etheric place that the spirits of the deceased, those souls who have passed with ease into their discarnate state, travel to. I have chosen the poetic title of the Summerlands as it gives a sense of the wonder, comfort and joy we experience in this state of being, for (just like all other astral realms) it really is a state, a *point of perception*, rather than a place. It is a blissful state of union that we journey to in the ultimate 'out of body experience'.

In the classic near-death experience, the vast majority of people (regardless of race or religious persuasion) recall a sensation of moving through a tunnel towards intense bright light. This symbolic re-birthing journey expresses our soul movement from incarnate to discarnate being, just as when we incarnate we also experience moving along a tunnel into light, journeying down the birth canal. What these experiences give us is an understanding of moving from one condition to another via a link or passageway. This passage is an inter-dimensional highway, a portal between two energetic states of being.

We can effectively use the analogy of computer technology to help us to grasp this energy transference. We can witness our soul as unseen information that is downloaded through a cable or wire into our body when we are born into the physical. We can then say that when we leave our body at death this upgraded information is then uploaded into the spiritual, etheric realm using the same process, only through an energetic wire, or connection, as opposed to our mother's body. When we make this transition into discarnate existence we move through space and perceived time to enter the state of life-between-lives of the Summerlands.

When we ourselves are 'in spirit', as pure soul energy, then here we may re-connect with loved ones who are also discarnate, meet with our soul types/groups and undertake 'debriefing' from the incarnate experience we have just had. To use our computer analogy we could say that we have our hard drive, the soul, defragmented and scanned for viruses etc. We may, after a process of assimilation, re-assessment and rejuvenation, undergo 'upgrading' via creative learning programmes, whether on our own or in affinity groups.

These soul or affinity groups are rather like mega or gigabytes – clusters of energetic information held together – or, to return to our organic analogy, they are as cells working together. Although we are all 'cells in the body of Creation' some cells work in tandem better than others – for example, cells that have worked together in a heart will be more compatible by nature than those who worked in both an eye and a hair, even though they are ultimately all related. The analogy of us being like cells is one we can return to time and again to show that we all have interconnected status even as we simultaneously all have our own individual preferences and skills. Souls that return to the Summerlands may, at least at first, prefer to remain with those that they work well with in the physical world –

sticking with their cell. It is interesting to note here that 'cell' not only refers to a singular molecular part of the body but also to a small group or unit that in itself is the sum of several individual parts.

In this convivial atmosphere of reunion and enlightenment the Summerlands are a far cry from the hellish state of the lost/trapped soul which is the human astral. Energetic existence in the Land of the Dead is, if we allow it to be so, like having an eternal summer in the company of those we love and find stimulating, without any of the confusion and stress of manifest life. In this we are just pure awareness with none of the pain and preoccupations of the physical, able to 'follow our bliss' free of the distractions that divert us when we are in a body. Many of the witnesses of near death experiences who have briefly caught sight of this wondrous level of existence have described variations on a beautiful, tranquil garden in summertime although ultimately we will all affect our own energetic reality – one that will reflect our souls's needs at that time. These variations on 'paradise' are all conducive to the re-connection, recuperation and renewal that we experience in between lives. This is the nurturing space from which we consider embarking on further incarnations, be they on Earth or elsewhere.

We say that we consider embarking, as there is no external regulator ready to push us into other physical experiences. We do not get forced into incarnation and there is no time limit on how long we may stay in this state of awareness – in fact *there is no time*! We are, as ever, in control of our destiny and whatever we deem as valuable experience is up to us. Similarly there is no judgement save the self-assessment that we experience during our time de-fragmenting the hard drive of the soul. We are always self-regulating as well as having that omnipresent sense of connection and collective responsibility.

When we are incarnate in a physical form we cannot readily travel into this ethereal realm of the dead. As we have said, it is a defined state of existence and is not in our current plane of being. It is not advisable to journey into this level unless with a trusted and competent companion who thinks that it is vital or valid for us to do so. It is not a level of existence to be 'day-tripped' to or dabbled in. However, the spirits of this level can sometimes travel to us...*but only for specific purposes.*

When a balanced soul is accepting of its new non-manifest state of being then they may wilfully visit the physical plane for a time after their own bodily demise. The spirit, knowing that they themselves are energetically safe and well, may wish to comfort and reassure any affected parties left mourning for them on the Earth-level. As they are not wishing to return to physical life, and are confident in their newfound condition, they will be able to travel back to our dense level of being without too many problems. This they will do with their attendant companion spirits who will act as bridge-builders to our 'solid' realm so that the departed soul may make their etheric presence felt to the relative or friend left behind. However, even if a spirit does choose to make a foray back to the Earth-level in this way it is only *temporary* and after any comfort has been given the soul is once more escorted back to the Summerlands by their companion. After this transitional period such trans-dimensional journeying of the departed soul will cease and, although it may seem harsh to those of us who mourn deeply, it is *right* that it ceases.

Often the spirits of our dead friends and relatives do not journey to us at all, rather our trusted companion spirits are dispatched back to us to bring us comforting gestures without the newly deceased spirit having to do this themselves. We still receive the good tidings/feelings/messages which we assume to be from our dear departed without them having to make the journey back – a journey which may seem daunting or even distressing. This reluctance to return to our dense level of being can be due to the soul concerned being glad to be free of their elderly or pain-filled body, or their difficult life circumstances, and not wish to revisit the scene of their last incarnation. It may also be due to the fact that once a spirit is in the wonderful, peaceful Summerlands such worldly concern and a desire for physical human contact fades away – although clearly the love that underlies all experience, be that incarnate or discarnate, never fades. Love is an indefatigable energy, the 'fuel' of Creation that knows no divides nor limits . It is love that sustains the faith that we shall always be reunited with those who pass on before us and in this there is no need for us to try and hasten contact. We should trust, as do they, that we will meet them again soon enough.

As regards to our meeting again we should take on board that in their discarnate state of awareness there truly is no time. In the Summerlands we are not governed by human years or by a human longing for time to pass. For spirit all time is in the eternal *Now* and so that desperate need to see loved ones again diminishes as it will only be a moment before we are together again in spirit. In our own pain we can take comfort that it is only our human selves which feel the separation of death as being a indeterminably lengthy one and that our dear departed have no such perceptions. They are free of the limits three-dimensional being and its (apparent) governing factors of time and space. Their experience is indescribably different to ours here on Earth.

Saying all this we should not feel that the Land of the Dead, or the dead themselves, are far way. On the contrary, they are but a breath, or, more accurately, a *vibration*, away. Our thoughts are with them, literally, just as their memory will remain with us until we meet again. The living, the dead and indeed all created energies unavoidably share the same *Now* only with different points of perception. The veil of separation that we experience from the One-ness of All, including those who have passed over, is only an illusion – but a necessary illusion if we are to continue to live in human form. As we have said before, these bodies of ours can only cope with so much information at this present time and to perceive all levels of the unseen would be extreme sensory overload, a computer crash of the senses, at this stage in our human development. However, we can expand our awareness as spiritwalkers to a degree where we can accept and understand the other energies that are around us. We just do not need to try and cross over and be with those in a different vibratory level to our own – our job is to stay with our current point of perception and learn by it. We will 'pass over' soon enough ourselves!

So, in the energetic sea beyond the local astral there is the Summerlands where our souls go to between lives. Of course, there are many other levels, or dimensions, of existence in the greater astral that would perhaps be more at home in a book on advanced spiritwalking. It is certainly beneficial to consider such concepts as parallel universes and multi-dimensional existences, as they are undoubtedly part of the eternal *Now*, but an in-depth study of such matters is more than an introduction to spiritwalking can contain within its pages. For now let us have a brief look at what else lies beyond the last stepping-stone on the fringes of the local astral as we move from that which is appreciable into what is presently unfathomable to us as limited human beings.

The Greater Astral – The Cosmic Sea of the Beyond.

The inaccessible etheric environment that stretches away from the specific energetic state of the Summerlands is truly unknowable and untameable, extending off far away from where our human understanding can let us explore. We are, after all, limited by what our brain can transmit or translate for us and so we should accept that our astral travelling will stop at some boundary. The place where the river of the local astral meets the sea of the greater astral is usually this border of human understanding. Beyond lie things we cannot possibly hope to interpret, inhabiting restricted human bodies as we do at this present time. All we need do is acknowledge that there are unseen regions, or levels of existence, out there that hold energies and influences beyond our human faculties.

However, saying this there are those of us who may like to try to expand our horizons beyond these accepted margins, although this is certainly not obligatory and definitely not always feasible. Even though we cannot hope to charter all the depths of the great astral seas we can consider the words of the Nineteenth Century scientist and adherent of Darwin, T.H. Huxley, when he said '*the known is finite, the unknown infinite; intellectually we stand on an islet in the midst of an illimitable ocean on inexplicability. Our business in every generation is to reclaim a little more land.*' Maybe part of our role as spiritwalkers is to stretch ourselves to our full capacity, gaining an understanding, inch by metaphorical inch, of the unseen realms beyond our present horizons. Perhaps we can then begin to evolve to a point where we can comprehend such mystery. Or conversely perhaps we will simply be able to begin using the parts of ourselves, of the body, mind and the soul, that have long since become dormant from lack of exercise. In reaching out little by little into the *wild beyond* on behalf of others we allow ourselves to gently stretch those parts of our selves that could accommodate such mysteries.

Undoubtedly it has always been the role of the spiritwalker to push boundaries and to act as the equivalent of a researcher or explorer, asking '*what if?*' as a matter of course. If we persevere then we will experience insights into the unseen and the unknown on behalf of those who are less intrepid, or who have other roles in life besides that of spiritwalker. In so doing we can expand the human experience of reality for the good of the All, just as a mountaineer does. And, like mountaineering, this work is not without its dangers and is certainly to be taken seriously, with commitment.

Let's now leave the idea of the unchartered terrain of the wild cosmic sea and move on again to an ever greater concept. Continuing with our watery analogy for a moment, let us consider the source from which all water comes, be it in a fish tank, river or untamed sea. This metaphorical water, which moves around and across even the most unknowable shores, is the ocean. All water simultaneously comes from this and *is* this, for once again we find the inevitable interconnected independence in our naturalistic analogy. How indeed may we draw the line between the singular droplet and the collective body of water; where is the place where they divide? If we again acknowledge this vast flow of wild water symbolically as unseen etheric spirit-energy then we may witness this as the *boundless etheric ocean*, made of countless tiny singular 'droplets', or cells, yet encompassing them all.

The Endless Ocean of One-ness

The spiritual ocean of which we speak is the far-flung astral environment that we humans cannot easily traverse (as we have no way of interpreting it) whilst simultaneously being *beyond* it and also omnipresent in our daily experience. By this we mean that this energetic ocean is *everywhere and everything* and we now know it as the *One-ness* of Creation. The endless etheric ocean of One-ness is the Great Mystery, or Greater Spirit – the Source of Life that suffuses all things and *is* all things at the same time. This ocean is to be observed in the man-made microcosm of the fish tank as well as in the fabulous macrocosm of the cosmological All. There can be no division of One-ness and one, Creator and created, yet there is always individualism within the whole. It is the Way and as spirit-walkers it is both our journey and our destination – both where we walk and how we walk. It is a state we can visit without it ever becoming a realm; indeed it encompasses all realms and levels within itself at once whilst being none of them.

This One-ness contains the divine paradox which lies at the heart of spiritual understanding and the more we connect with the essence of being through the process of our daily practice, as discussed in our last chapter, the more we will come to witness this eternal truth in our blood and bones, as naturally as breathing. It is this – *the farther we travel astrally or etherically the closer we come to the heart of the matter.* We will come to experience, through our own connection, that by going within (at what is, in universal terms, our infinitesimally small individual level) we may experience ourselves as the overwhelmingly vast All. Reaching this state is rather like travelling rapidly out to the unimaginable reaches of all universes whist discovering simultaneously that we are merely looking inside microscopic atoms in our own body. The ultimate in cosmic exploration is actually within us at a quantum level!

Let's expand on this idea for a moment. Through our learned perception of the 'real' (or manifest, seen) world, we expect for things to become weaker or lesser the smaller, and therefore less seen, they become. Therefore as we travel deep *within* the molecular building blocks of life, viewing them through a microscope at an infinitesimal level, we expect to find something insubstantial and rather puny. Yet this is not the case. In fact, investigations of the most imperceptible unseen core of a molecule have just taken researchers straight back into the all-powerful, all-pervading *without* aspect of being which holds infinite energy! As quantum physicists have observed, the further we zoom in to observe miniscule inner workings of a sub-atomic particle, the more powerful what we witness becomes until *what we see is what we are.* In the unseen is mirrored the seen and at the centre of one tiny cell is found the All. Truly mind-blowing yet we are all capable, with a little effort, of assimilating this information and relating to it in whatever way serves us best.

For example, this process of simultaneous connection could be compared to watching a flower unfold its beautiful petals and fold them closed again in extremely rapid endless succession ...*what we think is open is in fact closed* and *what we think is within is also without*...and so on. The bloom of our imagined example is in constant undetectable motion, being both extremes of itself at once, yet we only see an aspect of its entirety at any one time. When we begin to consider life as a circle and not a straight line, as indeed we must if we are to begin assimilating these concepts, then one extreme always becomes its opposite within the endless looping cycle of existence.

In short, the more we push ourselves to witness external truth, or Truth with a capital T, the more we must go deep inside to experience it. As I observed in 'Craft of the Wild Witch' *(Llewellyn 2004)* we will not come to this realisation through a temple or a church but rather '*within the deepest fathomless places of our own souls...places that echo the furthest reaches of the starry veiled cosmos*'. And similarly the unknown dark depths of the physical ocean, illuminated by almost alien beings lit by bioluminescence. The ocean of unlimited being that we find within as well as without is the *dazzling darkness* – the place that is so hidden that it has glorious eternal truths shining in its shadows. In what seems like a void, a black *nothingness*, we discover *everything*. We will find it in the farthest reaches of being and know we held it within us all along, like an oyster holds a pearl inside. We know how to do this by plugging into the limitless, generous and *neutral* Creator-power and we should now make sure that we are doing this regularly so that we may become the most adept and fulfilled spiritwalkers we can be.

To further explain what we have been discussing, here is a new analogy. We have already established that the astral, or etheric, levels operate concurrently to ours and in this we can observe that they are like the layers of an onion. As such they can be separated, or peeled away, but they also sit together to give form to the whole onion, giving it the overall appearance of an entire sphere whilst still being made up of the sum of many interrelated (unseen) parts within. Just as with our previous analogies of electrical energy, cells and water, who can say at which point the layers of the onion end and the whole onion begins? Does not each layer connect itself to the last to be witnessed as both a complete sphere and a series of rings simultaneously? We may not be able to categorically state where one level ends and another begins but can sense their seamless *merging*. In the diagram below we may witness this simultaneous being that creates a whole.

Here we witness the whole sphere of the etheric onion, made up

Diag.8 *Layers of the Etheric Onion – Astral Levels of Being*

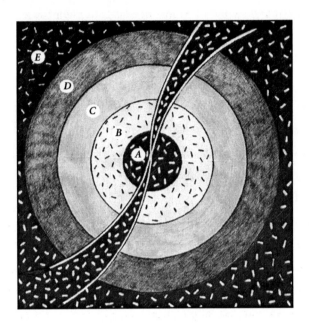

A (black with white shading) shows us the heart of the matter, the spirit at the centre of all creation, including ourselves - the within

B (white with black shading) reveals to us the human astral layer that is the unseen realm closest to our current manifest realm

C (light grey shading) shows us the local astral level where we may meet our companion guides on trance journeys

D (darker grey shading) shows us the greater astral which includes the realms of the Summerlands and the Otherworld

E (black with white shading) depicts the One-ness of being as it lies without yet within simultaneously, flowing through all whilst being the All.

of concentric rings or concurrent levels of existence. This also includes unmarked multi-dimensional and parallel states of being – it is a solid shere not a 2-D image. Yet our onion analogy, although excellent for expressing a composite round All made up of many interrelated separate skins, or energetic membranes, does not perhaps allow us to truly grasp the endless cycling/flowing of the etheric. Unlike real onions, some things cannot be neatly sliced up into readily identifiable chunks with a cold human blade and energy is one of them. Energy flows and cycles, it does not have a readily identifiable beginning, middle and end and this is why we have primarily used the analogy of water to explain the astral realms.

The onion analogy is useful but, like all such analogies, it has only a limited place in our overall understanding of what is a multifaceted, richly layered and infinitely deep subject. It is well for us now to try and not get too stuck on one viewpoint but to witness astral existence, and indeed energetic being, from as many different angles as possible, using as many different analogous tools as we can. With the concepts of electricity, cells, water and now the onion we should be getting closer to an overall understanding which has breadth and depth.

Finally, let's use a different kind of analogy so that we are able to consider this idea of astral states in a variety of ways. As we are discussing states of being then it is obvious to draw a parallel with America. Let us think about our living a rather parochial existence in a house in Akron, Ohio. We can imagine that human astral is what we experience all around us every day in our town of Akron and as such we understand that we can have an influence on this area. We are happy to venture across Akron into the neighbouring towns, as they also share this same human astral ambience and everything is familiar to us, and we may even feel that we may have some influence there too. On occasion we have travelled as far as Cleveland to the north or Columbus further south but we don't really know these places and they don't affect our lives; we feel as if we have no influence there. They are on the very fringes of our experience and for us they are the equivalent of the edges of the human astral. Beyond these outlying cities there seems to us to be the unknown and, being pretty cautious, we have never wanted to go out of our state of Ohio.

However, all around Ohio are other states, the nearest being Indiana, West Virginia and Pennsylvania, places where people are no doubt friendly although they are mostly strangers and so a little off-putting. These neighbouring states we can liken to the local astral. If we were able, and we knew what we were doing we could probably get to visit the nearest parts of these neighbour states without too much trouble – especially if we had a trustworthy guide to help us cope with all those strangers.

Meanwhile outside of Ohio's neighbouring states there is, of course, the rest of the vast United States of America. This is like the greater astral which encompasses both the local and the human astrals within it. These places are full of unfamiliar things. We do not know these far-flung regions and will never visit them, although we are aware that they are there. And outside the US? Well, there is the world – the *beyond*. We can know we are a part of this when we are at home in Akron looking at a map but find it impossible to imagine how. They are as unknowable to us at home in Akron as the stars and planets above us or the hot magma miles below our feet, even though we acknowledge that these aspects exist. We can accept, even appreciate, their presence but little more.

So, we have a basic view of the levels that the spiritwalker may experience which will of course be enhanced as we work through this book, along with our introducing another layer, *the Otherworld,* which will be covered in Chapter Twelve. At this stage it is enough for us be able to understand the unseen astral realms as defined regions, or states, although we should not make the mistake of thinking that this is the literal way the unseen works. Our delineating them is acceptable for now, for learning's sake, as long as we can then take on board that in fact there are no walls between them and their boundaries are very blurred. The astral levels are not countries with borders, as such, rather when we speak of realms we are not talking of man-made linear divisions but instead of spirals and concentric rings, one aspect overlapping and interlocking with the next with imprecise edges.

As we now have a much better idea of where we are walking to, and a firmer grasp of why, let us return to developing our skills as spiritwalkers, working with the etheric essence of the local astral in order that we may start to interact more fully with energies in a safe place. To take ourselves back in a loop, as spiritwalkers are wont to do on their travels, we should now consider that as well as our regularly connecting with the All we shall also need to begin to undertake spiritual expeditions to the local astral, the etheric level that lies just outside of our human astral condition, or state. These local astral expeditions we may call *trance journeys,* or *pathworkings,* and are undertaken for the sake of obtaining guidance, healing or experience. We will begin discussing the practice and application of this vital part of the spiritwalkers' work in our next chapter.

CHAPTER SEVEN

THERE'S NO PLACE LIKE HOME

'No thing is permanent and yet the Creator does not engage in half-hearted measures, based on the knowing that the being that is fashioned will only exist in dense form for a few months or years. By no means! As co-creators we are here to make every action count, to make it *resonant*, so that even when the last cell of our bodies has broken down, as surely it will, the things that we have created will sing on strongly in the ether, like the lingering trace of birdsong as night falls. We are here to do great things, in beauty. Let the thought of impermanence now leave our consciousness for good and all, for no flower considers whether to bloom, knowing that it will only become mulch in the end! Create well, with loving conviction, and all worlds will change.'

From Guidance

Here begins our active work as a spiritwalker and as with any work we need to find a place to work from. Because we are talking about the work of one who moves between worlds, or levels of existence, we will need both a physical place and an unseen place – as without, so within – to work in conjunction. The former is simply a place inside our manifest earthly home, garden or environs where we are able to engage with spirit undisturbed. The latter I will refer to as our *astral office*, the safe place in the universe where we may conduct our unseen business safely and efficiently. This is something we ourselves must create using the etheric energy of the local astral region that we discussed in the last chapter.

But before we embark on our first conscious astral creation let us first prepare ourselves by considering where we will work *manifestly*, in the physical world – our seen sacred space.

Physical Sacred Space – A Safe Haven

Spiritwalking, like so many other creative disciplines, requires a secure place that allows for uninterrupted working. By this juncture it should be clear for us as individuals that we will require such a safe haven for prolonged periods of protection, reflection and connection, as well as the subsequent grounding and note-making that is such a valuable part of our work. It is common sense to consider somewhere that is within easy access for us that will reliably afford us a great degree of privacy and peace and so our own homes, gardens or immediate neighbourhood are the most obvious places for us to start. Perhaps we already have our place in use or have one in mind ready to work in. Whichever, we will need a way of ascertaining if this place is the best one for us.

Choosing Physical Sacred Space

Here is a checklist for those crucial things we are looking for in our manifest place:

- Somewhere which is *comfortable physically* in terms of temperature etc.
- Somewhere where we can easily *sit or lie down,* performing our protective routine and our relaxation postures etc. for sustained periods
- Somewhere where we can safely gain *prolonged stretches of*

peaceful time

- Somewhere where we can *safely have darkness if we so choose*
- Somewhere which allows us to feel at ease where we *fear no physical interruption*
- Somewhere we are *free to visit* when we so choose
- Somewhere which will allow us to *build up a resonance,* forming a relationship with peace that co-creates a conducive space
- Somewhere where we can symbolically *draw the line* between this world and the unseen worlds

Firstly let's consider our primary physical needs that are to have somewhere that is comfortable for our bodies. The place we choose has to be dry, or at least to provide shelter for us if needed. Being buffeted by wind may seem invigorating at first but will end up being distracting while prolonged exposure to damp conditions is not wise when we are in positions that necessitate stillness and physical contact with the ground. Our space also needs to be of an adequate temperature that we can adjust if necessary. We simply won't be able to concentrate on our spiritwalking working in a place with ice on the windows, especially as our body temperature generally falls as we go into trance. Maintaining adequate warmth and dryness is a prerequisite of the place we choose to work in. As is having enough room to comfortably adopt our chosen posture/s for spiritwalking, as discussed in Chapter Four. There is no point in having a high ceiling but only a metre or so of floor space if we prefer to work lying down.

Once these matters of bodily comfort and ease are attended to we need to consider the other physical necessities – peace and quiet and the ability to have darkness if we need it.

The issue of noise pollution and gaining peaceful time in our chosen environment is an important one. Of course, noise may not be an issue for us if we may be lucky enough to live in a rural place where the only intervening sounds arise from the odd passing tractor or rampant cockerel. Or perhaps we live alone in a quiet detached house away from traffic or many passers by. I myself have lived in urban environments for most of my life and have had rooms in unpredictable shared houses and flats situated on main roads. Through these less than peaceful circumstances I have found that a standard pair of earplugs have been an invaluable aid to artificially creating silence for spiritwalking. The foam or wax variety, bought readily at any pharmacy, block out input from the physical senses and allow our innate spiritual sense, our inner seeing and knowing, to come to the fore. Even the seemingly mundane act of putting them into our ears can be a statement of intent – *I am now filtering out the manifest and tuning into the ethereal.*

For particularly stubborn sounds, such as a neighbour's music reverberating around my room when I wanted to go spiritwalking, I have put headphones on top of the earplugs and played suitably soothing music to journey to. Something purely instrumental with no distracting words, or a piece that fits the mood of the journey I am to undertake, usually does the trick. This doubling up on aural protection isn't ideal but it is a working solution for those of us who value regular practice. In the long run we could also pray for a quieter home!

Equally we need the option to work in darkness, as well as silence, if we so choose. Closing our eyes isn't always enough to give us the true darkness we may crave for really deep work. If we are working at night the simplest solution is of course to turn off the light, which disconnects us from the seemingly omnipresent effect of electrical illumination, automatically taking us into another, more primal, way of seeing and being. Yet if we are to work most often in the daytime we need to find other solutions. Closing the curtains may be fine if we have heavy velvet drapes but not so effective if we have unlined cotton at our windows. Here we may like to resort to the commonly available black-out mask to give us that extra layer of darkness. These masks can take us from the busy surroundings of our family home or our less than aesthetically pleasing environs into a darkness that can make us more amenable to the mysterious unseen realms 'behind the sun'. There is something satisfying about placing a cover over our physical sight that makes the definite statement of intent – *now I have to look within.*

I would add here, although it may seem obvious, that earplugs and black out masks cannot stop us from feeling *vibrations.* If our circumstances are compromised by noisy family and friends then it may be well for us to conduct our spiritwalking at roughly the same time each day and ask them to respectfully refrain from their vigorous activities then, promising them to do something for them in return. Activities such as door slamming or vacuuming can clearly be felt as vibrations whilst stronger sensations like being physically touched or shaken should definitely be avoided. It may also be well for those around us also from creating strong smells, like frying food, which may divert us although it is easier to gently incorporate a smell into spiritwalking than it is to be jarred out of a deep state of trance by a physical sensation.

Clearly it is not advisable to sit with earplugs in and a blindfold on in a public place but that does not mean we should avoid public places altogether. We should feel free to walk with spirit whenever we feel like it and no doubt we will find suitably quiet times in public parks or gardens, on the beach, or even on a train journey. These occasions should be utilised and treasured as gifts, especially if we are with others who can 'keep an eye on us' while we do our spiritwalking. Indeed, we should aim to be ready to practice our spirit craft in any and every situation, from café to secluded glade. But we cannot rely on there being solitude, silence or safety every time we visit a favourite public garden or well-known beauty spot and therefore picking such a place as our own sacred space is not conducive. As we know, spiritwalking requires of us that we make contact with the unseen every day if possible and therefore we need a regular 'haunt' that we can guarantee won't have a group of picnickers on it. While it is beneficial to do the work in an ad hoc way while we are out walking, for instance, this is not the way to choose our special place for daily working as this needs to be quite distinct from places we, and many others, enjoy visiting. We would not want to go to our job in an office to find someone else using our desk and so we need to ascertain that our spiritwalking space will also be ours alone.

As well as the issues of privacy and security regarding a public place we cannot really expect to build up a strong personal resonance in a place where many other people pass through. Such movement will cause the energy we have stored there to be disturbed and dissipated, even overlaid by others. As spiritwalkers we understand that we need to work in a singular place regularly, and in an uninterrupted fashion, in order to build up an appropriate atmosphere – in this case an unseen resonance of respectful intent that proclaims *this is my space, I am protected here!* This deliberate creation of an ambience we may also call an energetic *imprinting*. When we repeatedly frequent a place we imprint upon it our desires, attitudes and our innate individual essence and this becomes even more pronounced when we actively aim to do this. There will be more on the idea of energetic imprinting in Chapter Fifteen.

Going back to our electrical analogy, we will be *charging up* our sacred space so that it will be topped up with our particular energy for when we come to work with it again. A place that is already 'charged up' is much easier to 'switch on'. Thus if we have a good relationship with a well chosen working area we can hope to have achieved a *living* space - a place which is an enlivened and able to support, if not contribute to, the proceedings. Clearly if we are able to work outside we will also have all the natural wild green energy of the area to incorporate into our spiritwalking too but this idea of a living, or enlivened space, goes as much for if we are sitting in a locked spare room at home as if we are spending time in a tree house. As we know, the life-force energy of the Source is everywhere for us to connect with, not just in wild places, and we only need to do this with our directed will to make what we desire a reality.

So, we can enliven our space deliberately and utilise any energy already available there to us to charge it up. But what kind of space is best? Well, depending on our soul's preferences (as discerned in our looking at our soul traits, previously) our special space could be in any of the following:

- A shelter at the bottom of our allotment
- An unused spare room in a friend's house

- A reclaimed walk-in cupboard under the stairs
- A cosy garden shed with its own woodstove
- A peaceful attic space in our family home
- A 'bender' or Yurt on a (private) plot of ground
- A summerhouse conservatory in a suburban garden

We are aiming to work in, and *with*, a place that will become a valued part of what we do and so it should be anywhere that makes us feel safe, positive and inspired. All we need are our physical pre-requisites met in an atmosphere of serenity, somewhere where we can build up a relationship without anxiety or distraction.

If we have not already found a perfect, undisturbed place, perhaps due to a lack of privacy or freedom in our lives, or due to restrictions of money or disability, then the solution to this may be our drawing a line quite literally in the space that we occupy right now. Having myself lived in cramped, gardenless, rented accommodation for many years I fully understand how any indoor modification or utilisation of outside space can seem nigh on impossible. But there are always ways of drawing a symbolic boundary between one realm and the next that can help transform the most tiny, cluttered environment into one of peace and space, effectively creating an everyday sanctuary.

Partitioning a room off with an attractive curtain found in a second-hand shop is one such means of creating a haven that is not of the hectic manifest world whilst remaining in it. It draws the line for us between 'ordinary' reality and otherworldly consciousness whilst not making a real structural change to our environment or requiring much financial or physical input. Similarly we could sit inside our bedroom within a circle of pebbles, with our or on the kitchen floor in a circle of chalk or salt. We can even prop ourselves up in bed on cushions and simply visualise a line of blue cold flame moving around the walls – behind us, to the left of us, to the front of us over the door and to the right, meeting back behind us. We can be bed-bound, incapacitated or have limited resources and still have the power to 'draw the line'.

Likewise, indoors or out, a piece of coloured ribbon or tape which can be strung across to cordon our space off, creating a boundary between this world and all others, is a very helpful ally. The ribbon can be stretched, for example, between a door handle and the back a chair, or tied between a table leg and a window frame, dividing the room into ordinary (five sense reality) space and spirit-space. Perhaps we can arrange it so that the ribbon loops around us on four sides, surrounding us, creating a new area within a familiar one. We can even just tie a piece of ribbon straight across part of a room, declaring one part to be our sacred area and the other our living area. We can unpin this ribbon when we finish and re-pin it the next time we go spiritwalking. No matter how basic this may seem if we do it with intent *then it is so*!

We may also like to consider other tools that can make a space temporarily special for us. We could have a cushion or rug that we use only for sitting on to do our spiritwalking work. Or we may bring out precious objects to have near us, like found stones, crystals, feathers, pinecones, bones or shells – things which make us feel a connection to the greater sacred All. Plants will help bring a wild green energy indoors. Perhaps we may like to burn a particular kind of essential oil or incense in our space to draw the line between what we usually do there and what we are to do now, letting the scent create an ambience that we immediately associate with spiritwalking. Likewise we may find that lighting candles, even a tea-light in a hand-painted jar, can evoke a particular feeling in us that is conducive to our working with the unseen. The point is that our psychic aids or tools need not be expensive or showy props but simple things that help us to evoke the necessary feelings we correlate with spiritwalking. We do not need shrines or altars to direct our devotions but we but we can utilise the idea of working with objects that help focus us on our intention, inspiring us to leave behind our cares and *look beyond.*

If we are prepared to be resourceful then we all have the creative ability to make the 'temporary temple' of which we have been speaking, no matter what our circumstances. This is *magic in the midst of life*, walking with spirit even as we walk in the world.

Unseen Sacred Space – Creating the Astral Office

As we now have a manifest place from which to work let us move on to the unseen part of our spiritwalking space – the astral office. The term office may strike us as rather coldly formal and it is certainly not to be taken literally as a room filled with filing cabinets, rather it gives us the impression of a secure working space in which we may take what we do seriously. Because we are used to thinking of offices as places where important business conducted it gives us a sense of the value of what we do there yet our office need not retain any of the negative connotations we may associate with places of business. We will find that instead of harsh strip lighting and insistently bleeping computers we will have a workplace of great beauty that blends with our own unique resonance as an eternal being. This office is a sanctuary for us, a place of safety that is also stimulating and satisfying to be around. It is for us to decide what sort of a place would offer us this kind of experience.

The best approach for this particular process is 'part Alice in Wonderland', part 'National Geographic' – employing both a lively mixture of fantasy and natural realism to the creation of our working space. By this we mean that it is appropriate for us to let our imaginations run riot with the things that we choose, perhaps designing an astral place that includes rivers of gold, talking trees and mountains of sparkling crystal as well as familiar features from our 'ordinary' natural world, such as a heather covered hillside or a wildflower meadow. Our astral office could feature a musical waterfall surrounded by windswept granite moors under which there lies a chamber that is a friendly dragon's lair or perhaps it is within a very ordinary seeming bluebell wood which has a shimmering silver pool and an enchanted fairy ring at its hidden heart. We are simply choosing all the places and features that we love in life, or have enjoyed in fairytales, and mixing them on the palette of our infinitely creative mind, a mind in which nothing is impossible. The key is for us to feel passionate or enthusiastic about the things we choose to include as the more feeling we have for our creation the more energised, and therefore real – ethe*real* – they will become for us.

It is important to stress here that this astral place is best based on the natural and the mythical *but not the modern man-made*. Although we may well see golden castles or sparkling glass towers in our astral office area it is advisable not to include the concrete and steel trappings of society in our astral office. This is because we are leaving that rather soulless reality far behind us and dealing solely with that which is gloriously magical, wholly natural or fantastically inspiring. We do not want attachments to anything of the lower/human astral and so all visual connections with modern Western society, and all its attendant destruction, stress and pollution, should not be brought, if at all possible, into this dimension of being. Our astral domain should be balanced and wholesome, an elemental celebration of all that is wild and wonderful. Think *otherworldly* and *olde worlde*, with natural stone, babbling brooks, creaking wooden gates and old orchards instead of bricks, tarmac, plastic and mobile phone masts...and don't forget a heavy pinch of stardust and whimsy!

Now that we have gathered a few of our favourite places and features together in our mind, making a mental list of them for reference, we are ready use our innate creative skills as co-creators of the universe. By this we will bring together all the concepts we have so far covered as we literally fashion energy in accordance with our own will. But before we continue we should now go forward a few pages and read through the process under the heading of *Directions for Creating an Astral Office* so that we are familiar with what will be required of us once we are in trance and spiritwalking.

As we are working with energies we will now need to put into practice our positioning, grounding and protective measures as discussed in Chapter Four. These are measures we should now be familiar with, as we have been utilising them during our daily connection to the Source. From now on whenever we are to undertake any unseen, or psychic, work we will use our protective routine in our physical sacred space. *It will be assumed that the reader understands this, and observes its practice, from here on in.*

So let us enter our physical sacred space now in order create our astral office. This we are to do by means of a *trance journey*.

Trance Journeying

Trance journeying is a method by which we may access the astral levels we have previously discussed – specifically, in this case, the local astral – and is a controlled, safe and legitimate way of gaining information, insight and inner vision. To some, the word trance implies that someone has gone into a state where he or she is out of control. In the case of spiritwalking this is never the case. When we are Trance journeying we are just as aware of ourselves, what we are doing, and why we are doing it as we are when we undertake a physical journey. We know who we are and what we are doing, as well as why we are doing it. The word trance merely denotes that we are not functioning in 'ordinary' five-sense reality, rather *beyond* it, at a profound level. We are using our inner sight and deep knowing, rather than our physical eyes and intellect, and therefore we may indeed appear to be 'out of it' to someone observing our closed eyes and serene demeanour. In fact to be en-*trance*-d in this sense is to be led by our eternal soul-selves, not our temporary human shells, and therefore is an act of empowerment, born of timeless wisdom and not of a senseless abandonment of out wits.

The Journey

When we are comfortable in our manifest sacred space, and are positioned, grounded, protected and ready to journey we can begin to deepen our trance state in the same way as we do when getting connected to Source. We slow our breathing and relax into a state in which there are no thoughts to distract us. There is nothing but breath, breath is life – *life-force*. Our breath is advancing and receding, expanding and contracting, filling and emptying. In and out...deeper and deeper...as natural and as rhythmic as the tides.

Keeping this rhythm going we can become aware of any thoughts that do pop up to interrupt our flow. If a thought crosses our mind then we should observe it as something that is of us but *it is not us*. Our thoughts are as flies at a summer picnic, unwanted but part of the natural order of life on Earth. It is for us to release the thoughts and watch them dissolve into the ocean of breath. It is not for us to catch the thoughts and worry at them. Let them go. Let the body go, limp and slack. Let all things go save breath. Deeper and deeper. In and out.

When we have reached a place of deep calm we can bring our spirit back to a place of awareness. This place is dark, endless, blissful, and peaceful – the dazzling darkness where we enter the silence and connect. As we do this we may have the sensation of tumbling over and over, a feeling of great freedom or weightlessness, yet we know our bodies are safely grounded in the manifest realm of Earth. The true essential eternal essence of our being is floating in the ether, between worlds, in a position of power and connection with all existence. We reach out towards the local astral, beyond human mores and influences. Out…beyond…and we are at an astral level beyond the lower human spheres of influence, in a realm where all things are possible. It is the place where we can begin to create – to actively intend.

What follows are the directions to help us to build our first conscious astral creation. It is hoped that we will have already read the following set through to familiarise ourselves with the format. We could then compile ourselves an audio cassette of the relevant directions that we can play back to ourselves once we are in the deeply relaxed trance state we have previously discussed and ready to begin the journey. Or, if it is possible, we could have a reliable person read us the directions as we sit in trance.

We will now continue from the place of deep connectedness we have reached in our well-protected meditative state. We should draw our attention back to the mental list of desirable geographical features we have compiled and have them ready to apply to the following process.

Directions for Creating an Astral Office.

1. **From the dazzling darkness of deep calm, the ocean of all potentiality, a vision begins to form**. From our position of power we look down into this fertile void. We look down to where our feet would be if we were standing on the land. But we find we are indeed standing on the land! Beneath our feet we feel contact with something solid or, at least, tangible. It has a temperature and a texture. Looking down to see what we are standing on our mind's eye beholds an image that is resonant to us, an image of something from the world of human beings that we hold sacred and dear – an image from our list. This image could be of cold flat stone, of lush grass, a clear pool or a tangled system of roots, of hot sand or of a tract of glittering blue-white ice. It is up to us to decide what it is. *What can we see in the down direction?*

2. **We expand our awareness now from the small patch we are standing on to what lies directly before it.** As we focus we can bring into being what we desire to see projected there. Whatever we are standing on unfolds before us like a beautiful rich tapestry, revealing more and more of itself until before long we are able to discern a full vista, coming into clarity. We can simply see the image spread, as the cinematic camera of our

intent pans out from our feet into the far distance. This is our northerly direction. *What can we see to the north?*

(Note: *If this process does not work for us immediately, with a scene building itself naturally from the ether in accordance with our own innate library of pleasing imagery, then let us actively paint the details of what we want to see on the blank canvas facing us. If we cannot imagine ourselves painting then we can use a collage technique, cutting and pasting imagery from our imaginings and layering them in to form a scene. And if we still cannot adequately see this then we may simply tell ourselves what lies ahead, allowing our visual references to follow our instructions gradually. Have no fear, for this is a magical reality in which all creation is possible. The astral/ether is the energy of creation, it cannot resist our instructions!*)

3. **With this clarity of vision, or with our focussed intent, now come sound, scent, and sensation**. We feel the presence of this northerly vista before us, becoming fully aware of each movement, atmospheric change, impression, hue, tone or fragrance. *What is the ambience of this direction?* Whatever there is we experience it fully. The things we have created now cease to be part of a two-dimensional 'carpet' or 'canvas' and come alive! We are in a living landscape, surrounded by all manner of growing things.

4. **From where we stand, facing forwards to the north, we look up and now observe what we may know as our above direction**. *What is above our heads if we extend our gaze to the skies?* Do we see clear colour or cloud; are there stars or planets to be seen even in this light? Can we see a source of illumination? Are there birds or any other creatures winging overhead?

5. **Now we may turn to our right. This is our easterly direction**. *What lies there to our east?* Let our gaze extend outwards, allowing ourselves time to savour the sensations that come with this direction.

6. **Now we turn again to our right, standing with our backs to our original northerly direction**. *What lies in the region that is behind our initial scene, our southerly direction?* Is the northerly panorama continued at 180 degrees or is the something quite different in the direction we now face? Perhaps in the north we were facing the sea whilst now in the southerly direction we are facing a cave mouth whilst above it are cliffs topped with scrubland. Breathe in this direction and reach to its furthest limits, painting in or describing all that we feel should be present there.

7. **Now of course we will turn again and be facing what will be our westerly direction**. *What lies to the west?* What is the ambience of this direction? (Note: *It is easy to get a little blasé at this stage and to skip on some of the detail in order to rush on with the experience but this is a crucial part of the creation process and we should be prepared to devote an ample amount of attention to seeing both the detail and the broader impression, like an artist wanting to present a believable three-dimensional representation of something he or she sees. In artistic terms we are not looking for abstract impressionism but rather photo-realism, a detailed study rather than a quick sketch. After all, we have to believe in this reality just as much as we believe in the one we experience when we open our eyes or ears each morning.*)

8. **When we have turned once through this cycle we can turn once more through 360 degrees to reaffirm, or add into,**

any area that seemed unclear or less 'lifelike' than another.
When we have made this secondary observation with all our
senses we now have a pretty much complete idea of what lies
all around us, above and below us. We will naturally have a
predilection for some directions more than others and so some
areas may be weak. They will, if the other areas remain 'fed' by
our input, gain their own strength and fill in the gaps for us.
Nature, and especially the 'super-nature' of our astral creation,
does not tolerate a vacuum for long and we will find that images
naturally 'bleed' into each other as does paint, creating their own
interesting features. Creation is the motivating force of the universe and so energy will expand creatively around us if we give
it enough impetus. We will, no doubt, be surprised by what we
come up with, even without consciously meaning to.

9. **When we have assessed the astral region from our
initial position we should make an exploration of the one
direction that pulls us most strongly.** *This is the direction
that we will want to spend the most time in and so it is the
best choice for creating our special office area – our unseen
sanctuary.* Although all of our astral landscape should feel secure
to us this is one area that needs to feel like our true refuge or
haven, as we are going to be engaging with, and opening up to,
other spirits here. We should ensure that this area has any special
features that particularly attract us and afford us a sense of
well-being – a clear bubbling stream perhaps, a rose garden in
full bloom, a grove of nodding palms or a stone circle built of
quartz that glitters in the permanent sunshine. Perhaps it simply
consists of pale rolling sandy dunes, a plateau overlooking
snow-capped peaks or a field of waving golden corn. Whatever it

contains it is special to us, moving us in a way that is deeper than the other directions we have experienced so far.

10. **When we have identified a particular spot in our astral landscape that will be our special office area then we need to fashion a doorway, or portal, to it.** Like any entrance way this signifies the move from one kind of space into another and this particular door/portal will signify a transition into an even deeper level of awareness. *It is a symbol of moving further into the beyond and away from 'ordinary' reality so that we may commune more readily with spirit there.* If we want to literally put a door or a gate in the middle of the landscape then so be it but the doorway/portal is, like so many things in spiritwalking, purely a metaphor. For example, we may prefer to utilise a natural portal, such as a hollow tree that enables us to move *through* it, rather than creating an actual gateway in a wall. Alternatively we can consider a portal to be a passing place, like a row of stepping-stones or a bridge – a means by which we can cross *over*. Or we may prefer to move *under* to the other side of awareness, using any structure with a tunnel-like quality such as two trees bowing together to form an arch. As long as we have somewhere that allows us to make a transition from our current state of awareness to an even deeper one then we have been successful in our choice.

11. **We should then always pass through the doorway or portal we have created as we approach our astral workspace.** *Therefore we should always follow the same route.*

12. **We can now spend time in our special area, refining it, making it as we wish it to be.** This is where we come into our own as creators, effectively pouring our energy into pleasing

forms, moulding it like sculptors into that which we desire whilst using all our senses to make the experience entirely real to us. This is our space, the one place in Creation that is ours alone to colour, and we can make it as vibrant as we choose. Of course, the more we visit this special place the more we will be able to energise and enhance what we initially intend into being.

13. **As we create we may wish to consider our guests that are to visit us here in the future.** As within an earthly office, that we need seating – or at least somewhere where we can offer our spirit guests a place to rest and commune with us. Although they will not have made a hard physical journey they have still (astrally) travelled to see us and are still our guests, therefore we can still behave accordingly. Perhaps a few old logs covered in ivy would serve as a seating area or maybe we would prefer a natural depression in a rock, a bench woven from living willow branches or simply a patch of springy moss.

14. **We may finally consider that it is beneficial to maintain an open meeting/working space**. By this we may see the comings and goings around us rather than our trying to create a sheltered or closed in area, separate from the environment. We should take care to remember that here in this astral place we can work 'outdoors' without fear of rain or cold and we have our psychic protection to cover us from any unwanted intrusions, therefore we do not need to have a roof or walls between our surroundings and us. The climate, as with everything else in our astral place, is within our power and we can have the pleasure of an exposed working space that is not subject to the vagaries of anyone's weather but our own! In the case of the astral office we always bring the weather we want with us. Also it is well for us

to keep a three hundred and sixty degree outlook from our astral office if at all possible. This not only gives us a sense of place within the astral landscape we have created but it also empowers us as we will always have the ability to witness any incomer who has not been invited into our realm.

15. **We can now leave the astral office**; retracing our steps through the doorway/portal etc and following the same route back to our starting point, and then back to 'ordinary' reality.

16. **On our return into 'ordinary' reality we need to ground ourselves.**

Grounding – Coming Back to Earth

Grounding is as valid a part of the process as is protection and no spiritwalking session is complete without it at its conclusion. As we have suggested previously, we can do this grounding in basic physical ways – by rubbing our hands, stretching and stamping our feet, as well as by taking a little light refreshment – but the most important aspect of grounding ourselves is by keeping a record of all that has just happened.

The most common way of record keeping is by the use of a journal. The actual creation of our own journal can be a valuable part of the process of dedication to our life and work as a spiritwalker. We can either do this by customising a notebook, perhaps using a scrap-booking style, or by actually fashioning our own paper and binding it. Making our own paper obviously means we can imbue each page with our intent and can give it our vital energy. The very act of pressing pulp to make a new material is an act of transfomative sympathetic magic in itself, one that binds us together with our purpose even as we bind the freshly made pages. Perhaps

as we press the pages together we could be focussing on such vows
as:

- *'May I travel well, in safety, for the good of the All'*
- *'May I journey deeply for inner wisdom and outer clarity'* or
- *'May I follow the sacred ways of the spiritwalker, in truth
  and beauty'*

Also, of course, the process of paper making is an ethical act that tie
us into the cycles of existence, linking us with donor trees and
giving us respect for the resources the Earth bequeaths to us –
bringing us into closer harmony with the All. Such caring acts, filled
with positive intent, reaffirm what we spiritwalkers do as being
relevant, and indeed essential, for the Twenty First Century. I give
instructions on how to make paper in my book *Green Spirituality*
(Green Magic, 2004) written under the pseudonym of Rosa Romani.

Another advantage of creating our own journal is that writing on
handmade paper can be a deeply sensuous experience to be
savoured, not rushed. The extra effort it requires to write on the
slightly uneven surface stops us from hastening through our
journaling process, ensuring we adopt a more conscientious
approach. There is something deliciously arcane about the leisurely
process of writing in a handmade journal – it is an act that is in the
world but not fully of modern society. Yet although it is precious it
is not the only way to keep spiritwalking records. Taking into
account some of us are not at our best with the written word we
could utilise a more contemporary method, speaking into a
Dictaphone instead of transcribing our journeys. By this we can
aurally note our experiences and findings onto tape. This method,

although more prosaic, has the advantage that we can carry a Dictaphone discretely with us in a pocket and record any feelings or insights when we are on the go.

The main thing is that we engage with the grounding process of recording our findings, understanding that there is no right or wrong way means to do this. However, there *are* rules we can apply from the outset to ensure that we get the most from our annotations, both now and in the future. One such rule is that we should never overlook any detail, no matter how random or ridiculous it seems. All information we psychically receive in trance, or all that we experience as intuitions or dreams, should always be noted and never discarded as a tedious irrelevance. Such attention to detail strengthens our ability to witness the unseen with greater clarity, leading us away from the laziness of generalisation. I can vouch for the need to note even the silliest seeming details of a trance journey or communication as later they will always prove interesting, if not important. Even this week I have been alerted to a simple piece of symbolism, a single shining sword, which I received in a trance seven years ago. Thankfully I noted this seemingly minor detail down at the time, in the context in which it was originally given, which has enabled me to look back and understand why it is relevant to me today.

As a further example, perhaps when we are recording our experiences of creating our astral office we may have witnessed small anomalies that appear as trivia within the exciting whole. Such points may be things like *'the row of poplar trees which I wanted in my special astral place would always bend over to the left when I tried to focus on them'* or *' try as I might I simply could not visualise the sand as pearly white as I wanted but only as a kind of deep terracotta colour'*. Who knows what symbology these two pieces of anomalous material will have for us at a later date? There are no coincidences in spiritwalking and the more we connect to the All we will realise that, everything has a meaning and is relevant somehow, even if how is not clear to us yet.

Later in our spiritwalking journeys, when we are meeting other beings in our astral office, we may want to note down such seemingly trivial, but undoubtedly irregular, things as *'he was wearing green shoes when previously he has professed to find the colour unpleasant'* or *'I overheard the name Emmeline three times on my journey although I know no one of that name.'* These remarks may seem impenetrable or even as superfluous nonsense now but there are usually little gems hidden within even the most mystifying or banal material that we come across on our journeys.

Another rule is for us to say what we actually saw, or heard, *not what we think we should have seen or heard.* When we work as spiritwalkers we experience things on many levels, often receiving symbolic imagery as part of our experiences, and just because something seems bizarre or improbable it doesn't mean that we should second-guess what it was really mean to be and override the original image or statement given to us. Our conscious mind always has the most logical explanation that may completely go against the subtle symbolism or lilting lyricism of what was intended for us. For example, we go to our astral office one day and find an old fashioned golden key, its top shaped like an Ace of Clubs, sticking out of a large rock where we usually sit. As we stand looking at this key in the stone a large flock of geese fly honking overhead. Afterwards we should make a note of this event *exactly as it we saw it* and not simply write up an analysis of what we think it means. By keeping a clear record we have a much better chance of recognising its true meaning when the time is right. By just writing a lot of speculation we may be way off beam and so lose sight of the core message. For instance, I recently witnessed a Spiritwalker interpret 'men in white' as cricketers when it actually turned out to refer to men on a spiritual pilgrimage overseas!

Once we have completed our journaling or recording process, along with other grounding activities such as eating, drinking, making bodily movements or sounds, then we can then relax or simply carry on with our day.

In future we can utilise a ready-made journey as either a framework or just a guiding example for us to study in order to see if we have the right idea. If we do go for this option then we must be sure to add a little, or a lot, of ourselves into what has been given to us, customising it in the same way one may liven up a jacket bought straight from the rack with a pocket handkerchief, row of new buttons or decorative brooch on the lapel. Even when we are using someone else's framework our spiritwalking really does require effort, or an input of energy, from us. Such 'ready-made' trance journeys will be known, from hereon in, as *pathworkings*.

Pathworkings are rather like focussed teachers who can lead us through the labyrinth of the Otherworlds, or unseen realms, to enable us to reach a certain point, level or lesson. Because of this we may find it useful to record ourselves reading all subsequent pathworkings so that we may follow the instructions on a personal stereo, just as we would listen to and be guided by a tutor's voice. It is virtually impossible to memorise all such instructions without a photographic memory (although we can probably memorise a string of cues such as 'stream, hollow tree, flat plain, rocky outcrop' etc.)

and so it is by far the best method to have a taped voice to guide us, be that our own or of someone else reading the instructions. The pathworkings given in this book will have many evocative touches within their matrix and so it is well for us to have them read out so that we can make our journey rich and alive.

So, we are now able to trance journey in the local astral realm and have experience of deliberately creating with energy. Every time we wish to go and do our spiritwalking we can make this journey to our astral office, following the given procedure in our own unique way until it becomes second nature to us. We can, of course, over time and with experience, travel in all directions from this initial point of creation and get to know our etheric landscape in intimate detail. I would assume that eventually, as both our confidence and curiosity grow, that we would have such a need to get to know our fabulous realm.

As we become more and more familiar with our safe astral space we will no doubt begin to sense other presences there, or, indeed, to begin to desire their presence. Because of this in the next chapter we will begin to encounter other beings in a safe and enjoyable way, beginning with our most vital and valuable co-workers – our companion spirits.

CHAPTER EIGHT

A FRIEND IN NEED

'Your loneliness is an illusion, spiritwalker, and your sadness
only the cold fog of your *forgetting* that has been allowed to
settle for too long. When a daily connection is made to Source
then the light that results will burn this fog of separation and
doubt away, leaving only clarity and endless unity. When your
soul's light is as the noonday sun then we shall stand before
you, revealed as surely as are the shadows at your feet. And,
just as your shadow does, we pace you, unconditionally present,
feeling your joy, sharing your pain. Yet we are not servants,
only *waiters* – those who wait for you to *re-member* that
limitless love is the only reality and none stand alone when
there are no boundaries. Our ceaseless companionship is
indeed the quiet steadfast unity of a body and its shadow,
forever united in the light of One-ness. We are but a
particular point of re-membering for you, a way for you to
experience, one-on-one and day-to-day, an endless, marvellous
truth. Not alone, all One.'
From Guidance

In this chapter we begin to meet other spirits, which is one of
the most exciting and challenging aspects of our work as
spiritwalkers. Although some of us may already have a relationship
with other spirit-beings it is well to keep reading as even our current
associations can be deepened and a greater level of understanding
achieved. By going through the processes outlined in this chapter we

are able to attain the most effective relationship possible with those we work with at an unseen level.

Before we actively meet our companion spirits, let us consider the axiom '*may I keep what is mine and may you keep what is yours*'. This is an invaluable rule of thumb when meeting new beings. Because of the sentiments of this maxim it may well be relevant for us to refresh our memories on the information we gained in Chapter Two as regards knowing who and what we are, in terms of our essential energetic (soul) nature – *what is ours*. When we have once again considered our own true nature we will be in a stronger position to continue on the path of the spiritwalker, attaining successful contact with other essences and beings whilst always knowing what is energetically ours…*and what is not*. By this we will be able to come and go in safety, carrying no baggage save the knowledge we have gained and witnessing truth with the clarity of an authentic Seer – One who *looks beyond*.

So, with this ethos to the fore let us recap on the nature of our companion spirits, before engaging in a journey to meet them. To do this we will need to reinforce the principles we have previously touched upon, bringing the knowledge we have gained so far to the front of our awareness.

Our Friends in Need

We all have a need for friends and a friend who is unseen, with access to all the mysteries of life that we feel are denied to us as humans, is clearly a desirable proposition. Young children are seldom without their own 'invisible' friends and as adults there is no reason why we should be without ours. Our companions in spirit are just waiting to be contacted and worked with.

Firstly what, or more accurately, who are the companions? Well, as we have previously stated, companion spirits are wise and compassionate unseen beings that have elected to help us grow to our fullest capacity as spirits incarnate. Being discarnate themselves at present they exist as pure energy, as the individual expressions of life-force we have come to witness as souls.

These souls have all experienced life on Earth, or in a physical body elsewhere, which means that they can relate well to the dilemmas of being incarnate on a corporeal level. They may not have walked the Earth, or any other manifest place, for aeons (in our human reckoning) but as discarnate existence is but a point of perception, a state of awareness with no time attached to it, they are able to still relate to the trials and tribulations of incarnate being as if it were yesterday. They, as unique conscious beings, have opted to remain closely attuned to this dense level of being for the purpose of aiding others still caught in the diversions and illusions of manifest existence – and in this instance they have chosen to aid us personally.

By this they can empathise with us almost as well as if they were still 'of the flesh' but instead of being too grounded in human issues they have the benefit of the overview, or 'bigger picture', that they can share with us. They have the advantage of being in their pure soul-state, unencumbered by life-problems, yet have the ability to understand our current struggles at a human level – an important balance. They are able to straddle the divide between the manifest and the *beyond*, holding both spaces equally, acting as a bridge or link between the seen and unseen realities. This they do for the specific purpose of bring us deep insights into our current circumstances as they relate to the mysteries of existence. It is these insights that we will come to know as *guidance*.

Now we know of their role we can ask which particular groups of spirits are drawn to working with us as companions.

Who Makes a Good Companion?

Clearly there needs to be stability and maturity there for a soul to be adept at acting as such a bridge. The soul must be secure in their own advanced level of wisdom as well as being responsible, and selfless enough, to take on the mentoring of another soul. Companion spirits will need to be steadfast, willing to stick with their chosen protégé for the course of an incarnation, yet also responsive and flexible enough to cope with the unexpected that life inevitably throws at an individual. They will also need to show a marked degree of consideration and care for their protégé, displayed alongside a healthy objectivity. This may be the toughest balancing act of all for the companion spirits, keeping a deeply loving yet unsentimental attachment whilst practicing an essential detachment. Our clear, calm companions are certainly remarkable beings to achieve this blend, not infallible (for they are not gods) but unfailingly reliable and dedicated.

As well as the admirable personal soul-traits the companion must have there must also be a pronounced degree of empathy between the companion, or guide, and the person being guided. There would be no sense in a companion having a protégé that they find energetically repellent, dull or confusing – and vice versa. There must be a reason why the companion and the person they are to mentor are drawn together in the first instance. Clearly there needs to be some sort of etheric bond or vibrational match already in existence for a working relationship to be built upon. To explain this we will generally find that our companion spirits come from one of the following categories:

- **Ancestral** – these are the companions that are linked to our current physical body by a bloodline they have once shared with us. In this respect an ancestral companion guide can be a dead relative that we have known, although generally this link may be too emotionally fraught for the objectivity required in effective mentoring. More likely an ancestral guide may be one whose relation to our current body is from a more distant past. Indeed we need never have physically met, or even heard of, our companion as a physical part of our current family for them to forge an effective ancestral link. They will have an interest in us, as one of their old body's distant relatives, and therefore may feel the necessary empathy with our current plight or progress. We may even find that ancestral companions come from tribes or races that we have both shared when in physical life. For instance, our ancestral companion may have shared our African blood in many lifetimes even though we have not come from the same family directly. Or perhaps there is a strong Romany connection that, unbeknownst to us, we have in our body's heritage. Our soul often has a strong affinity with one particular ethnic group and our companion may reflect that deep soul pull to that way of being.
- **Soul-kin** – these are those who are from our own soul collective, or eternal affinity group. As we have previously discussed, our own soul characteristics may be shared by other cells in the greater body of Creation to some considerable degree. These single cells collect into wider cells of allegiance, what we

may call co-operatives, and they regroup again after death just as they may have worked together in life. It is to these that we refer when we speak of soul-kin – those who share our innate nature and perhaps come from a particular network of affiliated spirits. It is easy to see why our soul-kin would wish to help us. As part of their collective spiritual group our well-being whilst we are incarnate is of great interest and import to them. They want us to do well, and to learn successfully, whilst we have a body so that our experiences will filter back into the group more effectively.

• **Soul-tied** – these are those spirits who we have worked with us intensely, one-to-one, in other lives yet who are not necessarily of our soul group. These lives could have been on Earth or elsewhere and could be past (or, indeed, parallel or future) lives. We would have established a passionate or deeply felt bond of trust with this spirit whilst they, and we, lived. Now they dwell in spirit we are able to benefit once again from their trustworthy nature or caring approach towards us. Even though we are not of the same essential nature we may experience a harmonious balance when we work with them, a blend of energies that is conducive to learning. To this end we could be quite opposite on the energetic scale and, without friction and with respect, offer each other something we lack within.

• **Learning-based** – these relationships are with the highly advanced souls who have no particular tie or affinity to us but who want to expand their understanding of a particular trait or difficulty we have, such as an addiction or disability. They are wise and experienced enough to take us on in order to hone their already considerable skills and brush up on any soul-weaknesses they feel they may have. Also we may be drawn to them as we are in need of learning experiences in areas that are their specialties. We become, in the best possible sense, their project and we are in excellent hands even though they have no emotive, or motivating, soul-link with us. Such advanced souls do not need to have ties or links in order for them to feel a profound degree of affinity with us; they are simply compassionate and empathetic by nature.

• **Nature-linked** – the souls that are linked to us by nature are those who have a resonance with us even if they are not of our soul group or of our ancestral group. This would include any creatures or mythical beings that share our *essential* nature, for our companions are not always of a human soul-type. For example, if our soul is particularly 'Piscean' by nature we may attract 'watery' spirits as companions. These may be the souls of mythical mer-folk, sea serpents or selkies or they may be faery souls such as those of undines or sprites. Indeed our companion spirits may simply be those who have lived in or near water like seahorses, dolphins or gulls, or even human fisher folk. Less obviously they may be those souls who share the watery theme but rather *symbolically,* having qualities of water such as being deeply poetic, emotional or sensitive.

As usual this list is not exhaustive but it will give us a much better idea of why a companion may choose to work with us and who they may be.

Where for Art Thou, Companion?

So, where do these disembodied, yet communicative, companion spirits dwell? As we have previously suggested, they exist at an astral level that is *not* the one closest to humanity. Companion spirits need to be close to us, yes, but not as close as the collective energetic morass that is the human astral. We can locate them, if location can be pinpointed in such a way in etheric terms, in the next 'layer of the astral onion'. This is, as we have previously ascertained, is the local area of the greater astral, the unseen region where we have created our astral office. As we know, it is a place where independent and free-spirited souls can exercise their will for the greater good, having the benefit of far-sight yet the relative closeness, if they so choose, to human affairs.

We can now appreciate both who our companions may be in relation to us and where, metaphorically speaking, they can be found. Our next question should be what is their role? We have answered this by way of a brief introduction to our guiding spirits previously in Chapter Four but let's reiterate, and elaborate on, their function now.

The Job Description of a Companion Spirit

1. They are our most trustworthy *friends*, with us to give us comfort and invisible support whilst retaining that clear-headed objectivity that we so need from them. Theirs is the reassurance of an unseen presence that is benevolent and caring in a world that can seem, for us as human beings, quite the opposite. They are our supporters yet never sycophantic, continuing to 'root' for us through thick and thin whilst always offering us their unbiased, calm advice. They stand by us, often regardless of our circumstances or behaviours, and they will do this or whether we acknowledge them or not. Their air of gentle, but powerful, unconditional love may lead us to believe that they are our guardian angels.

2. They are our *guides*, not our controllers. They are not able to

intervene or make changes for us unless we ask them directly to do so, except for in exceptional circumstances (for example, a moment of extreme danger). They are not our ruling superiors, nor our manipulators pulling our strings, and therefore have no right to interfere in our choices. Their role is as our mentor who can advise and suggest, based on their experience and the 'bigger picture' that they have access to.

3. They are our *escorts*, acting as travel guides to enable us to traverse the Otherworlds in safety. They are also our instructors who share their in-depth knowledge of what we may, or will, find in 'foreign' unseen places. They are effective soul-couriers.

4. They are our *conduits*, our link between this dense earthly level and the faster, higher, more pure levels of existence that lie beyond them. They join with us so that our connection with the unseen may be strong and stable, as well as much more far reaching than it would be if we worked with spirit alone. Linked with them we can reach the *beyond* whilst alone we may only reach our nearest neighbours in the lower human astral who, as shall discover in Chapter Thirteen, can be very troublesome. To return to our trusty electrical analogy, the companions act as an extension lead that we may plug into, thus enabling us to stretch our own connective cable further.

5. They are our *transmitters,* broadcasting to us that which lies beyond normal human sight or knowing and giving us a wider transmission than we alone could pick up. To use analogy, they are on a 'broadband' connection, compared to our own 'dial-up' version, and have a digital capacity rather than our more limited analogue range.

6. They are our *bodyguards*, protecting us from any unnecessary harm and enabling us to protect ourselves. They will allow us to

experience hardship if it will have something to teach us but they tend to act as filters for any extraneous energy that will cause us gratuitous damage. This is intensified when we actively acknowledge their presence and work with them.

7. They will also act as *caretakers*, a practical healing presence that can help us to cleanse our energies (or auric field) and enabling us to fix physical ailments. They give us, or advise us on, the best tools for the job.

8. They are our *instructors*, giving us vital information for our spiritual growth and understanding. They have opted to teach us all they know and are willing to find out information for us if they cannot answer us immediately. Like all good teachers they are prepared to admit they don't know something and to go away and do some research of their own. Therefore are not perfect, just far more connected to the Source than we are at present. Our dense physical bodies hamper that connection by their very nature whilst the companions are free of this encumbrance.

As ever this list isn't conclusive and we can no doubt add to it ourselves as we go along.

And what lies outside their remit or is not their role? This is easy to answer as it is very clear.

What a Companion is Not

- A dictator seeking dominion
- A slave or servant
- A genie to grant us our wishes
- A beings with an agenda in opposition to our highest good
- A god or omnipotent
- Completely infallible

Our relationships with these uniquely benevolent souls should be treasured and, like the best friendships, never taken for granted or abused. The amount we put into this friendship will very much reflect what we receive, just as in 'ordinary' human reality. It must never be overlooked that these souls are just as much in need of love, respect and consideration as any other being. They are not exempt from the normal rules of existence, hence why they sometimes misinterpret things or present us with information that is, like anything else, subject to change. They may occasionally be less than a hundred percent accurate but their intention is never less than entirely genuine and they will always take the time to explain a process to us. Our courtesy and care means a great deal to them – as the metaphysical poet John Donne so famously observed, no man is an island and this applies just as much to those beings who are discarnate as to those who currently have physical form.

A Lasting Friendship?

We keep speaking of unique souls here and indeed all souls are unique. But are our companions also singularly special to us in that they are our one and only guide for a lifetime? And is this guiding spirit we get at birth the only one that we will ever know or do they indeed come and go throughout an incarnation? Indeed can there ever be more than one unseen companion at any one time?

Firstly there is no hard and fast ruling on the number of companion guides we may have, either at any one time or throughout a lifetime. We may find that one steadfast companion has decided to stay with us throughout all the seasons of our incarnation and will remain with us until we leave this physical life. We may also find that we have had more than one companion guide so far and that we may indeed have another one, or more, in the future. This is not because companions are fickle; rather they will come and go only if there are others who have opted to co-work with us for a period of time. In this instance the original companion will step aside while the guest companion, or companions, comes into our sphere of being for a while. Yet it is unlikely indeed that our original unseen mentor will disappear for good.

So, we definitely have one, and often two, key-workers, that is to say *core guides* who will remain present throughout our Earth-walk. However, there may be affiliated *guest guides* who step in to help us throughout a particular life-phase or problem. These secondary guides may have specialisms that we may benefit from, such as an ability to work with those who are physically sick or mentally traumatised, and so they come forward for a time when we are experiencing a testing time to give us the benefit of their own experience and skill. We may indeed be fortunate enough to have a team of such skilled souls with us from the beginning of our life, perhaps two or three companions who work well together and whose energy blend is exactly what we need.

At this juncture I hope that it will be useful, rather than confusing, to add this aside. My one of my own core companions has remained constant throughout my life so far yet has changed his appearance to suit any particular life-phase and all its attendant preferences. His root being, his *essence*, has kept our connection while the appearance he adopts for my benefit has altered, tailored to my prevailing energies. I have thought that he has gone away or been replaced when in fact it is only his packaging or costume that has morphed into something more resonant for me…his essence has remained the same. Thus far he has been a Native American elder, a

Welsh shepherd and a solitary Gypsy gentleman. This illustrates that the appearance of the companion is just cosmetic, a case of dressing up for our ease of recognition. But more on the appearances of our guides shortly.

I have yet to put a limit on the number of companion spirits we may have at any one instance. For example, at the moment my two core guides have stepped back to allow two specialist guest guides step in and help me through a particular life-phase. Along with them at the moment I have a spirit companion in the form of a mythical being (winged white horse) and two animal helpers (moon-pale snake and crow) who come and go. There really are no hard and fast rules. Only common sense dictates that we cannot possibly relate to a vast throng of spirits all at once. Perhaps three is a good number for us to work closely with at any one time, the optimum number for us to have a relationship with all at once. Yet this is only a guideline. We could in theory have a team of four or five core helpers that come and go and that we are perfectly happy to work with in rotation. It is as personal to us as our fingerprints and all variations are valid as long as they work well for all concerned.

When we develop a relationship with our companion spirits, as well as any other helpers, we will find that they will let us know if they have to step back for a while, and why. They will not simply leave us stranded or confused if we maintain that active interaction with them. Their role is not to make us uncomfortable and bewildered, rather to help us to maintain state of balance and harmony, and so it is highly unlikely a core guide would simply disappear. More likely, as with my own case, they will morph or shape-shift their appearance and we may believe that they have gone, when in fact they are still with us in another form. My own guide did this to test my ability to tune into energy beyond appearances. Yet before ruling out the rare scenario that they would leave us for good let us consider any exceptional circumstances that may necessitate this behaviour.

These may include:

- Our unexpectedly committing a murder
- Our engaging in a vicious assault
- Our suddenly becoming very mentally unstable
- Our having a dramatic physical accident or illness

These are scenarios which may prompt the guide's reluctant departure but *only because there will be another companion at hand who is more able to take on the role now needed.* At such a vulnerable time we would never be left bereft one with more experience of such energies would step in the role of a relief spirit worker. These are specialists who can cope much better with incidents of this nature which are unexpected and, perhaps, too much for our initial companion to take on board at that time. Remember companions are not infallible, just spirits who have the 'bigger picture' and a willingness to help, and therefore they may find that such circumstances are currently too much for them in terms of energy. They do have to come into close energetic contact with us after all and such an act may mean that they find it too difficult to get draw near. They may think they can cope but find that they cannot. In this we should not feel disappointment, only joy in the fact they have tried and trust that they will get a more appropriate replacement for us.

Let us state this loud and clear – a companion would not bale out on us because they found us distasteful or too much like hard work. They are simply wise enough to know their limits and they hand us over to other 'professional' spirits with the deepest love and regret. *We would never, ever be left without a companion.* As I am fond of saying in my work, just like belly buttons every one has a companion, no matter what. This is an immutable fact. It is nothing to do with our deserving one, nor does it have conditions on our exemplary behaviour. Who we work with only depends on their being able to work with us easily for the highest good, having a compatible or complementary energy.

Putting us at Ease – Our Companions in Costume

As I have already implied our companions are wont to disguise themselves to help us feel more at ease. It would obviously be counter-productive for a peace-loving person to have a companion who appeared to them in trance as a hard-nosed marine or S.A.S man. Just as it wouldn't be constructive for a frilly Little-Bo-Peep type character to introduce themselves as our guide if we like a no nonsense and practical approach. Similarly it wouldn't be the best idea for a Chinese Mandarin companion to appear for someone who has an overwhelming affinity for Ireland and an antipathy towards the Orient. Energetically the costume that is worn must be the most effective one for the job in hand – the appearance of our companion is tailored to our needs at any one time. We would not work as a chef in a crowded kitchen dressed in a voluminous floor-length ball gown and our companion would see it as similarly impractical to appear to us in a guise we found irritating, frightening or distracting.

With our own innate preferences in mind our companions are notorious for appearing as figures that they feel have a resonance with trustworthiness and wisdom, hence the proliferation of sages, wizards and monks etc. in the retinue of recorded spirit guides. This may be suitable when we are in our spiritual 'infancy', taking our first steps back into the unseen, as it has a tried and tested appeal and we may well feel safe with a wise Priestess of Isis, Native American Medicine Man, Poor Clare Nun or a Tibetan Lama – I know I did! All that is happening here is that our companion is dipping into the astral dressing up box and coming up with a guise that will please and reassure our psyche. This is not to say they are dishonest or trying to con us, rather they are just attempting to put us at our ease so that communication and trust can be established.

Sometimes the companion will revert to a form that we will recognise from another life or time with them. For example, perhaps we had a deep and trusted relationship with our companion when they taught us music in Eighteenth Century Germany, allowing us to go on and be highly successful. In this case our companion would don the guise of this persona of music teacher that would immediately instil a deep sense of confidence and happiness in us, even if we did not consciously recall that particular life at that time. Similarly we may have had an incarnation when our companion saved our life when we were both hunters in the last Ice Age and consequently, although it may seem a crude and unlikely disguise, a simple man dressed in skins would inspire great faith in us immediately. Or our companion may appear as a ragged child to us, which may seem like an unlikely choice when we ourselves are now adults and need someone to look up to and rely on. Yet this may be how we last saw them as a dear and trusted sibling who looked after us when we shared an incarnation as part of a large family who worked on the canals of Victorian England. How are companions appear may seem strange to some but will always be tailored to our specific needs.

It may seem rather a paradox to think about appearances at all when we are discussing the unseen. Our companions are in spirit, not in flesh, but as we are in flesh we prefer to meet with an apparently physical consort rather than with a puff of smoke, shimmering haze or a dancing light. We can relate better to a recognisable form, and preferably one that resonates with our current state of being, as opposed to a luminous, etheric miasma of some sort! Our companions are indeed but a light-form or vibrational etheric body in the unseen realms in which they dwell but this does not serve us when we have 'face to face' astral meetings. Perhaps as we progress we will become more willing to accept guidance from non-human, and even non-physical, beings – finding as easy to talk to a ray of light as it is to talk to the figure of a Siberian shaman. This would be a good aim for us to have, allowing ourselves to move away from human-centricity and into a more universal energetic awareness of being, using our inner wisdom to intuit a presence rather than our always relying blatantly visual cues.

For now our companion will certainly don an appropriate costume for us in trance journey. In all other communications with them they need not show themselves to us in any guise, rather using direct guidance which we hear or perceive. More on this in the next chapter.

How to Meet the Companions in the Astral Office

For this we need to embark on the journey to the special, safe area we created on the astral in Chapter Seven.

Before we begin we should, of course, prepare ourselves

appropriately for an otherworldly encounter, following our protective procedure for undertaking any spiritwalking. Then we need to follow the route of the trance journey as before until we come to our astral office.

Although we have already fashioned this special place we have not yet used it for a meeting. We should therefore take some time to bring this region into being as much as we can so that our encounter with our companion has as much energy and clarity behind it as possible. For this strengthening of our astral environs we employ our senses to their fullest – seeing each part of the office in minute detail, experiencing its light and shade, feeling its textures, scenting its particular fragrances, hearing any background sounds such as birdsong, running water or the wind in the trees. To ensure that our experience is of a panoramic place of three dimensions we should ensure that we turn slowly around all three hundred and sixty degrees. This is vital to the efficacy of our work as we need to be convinced that we are inviting guests into a living, breathing and authentic realm not a two dimensional backdrop that may melt away at any second. We should have all six directions in place and be centred at the seventh, within ourselves.

From this point we can proceed make a statement of intent, an invocation. Here we are to invoke for the presence of our true companion spirits (we can say spirits plural to cover the possibility of there being more than one, however this also covers them turning up as singular guides). We may say something like :

'*I stand now in my own secure office and ask that my working partner, or partners – my own true companions who come for my highest possible good – come to me*'

As we do this we should extend our forefinger of our favoured hand, the one that represents our will, and see a beam of purest blue-white light emit from it. This ray should be rather like a laser beam. Perhaps it will aid our imaginings if we consider our finger as being somewhat akin to the light-sabre used by the Jedi in the Star Wars films – only this is our *intent sabre*. We then point this beam downwards and trace a large figure of eight upon the ground. This should be big enough for us to stand in one of the loops whilst allowing enough room for others to gather in the other one. Do not be afraid of doing this – the beam is kind-light, or cold-fire, and cannot harm any plants that dwell on the surface or, indeed, us. In our realm we mean no harm and so no harm will come.

We then step into our chosen side of the loop and say:

'Here is a space between the worlds that I have prepared for you where both you and I will be safe. Please show your selves truly to me now and step into the loop!'

We can then wait for the arrival of our companions who have been called.

What happens next is, of course, a highly individual matter that will be tailored to our needs and means. A presence will become discernible within the other loop. Perhaps there will be a glow or light-form, or perhaps a fully-fledged figure with plainly distinguishable features. Perhaps we may get little impression of who is there but rather sense that someone now is. In order to get more clarity and to affirm our desire we then say:

'Show yourself, show yourself, show yourself!'

We then point our beam of light at the form/figure/presence. This is not a gesture of aggression but of affirmation – it is our way of testing and confirming the veracity of a being. If the guide is truly our own companion they will now become clearer and more visible to us. If they are not our true companion/s they will fade from the blaze of our kind-light/cold-fire and be replaced by our authentic companion. Obviously if there is more than one spirit then they will all become more tangible. None can resist the firm but fair command of our testing. This is our space with our rules!

We should then wait, and keep pointing until we are able to discern the companion as a verifiable reality in this unseen world. When we are certain of their validity then we can lower and retract our beam of light. If we are in need, at this early stage, of more proof of their true nature as our companion then we may hold up a 'truth mirror' to them. This mirror is something we can literally conjure up, having it in our hands even as we intend it in our thoughts. As we hold it up to this newcomer they must be revealed truly within it. We say:

'Now I ask again, show yourself truly to me and may only my true companion remain!'

If the companion is genuine then their reflection in the mirror will not worry them, as they have nothing to hide. However, if the spirit is an interloper then their reflection will reveal their duplicity and they will be forced to depart.

As we have been careful in our procedure and are well protected then there should be no problems at all here. The only difficulty we may find at this juncture is that we cannot discern who or what we are looking at clearly. This may be due to a little wariness on our part, or doubting of the validity of what we are doing. Or it may be because we have expected one sort of companion to appear (perhaps a glamorous elf or a gallant knight) and instead are seeing somebody quite different. Expectations can cloud our vision so try to remember that *the companion is a spirit and they are only wearing a costume*. Whatever they are wearing as a body is the best thing for us to see at this time. If possible we should try to remove any pre-conceived ideas from our heads and to just observe what we actually see rather than what we hoped to see.

Genuine companions may appear in the astral office as one thing, for instance a lynx or a red dragon, and then on our asking them to show themselves truly they will morph into a human form. As a further example, one of my companions would show himself as a playful white mouse and another as an eagle stretching its wings. This morphing process is the 'calling card' of our companion and is quite normal. The initial form expresses an aspect of their energy but is not the most convenient one for us to relate to. We, as humans incarnate, will usually find it easier to talk to a humanoid form than a creature, at least until we get well acquainted. The companions will always be amenable to what works best for us as individuals.

As we have protected ourselves well and have asked for a specific outcome then it is very unlikely at this stage that an unpleasant or unwelcome spirit will show themselves instead of the companion/s. However, if they do, and do not immediately respond to our mirroring technique – perhaps due to the fact we haven't enough confidence in our abilities yet and have made our gestures with half a mind on not succeeding – then we can still banish them. There are full details of how to go about this in Chapter Sixteen in the section on dealing with unwanted beings yet for now it is enough to say ' *I banish you to the place in the universe where you will best receive healing, for your place is not here with me. Go now and may my true companion be revealed!*'

Now we have our true companions before us the first thing to do, obviously, is to give them welcome and to thank them for being with us at this time. If we feel automatically at ease, or confident, we may invite them to sit with us in the special area we have prepared for such meetings. However, we may not feel so bold straight away and so until we are ready it is just as acceptable for us to remain standing, or sitting, within the figure of eight. This figure of eight acts as a barrier and also a portal, something akin to the transporters that used to be seen on episodes of Star Trek. It is a line we have drawn between our energy and external energies, and will be respected as such. If we choose to remain *in situ* within the figure of eight it will not be taken as an insult, rather our companions will be pleased that we acknowledge our feelings and know our own current level of expertise.

At this early point in our relationship our guiding spirits will not mind if we just want to stare at them or feel their energies. This is not the time for lengthy discussions on the meaning of existence but rather for us to get acquainted so that we can feel their presence and learn to recognise them again, either here or in our daily lives. Just because we specifically meet them in the astral office doesn't mean they aren't with us for most of the time when we are back in our day to day routine and so learning how to feel and sense their energy is a valid way to spend the first meeting. To use an analogy, let us think of this as a reunion of friends who have met over the Internet; there has been a 'virtual' friendship but this is the first time that we have met in person and so a time of just being together, or 'sussing each other out', is needed. This applies even more if we have more than one companion show up as each will deserve a little time spent on feeling their presence and observing their guise adequately.

From this we can go on to make introductions and invite our companion/s to share with us any brief snippet of information that we should know at this time. Certainly in the early stages of our relationship, and in the infancy of our spiritwalking, we should be careful not to get too much information all at once as we will be hard pushed to remember it when we return to 'ordinary' reality. Instead we can ask basic questions simply allowing the guide to tell us what they wish us to hear at this time. There is no rush and certainly we should keep the meeting as brief as we like at this stage. It should be considered that otherworldly, or energetic, work does use up a lot of our psychic force and until we can learn to moderate this and to walk with more ease between the worlds then we must be aware of our bodily limitations.

When we have concluded our initial introductions and enjoyed spending a little time with our mentor/s we can ask if we may consult them again in this place. This is a courtesy and starts us off as we mean to go on, by not taking our relationship for granted. We can then either ask them to step back into the loop of the figure of eight that they occupied or, if they are still in it, then continue from there. We can now bid them an *au revoir*, rather than a final goodbye, and establish that for the foreseeable future this is where we will meet. We can then say:

> '*May you keep what is yours and may I keep what is mine as you return to your realm and I to the manifest world. Until we meet*

again, go well spirit/s!'

This is our cue for them to leave and for us to retrace our steps from the astral office back through the terrain of our safe place to the start of our journey.

Normal spiritwalking rules apply on our return to this physical level of existence.

Deepening the Bond – Developing our Relationship

As we have said before, the spiritwalker/companion relationship is at the root of all we do and as such it needs to be fed and watered. We should not just be aiming for the bottom line of maintenance, just keeping it from dying off, but rather aiming to regularly nurture it, encouraging the friendship to grow, bloom and bear fruit on all levels of existence.

And how may we do this? Well, when we are initially opening the active connection with our companions then I advise a 'little and often' approach. This we can achieve in the form of a daily 'check in' – a short trance journey undertaken to the safe astral office for the purpose of saying hello, refreshing our connection and sharing/exchanging our energies. These are, I am sure you will agree, things that all close friends need to do and just because our companion is unseen rather than corporeal this need is not diminished.

This check-in exercise for this essential re-familiarisation can be done for around ten to fifteen minutes, morning or evening, and is the equivalent of making a regular catch-up phone call to a friend or relative on the physical level. Consequently we need not make this linking up any more complex or serious than picking up the phone.

A simple friendly exchange, informal but informative, is what we need to aim for. We can start by considering the following:

- *Courtesy* – asking how the companion is, thanking them for coming
- *Interest* – asking what they have been observing in spirit
- *Gossip* – seeing whether they have any 'local' news/views for us
- *Development* – asking if they can give us any feedback on our day

This may seem rather basic but we will find that if we ask more than this at first we will simply forget all the information by the time we return back to 'ordinary' reality. We shouldn't forget that we are new to journeying into other realms of existence and so the journey itself may be more than enough to try and remember for the time being. The main thing is that it we have a regular companionable session and what transpires in its duration is concise enough to remember. Just this short time of companionship offers us something dependable, yet magical, that we can build on.

It is well for us to mention here that this check-in, and indeed our whole relationship with the companion, is not a strictly two-sided affair. We can't really ask what the companions have been doing in the same way they can relate to what we have been doing, nor can we readily give an opinion on what they have been up to. However, we can be *reciprocal* of the care and attention they give to us. Giving our full attention to the matter in hand is as valuable as not letting our eyes wander or picking our nails when a friend is speaking with us one-to-one on the physical level. The companion won't mind talking constantly about us, in fact they will relish it, as long as we give them a respectful attentive presence in return and not have half a mind on getting back to watch a TV programme or making mental shopping lists.

We will not be able to progress to having a more protracted session with our companions unless we can become more adept at staying focussed on what is happening and at retaining the information we are given. A huge part of the spiritwalker's work is about remaining in the moment, being attentive to all that happens in the eternal *Now*, and this should be our long-term goal, both in our physical and in our unseen lives. This staying in the *Now* allows us to:

- Strengthen our ability to perceive what is truly before us, building on our ability to *see* that which is considered unseen
- Strengthen our discernment of any unseen information presented to us, building on our ability to *know* without being told

To See and to Know – The Seeing and the Knowing

Seeing and *knowing* are also vital qualities or attributes of a successful spiritwalker. *Seeing* can be defined as the ability to perceive what is actually being offered to us at an energetic level. This means that we have the ability to translate energetic input into imagery or creative dialogue or sound/scent/sensation. To *know*, on the other hand, is our ability to inherently witness the energy and to comprehend its implication and significance at a deep level. Seeing and knowing, along with use of intent (which blends these two key skills with our will) are essential skills. They must be developed through hands-on working such as the check-in and they can only be established when we resolutely stay in the moment with what is happening to us.

When we have proved that we can remain present and aware in the eternal *Now* and are ready to move on then we can conduct a lengthier journey and stay with the spirits for up to an hour, perhaps longer. By this we may extend our discussions and have more involved esoteric deliberations that consider more testing issues as regards our existence. Our companions will be happy to alert us when they deem us ready to do this, although we will no doubt get a sense of this ourselves, finding we are using our seeing and knowing effortlessly without being distracted. We will go on to discuss the asking of these deeper spiritual questions in the next chapter.

For now I will offer one vital piece of advice on questioning our companions during our check-in time. It is this: *the companions are always far more successful at their job when kept to personal subjects pertaining our energies, or to the energetic workings of Creation itself, and are not at their best when being pressed on the future of the planet or the outcome of a political or economic situation.* In short they are not great predictors and are much more qualified to discuss energies. They have the overview, yes, but not the *ultimate* view. This is why I have mentioned several times that our companions can, and will be, fallible if we push them to predict for us.

If we choose to ignore this advice, as it is just too tempting not to ask the spirits for prophetic insights on a global, or even universal, scale, then the companions will be forced to offer us their view on what they can see/feel at this time. There are the key words: *at this time*. All futures, and even realities, are subject to change. Other influences and energies, including random events, *always* affect the wider etheric flow and one decisive gesture or thought can be enough to tip the balance in any given moment. Because of this our companions are almost certain to offer us flawed information and then we will lose faith in their efficacy and discount their sound guidance on more localised esoteric issues. Yes, with their wisdom and experience they can certainly comment on an energetic trend, or speculate on the likely effects if a certain course of action is pursued, but they can only really make educated guesses based on their current perspective. We must remember this perspective allows them to see us, and our lives, much more clearly than we can but it does not give them the ability to witness *everything* – every eloquent curve in the wider energetic dance – in perfect detail.

If we think of the companions as satellites orbiting our physical realm then we can remember that there is a universe, and, in all probability *universes*, far beyond that little satellite. As satellites they can see us *and* they can see further out into outer space, or the *beyond*, than we can. Yet they cannot leave the orbit that they have opted to be in which allows them to zoom in on us, to track us and guide us – to teach us about ourselves and our place in the cosmological whole. Their role is to advise us on our individual purpose in relation to the general esoteric laws of creation, not to be our own all-seeing oracle.

There is a second reason why asking for great prophetic proclamations is not advisable. If the matter is dear to us, such as the future of our business or whether there will be a war in our country, then we will have a filter to put on the possible response – one of personal expectation. If a companion wishes to offer us an insight into our lives spontaneously, without being pushed into prediction, then we will have not expected anything and therefore our filter will be off. But if we go trying to wheedle information out of the companions then we already have our expectation as a filter and so what we hear may not even be correctly received. The companion is a good transmitter of (relatively) long-range frequencies and we can be skilled receivers if we don't put ourselves in a position of expecting to hear certain advice, or even of fearing hearing it. To make it plain, companions give spirit *guidance*, and guidance is counselling and support from the perspective of a non-physical experienced being. This is what we should be aiming for in our time together.

At this stage the more we use the check-in to meet our companion the better our chances are of becoming an effective spiritwalker. We can enthusiastically engage without putting any limiting human filter of cynicism, fear or expectation on the pro-ceedings and thus our experiences will be fresh and dynamic, enabling us to quickly grow in confidence. If we can consider this time to be one where we can relax and chat with a new and very exciting friend – one with amazing insights and a wonderful warm interest in all we do – then we will be doing really well. As this process of journeying becomes less intimidating and more like second nature we will find that we develop into being a competent spiritwalker whilst simply 'hanging out' with our companions. This, combined with our ongoing daily connection to Source, is enough for us to work on for now.

In the next chapter we will step out a little further with our companion spirits, continuing our journey towards soul-wisdom and spirit connection, this time by the use of *channelling*.

CHAPTER NINE

STEPPING OUT TOGETHER

'Spiritwalking is about having an active link – a direct line to universal wisdom. Our aim should be for total connection, enabling our recognition and assimilation of valuable unseen information to become as effortless as the constant transmission of our thoughts. Human beings have always thought with careless abandon, walking around casually projecting their individual energies and taking for granted their ability to send unseen signals into the ether. Indeed, for too long humanity has been tuned to its own low frequency, hearing only the echo of its own constant emissions like too many bats bouncing sonar in a sealed cave. Now is the time for us to practice discernment, both in what we transmit but also what we *receive*. Let us now deliberately shift up a pitch, senses honed, and discover that there are other worlds out there and, indeed, other words besides our own. The doors of perception always open both ways!'

From Guidance

In this chapter we will cover the means by which we may gain more detailed information from our companion guides. This means is *channelling*. We may well have already heard of this method of direct spirit communication and if so we shouldn't let any negative associations put us off what is a very effective method of attaining direct, reliable and informative contact with our unseen companions.

What is a Channel?

As we know a channel is a conduit or link. When we speak of a channel within the framework of spiritwalking we refer to a clear route or line through which energetic information may travel and consequently be received. We may also think of channel as a specific frequency that carries information broadcast by a transmitter.

As we know, when we tune in our radio this aligns us to the frequency of the transmission that we desire to receive – for example, we can't pick up a jazz station's signal if we are deliberately tuned in to a twenty-four hour news channel. Likewise, when we purposely tune into the broadcast of our companion guide we only receive their unique instructive dialogue, not extraneous nonsense. An astral broadcast by our companion is really no different to a transmission of radio waves by a local station only we are the instrument that channels and receives rather than a radio receiver. For spiritwalkers operating with full psychic protection, this channelling allows us to pre-select only information that comes from a trusted source and not to pick up interference from other frequencies broadcasting alternative programmes.

Let's consider this process of accessing information using another familiar analogy. We know that if we connect to our trusted Internet Service Provider we will be able to access a particular website to attain specific electronic information and that our computer's hard drive will interpret this received, or *downloaded*, electronic data for us. Similarly if we make our tried-and-tested connection to Source we will then be able to access our particular companion spirit/s to attain specific energetic information and our own brain will decipher this incoming material for us. If we are working on a PC we can then see information appear on our monitor screen and we can print it out. But how do we view, or print out, our energetic or spiritual downloads?

Cosmic Dictation

The information we download from our companions is translated onto paper via a good old-fashioned pen rather than an inkjet printer in a kind of cosmic dictation. We simply transcribe what is received, the signals from our companions being decoded and directly translated onto the page before us. As we are fortunate enough to live in this age of instant electronic communication, with unseen information travelling from one place to another via a variety of technologies, it is easier for us than for any generation before to appreciate that channelling information through this directed form of writing is not a far-fetched notion but rather a feasible method of communication. Once we get the hang of this way of exchanging energy then it can be just as straightforward and immediate a way of making contact as the mobile phone. Yet unlike the telephone we have the benefit of having a permanent textual recording of our communication by means of our writing it down automatically as we go.

The Value of Written Records

This documentation is the main reason why we may want to take part in a channelled communication with our companions as opposed to meeting them in the astral office. As we have stated several times previously, there is only so much information we can retain after an astral meeting, even when we become adept at trance journeying. We will by now be used to bringing back our findings and experiences in a kind of symbolic shorthand – storing only the key aspects of an encounter in our memory for ease of recollection. This approach is helpful for our general interaction with spirit, helping us to understand energies and patterns and equipping us to interact with beings that are different from us. Yet for us to be able to recall each twist and turn of the discussion we need another way of approaching guidance, one which allows us to dictate directly what is being said to us as well as recording our own immediate responses.

Because of the inevitable limits on what we can remember we are destined to be frustrated by any kind of in-depth philosophical debate that may naturally arise with our companion spirits in the astral office. Although we may certainly engage in such lengthy discourses, and get a great deal out of it at the time, any intricacy will be lost by the time we come to recollect the interaction. Channelling directly onto paper is the answer if we wish to engage with our companions in a much more comprehensive and thoughtful way. By this we don't lose a great deal in the translation and can hope to read our discourse over and over as a means of learning and growing.

But what is the nature of these downloaded discussions?

Channelling Guidance

When we talk about a discussion or discourse in this context we are referring to spirit guidance – that is to say the advice and insights offered to us by an unseen companionable guide, one who cares about us enough to want to help us develop and grow. Spirit guidance is that which our companions give us when we meet them in the astral office as well as when we tune in and channel their wisdom directly onto paper.

This given material will only ever consist of suggestions by which we may live well and so spirit guidance is never dictatorial or controlling in any way – it is purely the friendly advice of one who has an overview of existence. Our welfare and spiritual growth always lie at the heart of good guidance and, although it may push us beyond our present boundaries for the sake of our development, *it will never tell us what to do.* If we ever receive a channelled dialogue that is domineering, threatening, demeaning or abusive in any way, then we should seriously check our levels of protection as we have probably attuned to the wrong frequency in our careless-ness. If we are well protected and aimed with intent at our compan-ions then the guidance we receive in their discussions with us will only ever be informative and considerate. Guidance should make us feel empowered and supported, never the opposite.

But what do we discuss?

Forget the Small Talk – Subjects for Channelled Guidance

Here we are not alluding to great predictions or specific foretellings, as we mentioned in the previous chapter, but rather the matters that a spiritwalker may wish to discuss with their companions that are, quite literally, of life and death. These include:

- The nature of reality – *looking at issues such as time, space, matter, other dimensions and the nature of perception*
- The nature of the self – *looking at issues such as other lives, simultaneous incarnations and the idea of the 'higher' self*
- The nature of incarnation – *looking at the process/meaning of death and rebirth and our continued existence between incarnations etc.*
- The nature of the soul – *looking at such issues as soul*

types, soul groups, soul mates and soul retrieval

- The nature of energy – *looking at the Source of Creation, the Creator, and the creative (life) force behind all existence*
- The nature of good and evil – *looking at the positive and negative forces of Creation both in cosmic and very personal ways*

Channelled writing is for answering all those big pertinent questions like '*what are we doing here?*' and '*why does that happen?*' and '*have I done this before?*' It is for getting the 'bigger picture' from a trusted source that is once-removed from our current level of experience and perception.

Now we know why we need it and, indeed, when we may use it we can now look at how to go about doing it.

Connecting Up to Our Direct Link

We have so far established that we need three things to be in place:

1. A desire to link with a known companion spirit for the purpose of gaining particular insights – *selecting the broadcast*
2. A connection made to them by our awareness that then acts as a channel for whatever may be passed between us – *tuning in*
3. A way of translating their broadcast or information into a readily understandable and accessible form, i.e. pen and paper – *receiving the transmission.*

Of course we will need the pen and paper on hand before we begin in order to receive the transmission. The best idea is to have a large jotter of plain paper that has pages that will turn easily. We do not want to be worried about pages that become loose or flop backwards constantly when we are focussed on writing the guidance that flows through us. Cosmic dictation generally comes through at a speed that is far quicker than the pace at which most of us usually write. It does not rely on us pausing for thought and comes from a realm where physical constraints are not an issue. Therefore we need to be unimpeded to let the words pour through us as swiftly as they wish. A reliable pen that doesn't rely on refilling or sharpening and a good supply of large unlined paper, preferably loosely bound, are the prerequisites.

Now all we need is somewhere to sit quietly, be that at a table or on the floor, and we may engage with the process of channelling.

Selecting the Broadcast

To begin we need to notice that in point 1. we say *particular* insights. Just as we need to know what kind of radio station we require or which website we need to visit we really do need to have a focussed question, or set of questions, in mind before we engage in this process. It is the question is that which keeps us aligned to the companion's particular broadcast, allowing the information to flow freely but in an orderly fashion. Without a question, at least one to start us off on a particular discussion, then we are likely to 'slip off signal'.

This is not necessarily due to our own lack of focus but more in respect to the fact that companions are discarnate, not limited by the concerns of this physical world, and without a direction they can become distracted by issues that they find fascinating and discuss all matters spiritual *ad infinitum*. We do have to bear in mind that our dear companions haven't our time constraints, or our more grounded concerns, and so they can easily digress, leaving us feeling bewildered or annoyed. This confusion or dissatisfaction can then lead to us losing the necessary concentration required for receiving an appropriate broadcast. The intention of our companions isn't to make us disgruntled, rather they love to talk to us about all things unseen and esoteric and if we don't keep them 'on task' then they may well ramble on obliquely.

Philosophical questions of the kind we discussed in the previous section are the best way to ensure we do not end up receiving a one-sided exposition, keeping us within the parameters of the channel we have set. If we have not got any specific questions about (for example) the nature of reality, or life after death, at any particular time then we can ask one straightforward guiding question that helps us to establish what kind of broadcast we want. This question is *'what is it that I should know this day as to enhance my understanding of Creation at this specific time?'* This allows us to keep the transmission we receive within certain established boundaries without limiting us to any one pre-defined subject. It sets us in the right channel.

Once we have the question, or set of questions pertaining to a subject area, that we need answering all we need is our companion spirit to aim them at. If we have more than one guiding spirit we may like to be specific in choosing one of them to come forward. Or perhaps, as is my own particular way, I will expect the companion who feels best qualified to answer me to volunteer themselves if I present the matter to them all. So, we can name a particular companion or leave it open as a request to all our true companion spirits. This selection is the equivalent of phoning the correct number rather than dialling a number at random and then expecting our friend to answer. There are many, many spirits out there just as there are many broadcasts on long wave or medium wave, and we need to be very specific lest we receive something that is the equivalent of annoying static.

Tuning In

Now we need to actively make that link with our question/s as our purpose for doing so – we have chosen our station and need to turn the dial to receive it clearly. For this we need to follow all of the usual procedures for protecting ourselves before opening our awareness up to focus on the unseen presence of our (by now) familiar companion spirit/s.

To make this connection we need to do two things – invoke and experience. By invoke we mean ask for the companion/s presence to be with us for the purpose of answering our questions. The invocation could be something like:

> '*Dear true companion/s* (name them if preferred), *spirit/s who come for my highest possible good, I ask that you draw close to me now for the purpose of discussing* (name question/subject area). *I ask this so that I may learn and grow, becoming a more effective part of the All. Draw close now and be with me so that we may work together on this matter above all others.*'

Then, to experience their drawing close we can use our most honed psychic skill. If we are primarily a visual person then we can actively see the companion/s moving towards us in our mind's eye. If we are predominately sensitive we can feel their nearness or perhaps scent them or hear their approach. However we engage with our own innate abilities we should know the companions to be within our sphere of influence. This inner seeing and knowing comes from our experience of working with the companions many times on our astral journeys. We can feel their familiar affect on our energies and are fully aware of their own unique vibration. Remember, we have protected ourselves and so a false or confused spirit will not be able to harm us even if they are pretending to be our companion. However to ensure that this being is truly who they claim to be we should assert our astral authority over them in our own unseen space by saying something like:

> '*May only those who come for my highest possible good remain here, may any other be returned to the place in the universe where they should be at this time, for their place is not here with me!*'

As we say this last we should imagine, or feel, a huge flash of blue-white light flaring around us, rather like our being engulfed in the heart of a star for as moment. Then the light is gone and we are left with our true companion/s. We should know, and truly have faith in, the fact that what we declare as truth is truth in our own space. We have the ability, and the right, to banish anyone or anything that isn't the true spirit that we have asked for. Believing in our innate power, and our ability to use it wisely and well, is vital for all such working.

So, we are left with the authentic companion/s we have requested and it is now our place to continue to make their presence a vivid actuality by whatever means we favour – for example, by seeing them more clearly or feeling them more acutely. We should know the companions to be with us as strongly as any physical presence, such as the chair we sit upon. They must be real to us. Silently strengthen this working bond by sending them our affection and trust and, similarly, experience them return any feeling or thought us.

Receiving the Transmission

Once the companion/s presence is as strong as it can be for us then we can open our eyes and take up our paper and pen, holding the pen in our preferred, or *active*, hand. Now maintaining that link we can write down our question at the top of our first piece of paper.

When we have done this we should sit with the tip of the pen on the page and wait. What are we waiting for? Well, we are open as a channel and now the transmission will flow through us in a way that is entirely individual to us. This could happen in any of the following ways:

- We may hear the companion speaking to us and what we hear in our mind we should write down on the paper – *receiving dictated guidance*
- We may see something in the mind's eye, a scene or a symbol, and feel the need to describe it on paper – *receiving inspired guidance*
- We may feel the need to write something without consciously knowing what it will be, giving the companion the ability to write using our hand without our being in control – *receiving automatic guidance*

All of these are equally legitimate means of channelling information and it is no more convincing to have the words flow from our pen with no conscious effort than it is to be dictated to. The way we find ourselves channelling the offered information is simply a matter of how our spiritual mentors can best relate to our own energetic field. They will work with us in whichever way is the most effective for our particular partnership and this may take a little adjustment.

We should not worry if in the first few sessions we get little more than a few coherent lines or a page of barely formed scribble. The companion and ourselves will need to find a way of blending our energy in order to coordinate this procedure, rather like a horse and rider getting used to each other. Conversely we may find that this bonding happens immediately and we are left with a very sore hand after writing page after page of fascinating insights! If we hit our stride like this straight away we are the exception rather than the rule and most of us should be prepared for at least a few false starts before we really start to channel well.

If we still cannot get any results after trying this several times we may wish to consider another variation that some people prefer. This is swapping the pen to our less dominant, or *inactive*, hand. Because few of us write with both hands we will always have one that we feel we cannot manage easily and this means it will have more flexibility and less restraint. Using it allows us to make the break with our usual controlled and conscious *modus operandi* and gives our companion spirit/s another opportunity to interact with us, this time with us being less 'uptight'. Some people like to write the questions that they have in their active, dominant hand and then swap the pen to the inactive hand for the answers from spirit. Although this is not my own preferred method I know that it works very well indeed for some people and it is recommended if the original approach yields no desired results.

We will find that however the information comes to us that the process, once it gets going, is very quick. Ideas and thoughts are pure energy being translated through our flesh and blood and so it may take some time for us to get used to the sheer speed of the delivery. We are used to thinking and weighing concepts and statements up, placing value judgements upon them before we commit to them, and for us suddenly to be placed in a position where the information is pure and flowing can be surprising. If we have done our protection and connection properly then there should be nothing to feel wary about, it is simply a matter of getting used to the way spirit communicates.

It is well for us to bear in mind that it is only our human body and its attendant ego that stops us from communicating in this quicksilver way all the time. Without such human filters as *'will I look stupid if this isn't correct?'* there is only a steady stream of authentic observation and clear wisdom, a truly soul-full exchange of energy.

It may be hard for us to grasp exactly what to expect from written guidance if we have not previously witnessed it. It is definitely not 'possession' – we are simply being guided by greater or lesser means, depending on our own unique connection to the companions and our levels of receptivity to the process. We are *always* at liberty to set our own parameters before we take up the pen, stating the questions we have or the format we choose, including a time limit. Some people like to organise their session so that they have a running conversation with their companions, centred around one or more issues while others, like myself, prefer to keep the session down to one initial key question and make sure the communication is relatively concise.

To understand how this works in practice we will need to look at some examples and in the next section I will share some of my own previous guidance to reveal how I operate and how spirit communicates with me.

Before I do this I can only observe, through my many years experience, that the whole process is full of idiosyncrasies. Particular patterns of speech and ways of expressing have been established as my own energy interacts with my own very unique companions. The nature of the channelled guidance I receive will be very different to how anyone else's may come across, and that is as it should be. The important thing is not about any quirky turns of phrase our companions may use but rather about receiving accurate insights of the kind we do not normally have. Channelling is for us to be able to access truth that is currently hidden from us, either as a result of our own blinkered human attitude or by circumstances, and our written guidance should always be beyond that which we would normally think and not just a series of platitudes. The crucial thing is that we find ourselves with pages of interesting dialogue that give us food for thought and a new perspective, not the kind of trite material that gives channelling the negative association of fraudulence that we alluded to at the start of this chapter.

Yet what is fraudulence? Can we ever really receive 'hoax guidance'? Well, if the guidance itself is valuable and contains only constructive messages of an instructive nature then no. It may be well for us to consider that it matters not if we believe that the guidance comes from our companion/s, (an external being) or from deep within our own self, as long as the information we channel is inspiring, challenging and exciting. Such stimulating channelled guidance can offer us unlimited access to the wisdom of the unseen, or to the deep soul-self, in a way that we are unlikely to experience anywhere else in the modern world. Indeed effective channelling is one of the spiritwalkers most valuable ways of understanding the energetic universe in which we live. What follows are some examples of why I find it so invaluable...and so intriguing.

Receiving You Loud and Clear – Guidance Received by the Author

To make the channelling process plain I have placed the specific question that I put to the companion spirits in italics. Each question came from a separate session of channelling. The essence of the answer is given here, not the entire transcript.

Spirits that love me, tell me about the purpose of religion?

'Man-made religions and all their divisions and diversions have caused war and suffering, of course, but they have also always acted as a catalyst for the greatest human achievements. No travesty is without its equal in beauty! We can observe this in immense creative drive within the art and architecture of the churches and mosques, the temples and also those places of devotion that defy denomination. In each there is that tender expression of love towards that which gave us life, in each the revelation of our own greatness as experienced in this selfless giving of adoration. Religion has inspired the most exquisite works of painting, sculpture and masonry, as well as acts of kindness that can only ever be born from the losing of the self in the greater eternal Self. Whatever name is given to the Creator there will always be celebratory creation in Its honour. How can there not be? Within the greater the lesser is always found, and vice versa. And in this finding there will always be rejoicing, in one inspired way or another.

Because of this religion can never be witnessed entirely as blight upon the Earth for within its honoured precincts comes forth intense splendour. We do not need to destroy religion, rather all that is needed is a glorious collective re-membering of who we truly are and the desire for such walled institutions would vanish immediately. Then what creation there would be in this physical plane – unfettered and unified, it would be truly unstoppable! Have faith for you are a part of that waking up to your true unregimented and boundless Creator-nature. You are a part of the forward motion that topples walls for good and all. And for the good of the All.'

Spirits who come for my highest possible good, tell me why some of us are terribly physically handicapped or damaged?

'Only the strongest souls choose the weakest bodies. Why? Well, my friend, it is to teach us, their companions on the road of life. Those with the most startling infirmity or physical deficiency are not neccesarily teaching themselves a lesson, or being punished for some supposed misdemeanour in another life. By no means! They are often here because they are strong enough to be our greatest, wisest teachers, showing us how to look beyond the transient temporal into the *beyond* of spirit!

In your pity never overlook the fact that we are all, without exception, powerful beings that all have choices. Imagine the power of one who has knowingly come forth into human form with a severe handicap to their physical freedom. What courage, what beauty and what power this soul has to attempt this willingly as a point of re-membering for others. What awesome resilience and marvellous dexterity has the eternal essence of such a being! Let us value them beyond measure and in them know our own incredible ability to suffer temporary hardship whilst still shining so very brightly.

Again I say to you that nothing happens in isolation – there is meaning for us to find in the existence of all beings and lessons for us in all that unfolds. '

Here are some other quotes from guidance that the reader may find useful as they show typical responses to our key question. This is:

What is it that I should know this day?

'Creation is like a mirrorball and you are but one small tile of mirror in the middle of its curved surface.

There are some mirrors next to yours that you are aware of and you may be conscious of the tiles that border your neighbours. But there are, you realise, also points of perception on the other side from your own little area of reflection – mirrors which have a completely different aspect to your own and witness life in a very different way. Likewise there are those mirrors at the top and the bottom of this sphere of Being-ness that you have no contact with, yet you know they must be there as they play their part in holding the entire globe together. You cannot see what they can but you know that we are all equal in our role of making up a orb that reflects all aspects.

By this mirrorball analogy you can appreciate that all the perspectives, or reflections, make up the broader whole. And you can know that this Oneness of singular ones has an inner and outer aspect, as well as the space it occupies. Can you appreciate that this wonderful composite of differing viewpoints is *who we really are* and can you take on board that through these differing experiences this collective is always expanding? Can you feel how wonderful this is, see how beautiful We are together as One?'

And:

'Nothing is outside of your capability. Nothing! Given time and application there is no thing on this Earth that you cannot do or be. I hear your inevitable questions along the lines of 'but what if I have no arms and I want to play tennis?' With re-membering that you are the owner of the power to create worlds, the potential originator of milky nebulas and enigmatic oceans, then manifesting some nice new arms should not be too much of a problem. What is a problem is that we have forgotten the power and therefore we do not really apply ourselves to the creation. That is what it has not been done, not because it is impossible. Nothing is impossible! An unfailing connection to that very knowable Unknowable Source that forms universes will enable you to form your own universe. This is as it is. What have you to lose by trying it out?'

Other Means of Channelling

Before we move on we may like to consider that there is another way of gaining a record of our channelled guidance and that is by literally recording it. Not everyone will feel comfortable with a pen in their hand and for those people who will not, or cannot, take up written guidance then buying a small Dictaphone may be the answer. Then we can just speak our guidance directly onto tape as the information flows through us. Perhaps we will hear the words in our minds and be able to speak them out loud. Or perhaps we will see scenes in our mind's-eye and be able to describe them as they unfold. Our companions may be happy to speak through us directly if we are prepared to step back and allow them to do so. It goes without saying that all of these methods must be considered using the same safe practice as we have in all our spiritwalking.

Channelled guidance is always unique and surprising. Whatever our method or means of facilitating a channelled conversation we should treat this sacred process as a central part of our life as a spiritwalker. Once we have established an active line of communication on a regular basis we can then consider backing up what we learn by undertaking some related pathworking.

CHAPTER TEN

FURTHER ALONG THE PATH

'We want you to know that you are always journeying. Please accept that stasis is not a universal condition, no matter how stuck you may feel right now, and that expansion is the motivating force of creation just as a temporary contraction is its inevitable balancing force. Movement, endless cycling movement, is always the result. You, my friend, are a singular point of perception within the Creator's ceaseless quest for wholeness and are unavoidably part of the collective journey that is an eternal moment, born of the essential movement in and out. Even in your stillness it is so...*especially* in your stillness! Be still and you will travel far as all things can be witnessed as they bloom from the fertile void and die back in the same instant, between one breath and the next. Here, now and always in the space between we move as one with the One. Is it not better to be a traveller who is in awareness to enjoy this experience?'

From Guidance

As we now know, a pathworking is a guided trance journey that takes us to a particular destination for a specific purpose. By this directed means pathworkings can help us further understand the questions we have posed in our written guidance, backing up or augmenting any given concepts with first hand experience. With this approach we do not become too bogged down in philosophy, achieving a desirable balance of the practical and the theoretical to obtain the 'bigger picture'.

An example of using this dual approach would be combining channelled written guidance on the subject of reincarnation, or *other lives*, with a pathworking that helps us to explore the possibility our own alternative lives. This would be most effective if we singled out a life that has a specific relevance to us at this time. I have chosen this particular subject as our example as reincarnation is a popular theme in spiritual discourse and sooner or later it is inevitable that rebirth, or other existences and alternate selves, will come up for discussion. Therefore this chapter is primarily dedicated to a sample pathworking that explores this area. As well enabling us to tackle a key concept it will help us to understand how to conceive of, and subsequently structure, our own pathworkings for other purposes.

Choosing a Path Wisely

Before we begin to look at this pathworking let us just reiterate something here that is vital to the genuine spiritwalker. We are not 'spiritual tourists' who go around 'doing' subjects, rather like someone on a whistle-stop tour of the wonders of the ancient world who hops out of a coach with a camera and takes a snap of the Great Pyramid of Giza or the Parthenon. The pathworking in this chapter is not intended to encourage this kind of spiritual browsing, making us think we can just go off 'astral sightseeing' for the sake of collecting tales of our apparent 'past lives' like souvenirs. Any such superficiality or flippancy within spiritwalking is not particularly sensible as it is the antithesis of our safe, effective and deeply respectful practice. Without our ethical codes of conduct we are, frankly, at risk.

This is even more pertinent when it comes to the issue of other lives/selves and the nature of incarnation, as here is one area in which we are guaranteed to gain some incredible insights, many of them deeply emotive. Without a carefully chosen focus and a stable framework we are likely to be confused, upset or even disturbed by what we find for invariably we will find *something*.

As incarnation is such an interesting (and contentious) subject we may already have a personal motivation to explore its meaning and purpose. For example, these could be:

- Our having a compelling recurrent dream set in a past era or foreign place that we have no conscious knowledge of
- Our being haunted by a memory that, although potent, cannot be accounted for in this life
- Our experiencing disturbing slips in time when we appear to be, for seemingly endless seconds, somewhere else entirely, almost as if we are having a parallel existence

All of these moving, intriguing and sometimes distressing, experiences can reveal to us the genuine need to explore other lives.

However, a sound motivation for exploring this area can be less personal or affecting than the above reasons. Perhaps our aim is to learn more about the way our soul gains knowledge/experience through multiple incarnations and so (with the encouragement of the companion spirits) we wish to approach the possibility of our ongoing learning in a practical way. Or maybe the reason is as simple as that the issue of other selves has always been an area that has absorbed our attention and we now wish to have an actual insight into how the process of incarnation works.

If we do not have such a clear grounds for making this journey then we are putting ourselves at risk of becoming confused and disturbed by what we may find. Our companions will *always* intimate with us if we are ready for what the process entails and if we should be considering it at this time. They will also advise us of just what we should be focussing in on, making sure we have a clear objective. More of this in the next section.

Being Specific – Identifying our Purpose

Part of this pathworking is about our choice to witness another aspect of our eternal self as it exists in another layer of reality. These aspects of our eternal self include:

- Incarnations, or physical life-roles, that we have experienced *before* this one in relation to linear Earth-time – *past selves*
- Incarnations that we will experience *after* this one in relation to linear Earth-time – *future selves*
- Incarnations that we are experiencing *parallel* to the one that we currently know as our key physical reality – *alternative selves*
- Discarnate being that we experience *between* incarnations – *soul selves*

To this list we could also feasibly add in the experience of our *higher selves*. This is the part of our core soul self that does not incarnate but supervises the remainder of our soul that does. However, this is rather an advanced topic for this point in the proceedings and one we may like to consider, with the help of our companions, in the future.

As we can now more fully appreciate, many related areas of importance converge on this exploration of our other selves. The subject is connected intrinsically to our understanding of the nature of reality and the purpose of existence, not just to our having had different incarnations elsewhere. For example, the issue of time, and our limited human perception of it, is one important related topic. Likewise the notion of a pivotal persona, or awareness, around which all others orbit is another pertinent spiritual matter that stems from the root of incarnation. It is not an easy issue yet it is so fundamental to our development as it gives us so many opportunities to question and seek soul truths. There could be few more stimulating or multifaceted topics to lead us on in our spiritwalking.

For now we need to tackle this subject at the level we are currently at. We need to pinpoint which aspect we need to hone in on and define the most suitable question for us to ask at this time. Examples of such questions may be:

a) Does my irrational aversion to Spain and my reluctance to visit it in this life stem from another existence? Will my remembering the root cause of this fear help me?

b) I have unsettling 'far memories' of being chased through dense woodland. What life experience does this relate to? Why is it relevant to me today?

c) I do not feel as if I have ever experienced giving birth in a physical form. Is this true? Why has my soul avoided this experience so far?

d) I have a strong sense that I was once on another planet than Earth, one that felt more like my home. If so why did I incarnate on Earth and not there?

e) I often feel as if I am uncontrollably slipping away from this current life in an inner city into a rural scene where I am sitting with others around a farmhouse table. Why does this happen? What is the connection between 'now' and 'then'?

We can ascertain the suitability of such questions with our companions through our channelled written dialogue with them. Perhaps they will suggest a more suitable road of enquiry for us or maybe they will help us fine-tune our objective. Only when we have clarified our line of enquiry can we proceed to the next stage of preparing ourselves for the journey.

Preparing the Ground – Practical Considerations

To undertake our in-depth pathworking successfully we need to employ one of two things at the outset.
Either:

a) A pre-recording of the pathworking so that we may follow its instructions as it replays for us through the headphones of a personal stereo

Or

b) A person who is prepared to read the journey out for us so that we may follow the directions as they are given.

We cannot usually undertake a successful pathworking by any other means than the two given here. Unless we have a photographic memory we cannot hope to memorise the complex route of a specific journey and so we need an instructive voice to guide us. All pathworkings share this intricate aspect, regardless of their theme, and even if we ourselves create such journeys for our own use we will still need to record them or have someone read them aloud for us. We need to keep the flow smooth and not have to worry about remembering the next set of directions.

Usually either one of these methods for relaying instructions will suffice. However, due to the emotive nature of this particular pathworking journey it is preferable to have someone else with us even if we are simply listening to the pre-recorded instructions in their presence.

Although spiritwalking is primarily a solitary pursuit, excepting our companion spirits of course, there are times such as these when we need to enlist the help of another person. Another human presence is reassuring during our engaging in the pathworking but is especially helpful afterwards when we return to 'ordinary' reality as having someone listen to us recount our journey will help ground us. This ability to relate to a person who has remained resolutely in the *Now* is vital when we have been reliving a genuine soul experience through the pathworking we are discussing here. Our awareness been off somewhere that felt just as real to us as this present level of physical existence, even if our bodies remain present in this version of the *Now*, and having someone with us who has not been a part of this genuinely emotional experience is both reassuring and centring. Communicating with their very physical presence enables us to earth ourselves in the reality of our current bodies again.

If we choose to work with someone who reads our pathworking instructions to us then we will be able to utilise them in another capacity too. As we journey they can read us our instructions and we can speak our experiences out loud as we go, in response, rather than our just experiencing it all internally. The whole process can then be recorded as we go along so that we have an aural record of the pathworking experience. I myself have had my other life journeys tape-recorded by the person who read me my instructions and it has helped me enormously to assimilate the information afterwards. If we can get used to doing this oral recounting as we go along then it will prove an invaluable aid to our development.

So, if we have clarified our line of enquiry and have set up our method of following the pathworking instructions (preferably in this case in the presence of another adult) then we can begin this most enlightening of astral journeys. The journey should be read through several times in order that we become familiarised with it before we begin. Whoever is reading the instructions should be sure to leave enough time for each direction to be accomplished and not rush through them with little thought for what will be happening behind our closed eyes. In order for this pathworking to transport our awareness to another reality it should be taken steadily to allow all of the attendant sights and sensations of the journey to become real.

It is, of course, assumed that all the usual precautions and procedures will be undertaken before we start.

Pathworking to Experience Another Life/Self

1. In the fertile void behind our close eyes a picture begins to form. We find ourselves sitting in a small boat on a river. We are currently tethered to the bank and are waiting to begin our journey. As we sit in this moored position we have the time to establish ourselves in this reality, using our senses to absorb our immediate surroundings. We can ask ourselves how the surface of the boat feels under our hands or feet. What is it made of, what

are its colours and its state of repair?

2. We now notice a rope that extends from our boat and loops over a stake driven into the bank. We reach out and touch this tether, letting our fingers caress its contours. Then we bring our attention out and around us, observing the flow of the river and its level of clarity. We can reach over the side and feel the water, its temperature and speed. We can also see what is reflected in its surface.

3. Bringing our gaze up we can now see the very same sky, birds, trees, plants and grass that find their mirror image in the water. We can feel the heat or chill of this day, noting the wind's freshness. We now turn left and right, looking up and down and behind us, breathing in the scents, taking in the sights and sounds.

4. It is now time for us to move away from the bank towards the place where we may find the aspect of self that we seek so we reach over and unhook the rope from the stake. We feel the weight of the rope in our hands as we let it fall into the bottom of our boat.

5. We now ask to be taken to the place where we will access the specific other life that we seek. We can trust the flow of the water to take us to wherever this may be.

6. As allow ourselves to be propelled by the flow we keep our selves alert to the changes we see around us as we pass. Perhaps we can witness fellow travellers on the river, such as waterfowl, or fish leaping up from its depths. All the time we can hear the reassuring noise of the boat as it moves through the living water below us. It sets up a steady rhythm that takes us deeper into our journey.

7. For a moment we close our eyes, enjoying the sensation of

gliding through the river, at one with it. When we open our eyes we notice that there is a bridge coming up ahead. We study the bridge as we draw nearer to it, noting its own solidity in this landscape.

8. As we draw along side the bridge we find that we are slowing. We drift over to the bank. We are *meant* to stop here. As if to confirm this we see an iron ring protruding from the ground and reaching out we slip the rope through this to once again hold us fast. We are now ready to get out of the boat and begin the next part of the journey.

9. With care we step out of our vessel onto the bank, taking a moment to steady ourselves on dry land after the motion of the river. We ask that this little boat be there for us on our return before setting off in the direction that feels appropriate. We hear our feet touching the earth, displacing any soil or stones, gently flattening grass as we walk. Then we look up.

10. Before us we see a dense bank of tall trees – the outskirts of an enchanted wood. Despite the quality of light and the weather it looks dark and as we approach we wonder if this is a safe place for us to enter. Yet still we walk, slowly and deliberately, knowing that what we seek lies within, just as the Prince found Sleeping Beauty in the heart of such a place.

11. We stop on the edge of this great green living wall, gazing up at the branches that weave together above us and down at the gnarled roots that push up from the soil. We scent the air. This is a pace of intense power, ancient yet still very much alive. We know that we must state our purpose and clarify our good intent. We say:

'*Spirits of this primeval place of power, please let me enter your realm for the purpose of seeking an expression of my true self. This I endeavour to do for the sake of my own learning that will in turn contribute to the deeper understanding of the All.'* As we have approached the forest with a good grace then access will be granted to us. It us up to the trees themselves how they show us this. They do so now. We observe what they do and then walk in to their midst.

12. Entering the realm of the trees with a quiet thank you we immediately notice the change in temperature, scent and quality of light. In this forest it is colder, darker, *greener.* We feel we are being watched yet we proceed to move between the many trunks, ducking low to avoid branches. At first we walk using only instinct to guide us on, moving through a carpet of fallen leaves and twigs, hearing only our movements in the strange sylvan hush. Then we discern a path worn into sandy soil, opening before us and leading us more quickly onwards through the seemingly endless sea of trees. We take it eagerly.

13. As we walk on this winding path, we reaffirm our purpose. Even though we seem to arc and double back on ourselves we keep walking until we find that the space between the trees grows wider and the light let in above by the seemingly endless canopy of leaves gets stronger. The forest is thinning, at last.

14. We follow the path up a gentle incline that soon becomes a bank of earth, covered in woodland wildflowers. The light grows stronger as we proceed forward, spurred on by the fact we have nearly reached the place we seek. Climbing to the crest of this verdant slope we let out a gasp of surprise at what we see spread below.

15. Before us now lies a great grassy clearing and in the

centre of this clearing stands a building like something from a fairytale. The place is huge, built of soft grey stone that has a strange lilac tint to it, like no stone we can recognise from our current physical reality. This marvellous place has many tall chimneys and two graceful round turrets at each end with colourful pennants streaming from them in the breeze. Elegant arched windows with tiny leaded panes and elaborately carved mullions line the walls, their glass winking in the sun. An old weathervane turns slowly on the long tiled roof and doves fly from a cote on the far wall. Staring in admiration at this romantic place we see that its huge wooden door stands open.

16. Before we know it we are running down the bank and towards that open door which seems to want us to run into its embrace like a long lost friend. As we arrive we reach out to steady ourselves on the stone doorframe.

17. Feeling as if we are being called onwards we step through the arched doorway into an entrance hall. A steady resonant ticking comes from within this hall and as we look across the tiled floor we see a beautiful old grandfather clock standing against the far wall. Its hypnotic rhythm immediately captures our attention.

18. The clock keeps its mellow pace slowing our heart-rate as we look around us. There are portraits all over the walls here but somehow we cannot focus on who they may be. Even so, we feel the benign presence of each person in the portraits keenly, knowing that somehow they are watching us, supporting our endeavour.

19. We look to either side and take note of what else we can observe. Now we see several closed doors. An oak panelled stair-

case stands to our left and sweeps up out of sight. To our right another set of stairs descend steeply away into the calm, cool depths of this place. We now that these doors and these stairways are the means by which we may reach where we need to go. We know that for finding our apparent *past lives* we must go down the stairs. To find our *future lives*, or *higher self*, we must go up the stairs. To find our *parallel existences* we must walk through a doorway that lies on this level. Now we should move to the appropriate place for us and follow the set of instructions that suit our needs at this time.

i) If we are to climb the stairs we are to count ourselves up as we do so, '*one, two, three...higher and higher...four five six, higher and higher...*'etc. until we reach a level which feels comfortable to us at this time. When we do so we will find ourselves on a landing that has a number of doors to choose from. We should now stand outside this door and reaffirm our purpose for being in this place at this time and hold it uppermost in our consciousness. Then wait.

ii) If we need to descend the stairs then we should so slowly so whilst counting ourselves down from thirty, '*twenty nine, lower and lower, twenty eight, lower and lower, twenty seven...*' etc. until we feel we have reached the appropriate level for us at this time. There we will find we are in a corridor that has a number of doors in it. Move outside the door that feels like the right one for us and then reaffirm our purpose for being here now, holding it at the forefront of our attention. Then wait.

iii) If we need to go to a doorway on the ground floor level then we should count our measured steps as we walk over to the door, '*one, further and further, two, further and further, three...*'etc., then stand outside our chosen door and again make our reason for being in this particular place and time known to ourselves. Hold this thought clearly, and then wait.

20. Now we are ready to open the door that stands before us. When we step through the door we will find ourselves in the place where we are supposed to be in order to find out what it is we want to know about our selves and the aspect of incarnation that pertains to it. So, when we are ready we can reach out and grasp the door handle or knob and open the door, stepping through. This door will be there for us at all times – no matter where we find ourselves and no matter how out of context it may seem on the other side it will always be there. With this as our safety feature we may step through into another reality.

21. We now need to ask ourselves some questions as to get orientated in this new reality. These are as follows.

a) What am I wearing on my feet?

b) What is on the ground under my feet?

c) What are my hands like?

d) What is in front of me when I reach out?

e) What am I wearing?

f) What is around me when I look, from side to side?

g) What does my hair, head or face feel like?

h) What is above me when I reach, or look, upwards?

i) *Who* am I? Have I a name, a sense of purpose?

j) *Where* am I? Has it a name or a particular feel?

k) *When* am I? Do I have a date, a time or a general impression?

l) Am I aware of why I am in this place and what I am doing? What has lead me to this moment? Why is it important?

m) Is anyone there with me? If so can I see or feel them? Who are they and what are they doing?

n) Can I move around the scene and describe what is happening? Do I want to?

o) Do I know what happens next? Can I go on and experience it for a while?

22. When we have finished exploring this particular scene or event we may then turn back to the door that has remained present throughout all the interactions that have taken place. We can step through it and close it behind us. As we do so we leave that life experience behind completely, taking only any understanding that has been gained away with us.

23. We then find ourselves back in the corridor. We are now going to retrace our steps back to 'ordinary' reality. Firstly we have to either ascend or descend some stairs to reach the original entrance hallway. Or else we need to walk over to where we began. However we return to our original place in the entrance hall we should count our steps in a measured way, bringing ourselves either up, down or across.

24. From our place in the entrance hall we may now leave by the stone doorway by which we originally entered the building. We do not shut the great old door behind us as it always remains open for our return.

25. We then walk back across the grass in the direction of the great woodland that lies in the distance, towards the bank that is covered in wildflowers.

26. We climb the bank and then descend again into the trees below.

27. We find our way back through the woods on our winding

path with the intention to return to 'ordinary' reality clearly held in our minds.

28. We exit the enchanted wood, with thanks for our safe passage through, and see the little boat waiting for us beside the bridge where we moored it.

29. We climb into our boat, untie the rope and let ourselves move with the flow of the water to the place where we will re-enter our current physical life. We should hold this desire to move back into manifest existence clearly at the forefront of our awareness.

30. When we are ready we can open our eyes. The journey is over and we are home in our present body. We should now engage with any grounding activities.

It is more important than ever for us to be well grounded after this session, hence the need for a reassuring presence to be there when we get back from our astral travels. As we have said, this is due to the fact that there most likely will have been some dramatic or emotional aspect to our experience which we will need to express and process. We can be certain of there being this poignant or disconcerting aspect to our pathworking into other lives as it is always the emotional highs and lows that give our existences meaning and it is unlikely that we would visit a monotonous scenario when we could pick one which had a highly charged aspect that tells us something profound. However, I have heard of one particular, and very genuine, case where the person involved simply recollected a rural life which centred unswervingly around 'trimmin' the hedge' and having sex! By this example we can observe we can never be quite sure what our soul-self will deem relevant to us at the time of asking.

One thing we can be sure of is that any emotions that arise from an other-life encounter will be equally as valid as those we have in our currently perceived, or dominant, life. They are as real to us as our reading these words today and as with any trauma or excitement we should give ourselves time to assess how we feel afterwards. Playing back the recording we have made of the proceedings with our helper is also therapeutic as well as being a valuable way of clarifying and assimilating what really went on for us.

Another way of earthing ourselves is by discussing or noting down how exactly we witnessed the pathworking behind our closed eyes. Some people see their other life as if they were watching a film being projected on the screen behind their closed lids whilst others live it directly in the first person, as they would 'ordinary' physical life. No doubt there are other variations on these methods that will give us further insights into our soul selves and how we operate as human beings today. Are we detached or fully engaged in the process of living?

This pathworking, and its subsequent analysis, is filled with subsidiary meaning that engenders enhanced self-knowledge whilst enabling us to witness our own part in the 'bigger picture'. Its balance of inner and outer exploration, and its resultant knowing, is what practical spiritwalking is really all about. Now we have this framework, and an understanding of how a directed journey works, it is advised that we learn how to create our own pathworkings for a variety of purposes, the subjects of which will arise naturally from our channelled guidance as time goes by.

CHAPTER ELEVEN

WIDENING OUR CIRCLE

'As human beings we tend to draw our circles too tightly, delineating our world with a heavy hand and inscribing barriers
between that which we consider bad and that which we accept
as being good, or *right*, like ourselves. In this we set ourselves
up for limited, and ultimately lonely, lives as there are
inevitably many more on the outside of this rather brutal line
than there are within its confines. These outsiders stay on the
periphery of our lives making us feel frightened or dismissive
of their deviousness or their meanness...or any of the other
qualities we do not wish to own and acknowledge in ourselves.
And among these ranks of outsiders there are the unseen ones
who we've already set aside as being unlike us. They are the
ones that make us feel the particular fear and discomfort that
only comes from an unsettling familiarity. They are the ones
who won't be quiet, who whisper to us from outside the
boundaries that *what is without is always within*. Their embrace
is greater than any circle of division we could ever inscribe
because they know...they know that *we are in all things and all
things exist inside us.*'
From Guidance

In this chapter, and the next, we will concern ourselves with how
we may meet other helpful beings besides our (by now) trusted
companion spirits whilst in Chapter Thirteen through to Sixteen we
will look at beings or energies that we do not wish to share our space

with – and what to do about them.

The majority of unseen beings we will come across on our travels will be reasonable at worst, amiable and helpful at best. This is due to the fact that we are raising our energy to new levels all the time through daily connection, whilst keeping our thoughts positive, thus attracting the same high vibration as that which we put out. This is also due to our as keeping ourselves safe through our prudent spiritwalking practice, ensuring that we are always aiming to meet those who come for our highest good. Our attraction of other benign spirits will naturally come as we get more adept but we will also find that the more we make astral journeys the more likely it is we will 'bump into' other beings *in situ*. This is especially true if:

- Our astral safe space is becoming more of a firm reality in the ether of the local astral, offering an interesting location for other spirits to visit
- We travel beyond the astral office, to the far reaches at the borders of our created space and move into the as yet unexplored regions of the local astral
- We journey to the Otherworldly realms which are out of our sole jurisdiction
- We undertake pathworkings which will take us to unseen levels of existence that are open to other influences beside our own

As these things are inevitable, and desirable, as we progress then it is good for us to now look at just who is out there.

Other Benevolent Beings – A Spiritwalker's Guide

There are six main types of unseen being that we may want to meet as spiritwalkers. These are the already familiar companion spirits as well as angelic beings, collective beings, guardian ancestral presences (Watchers), avatars and faeries. As we have already established a strong bond with our companions, and know who and what they are, this chapter and the next will be dedicated to understanding the nature and purpose of the remaining five categories. Of these it is the latter two, the avatars and the faeries, that we will concentrate on in more detail being as these are the beings that we can most readily have a viable working relationship with, exchanging energies with them for positive purposes. We will be discussing how we may make contact, meet them and maintain beneficial relationships with their kind.

Before we begin it may be pertinent to address the issue of why we are not having a more in-depth look at angels when many people claim to have beneficial relationships with them. This is because in my experience the beings that people generally consider to be angels are more akin to companion spirits. As we have previously stated, companions are often perceived as *guardian angels* because of their compassion for us. Depending on the degree to which we have been conditioned, some of us in the West will feel the need to put a reassuringly Christian veneer on our generous spiritual friends and consequently those who appear helpful will, inevitably, be delegated angel status. This isn't detrimental, as the companions will operate no matter how we see them or what we call them (providing it is respectful), but doesn't really help us develop an understanding of the way spirits, and the astral levels, work. The avatars we are to discuss could also be mistaken for angelic beings, given their advanced status and supportive role. Yet they are quite different in their function and position to angels.

With this in mind let's begin by having a look at just what angels are, as well as what they are not.

Angelic Beings

Angels have an essence that is of such a refined vibration that they operate at a level that is far beyond humanity's daily experience. They are so light and fast it is hard for us to have direct contact with them. Indeed, to be close to them, at their level, would be rather like a human trying to stare directly at the sun. We need not attempt to dazzle ourselves in such a way, instead we can still experience their influence in our lives circuitously, as we shall discuss.

Angels are energetic *overseers* – ones who take in the biggest picture possible for the purpose of rebalancing distorted energies. In this they are powerful distance healers and weavers of great swathes of energy. Their high frequency healing influence can be observed by us as it touches, and transforms, global or cosmic events. This high energetic input will inevitably filter down, from the greatest to the smallest, where we may witness it as a force or presence in our local environs and ultimately in our individual lives. Consequently we may be aware of their potency and purpose without ever encountering them directly.

Angels do not orbit our manifest world as our companions do, nor do they have a personal relationship with humanity as the avatars do (albeit intermittently). They remain at their incredibly high, pure frequency out in the greater astral and allow us to feel their effect as it trickles down to us. This angelic effect is rather like our tasting like fresh spring water that has reached us after a long journey from its origins on a high, inaccessible mountain. A small amount of such pure, refreshing, healing energy goes a long way. We don't need to climb the mountain to acknowledge the free-flowing benefits.

We could, if highly determined, make a specific journey from the greater astral into the wild *beyond* to encounter the angelic beings themselves but this would be very advanced work and best considered with the advice of our protective companions. The companions would have to be our intermediaries to manage the high-energy of the encounter and so our relationship with them must be solid. For now we can ask the companions to intercede for us with the angels without our actually journeying to them. This would mean their requesting intercession in a matter that required profound healing or a positive energetic boost. As an example, our companions may pass on our request for the swift healing of a war-torn land or for the raising of the vibration in a troubled housing estate.

We do have one means of making contact with the angels safely and that is by praying for such matters as greater well-being for all. Fervent prayers will inevitably reach all levels of energetic existence, including the angelic realms, as prayer is (as we now know) pure directed energetic intention that is fired like a burning arrow into the heart of the matter. Such directing of the will for the greater good is above individual human mores and therefore is wholly angelic in nature, thus aligning us with the angels themselves. If our wish and will is strongly for the wider benefit, and we pray with wholehearted compassion for global healing/peace etc, then we will reach the higher vibrations of these shining beings automatically and join forces with them easily, even while never actually encountering them on a one-to-one basis.

Our constant elevation of our desires beyond petty human need and the actual focusing our own innate will for the collective good is certainly the most manageable, and effective, means of angelic contact. By this we form a circuit by which we will naturally receive a little of their awesome power even as we give of ourselves in our compassion – thus making us more effective in the process. In this a circuit of altruistic prayer acts rather like our daily 'top up' with Source, giving us an uplifting boost from a point of pure free-flowing power and reminding us of our blessed interconnectedness.

I myself was fortunate enough to witness an angelic force when working with a particularly gifted spiritualist healer. While he simply and effectively went about his task I tuned in to the benevolent unseen presences that his work attracted. After a short time I was awestruck to witness the appearance what seemed to me an enormous being, rather like a shimmering golden pylon, which towered over him in his little house while he worked on, blissfully unaware of the angelic presence that was now with him. Try as I might I could not connect directly with this huge presence, instead I felt as if all I could see of it directly was the (metaphorical) hem of its shining etheric garments whilst it stretched up and away from us into realms I could only guess at. Yet even though this incandescent non-human being was distant and awe-inspiring I knew that my healer friend had forged a beneficial chain with them simply by regularly applying his own generosity. This observation taught me that some of our contacts do not need to be personal, or even discernible, to be effective in the extreme. With trust and connection to Source, the pure generator of all compassion, we may link in with these true 'sub-stations' of energy without our ever even being fully aware of it.

So, to sum up angels are not religion-specific, nor are they humanoid, rather they are pure, raw power – higher expressions of life-force. Let us now briefly consider the other kind of higher force we may feel the presence of, if not directly encounter.

Collective Beings

When meditating one evening in the presence of someone who was a formidable spiritwalker I was suddenly in the presence of 'something' I had never seen before and had no words to describe adequately at the time. It was as if a huge undulating, rippling cloud of dazzling golden energy, too bright to properly witness, was passing by and I had caught its attention. It appeared to be made up of many individual essences but as it was perpetually in motion and without a recognisable shape I was not able to keep any sense of proportion or form. I was touched by a sense of *many* and of complete harmonious being as it viewed me in a detached, curious but infinitely compassionate sort of way. I had the impression it had come from an enormous distance and I would not see its like again. It simply passed through my awareness like a fabulous comet, transmitting a sense of peace and unity that was beyond any human notion…and then was gone.

I was entirely delighted to have witnessed this fabulous evolved energetic grouping although I had no real idea of what it was. It was only coming across the work of Esther and Jerry Hicks some years later that I realised that this was a *collective being*, one of the same genre as their multi-spirited contact which names itself Abraham. Abraham is made up of a variety of discarnate awarenesses, all of which are far removed enough from human life to be utterly ego-less and fully coherent in their cause to bring deeper understanding. They represent a natural stage in the re-amalgamation of the singular cell, or soul, back into the larger cell and, ultimately, the Source from which it originally came.

To explain this amalgamation, as we know we are all ones that come from the same One; drops from the ocean as well as the ocean itself. We only adopt the (apparent) singular form in this life to give us a particular point of view for the purpose of furthering our learning so that we may then feed that unique perspective back into the collective All. Once we, and other members of our soul affinity cell group, have completed our singular learning experiences on Earth (and elsewhere) we can begin, little by little, to return to the wholeness from which we originated. We can stop having a singular experience and instead have a more collective experience with all the learning that more unified perspective then brings. We re-group bit by bit, droplets forming a puddle, then a stream, then a river, and expand our awareness back outwards towards the ocean of Oneness from which we came.

Collective beings simply show us the next stage in the natural process of re-amalgamation from where we are today as souls incarnating into singular forms. Such beings and their amalgamated soul-kin have learned enough to be able to shed their singular nature and join together to pool their resources for the greater good. Such a unified being has no more need of bodily learning and consequently no more need of individuality. They still maintain a unique presence or awareness (an I within the collective all-seeing Eye) but their essence merges selflessly and seamlessly into their neighbour's in a way that we find difficult when we are experiencing life from the perspective of our self-ish individual selves.

Of course, apart from the learning experience we also come into physical being for the purpose of actively expressing ourselves as creators through the medium of matter. We could observe that non-physical multi-conscious soul groups have moved away from the desire to create in material ways and have unified to be energetic co-creators of unseen wonders. As well as this they opt to share their own vibrant life-force to inspire us to create while we are in our physical forms. This is one of the key motivations of the Abraham collective that we have previously mentioned.

Although the Hicks have a wonderful contact with Abraham I feel that such an easy connection with such a highly advanced energetic assemblage is the exception rather than the rule and this is why I have chosen not to elaborate too much on the role of the collective being in the spiritwalker's work. Esther Hicks, the channel through which the Abraham energy collective communicates its incredible wisdom, is a very unusual person in that she has a nature that is open, optimistic and content in a way that most of us are not. She was specifically chosen for her lack of guile, strong negative opinions or even psychic experiences. Indeed, she was not someone who had been overtly interested in the unseen, nor had she any real previous spiritual/esoteric knowledge. The nature of the teachings that come through her from this evolved collective is so profound and of such a high vibration that it takes an exceptionally open-minded, uncluttered and loving individual like Esther to be the conduit.

As we spiritwalkers have already undoubtedly had experience of psychic phenomena and have also, to some degree or other, established firm views on the unseen from reading around the subject we ourselves do not fall into this totally neutral yet receptive category. However, it is well for us to be aware of the awesome evolved collectives that inhabit the greater astral and it is certainly healthy to have a desire to commune with them. Indeed, perhaps in time we will feel the need to pursue such fascinating unified beings and ask our companions to aid us in this process. If we choose to do this, and are able to raise our own vibration to a suitably high and pure resonance, then we will surely receive advanced guidance from a much wider universal perspective than our own guiding spirits currently have access to. Yet for now it is enough for us to know that these conglomerations are possible in the higher levels of the unseen and to appreciate how they came to be as they are.

Let's now move on to a category of being we could encounter more readily on our spiritwalking journey.

Ancestral Presences

We may well find, out in the sacred places of our native countryside, a very different kind of unseen being to the ones we have just been considering – these being the *ancestral presences* of those who once dwelled there.

When first faced with this reality of ancestral presences in the sacred landscape I was unconvinced of their authenticity. Surely such spirits had moved on when they had died many hundreds, even thousands, of human years ago? Wouldn't they have perhaps gone on to higher realms by now, perhaps even becoming part of a collective unseen being in the manner that we have previously been discussing? If not then wouldn't they still be reincarnating, having done so many times since their life as a Saxon Seer or Iron Age Smith? What on earth would someone who had passed on into the joy and harmony spirit want to be doing hanging around ancient sacred places as a kind of psychic tour guide or site guardian for future generations?

At that time I considered souls who simply hung around our human earth-level to be stuck or confused – these being the lost souls we shall be discussing in Chapter Fourteen. Failing this explanation perhaps these presences in the land were not ancestors at all but rather 'artificial' site guardians – energetic sentries created by the wise ancients out of the ether for the purpose of protecting their land etc. However, I was to learn that the venerable people of the past – such as those who built the chambered cairns, created the sacred land art or dug the ramparts and ditches of great earth-works – actually can consciously elect to remain *in situ*. This they do as wisdom keepers, guardians and as a link between our apparent human time and theirs. But how? I asked my own companions this question and received the following answer:

'After the death of our physical bodies we are offered to opportunity to move our awareness away from the Earth and on to the place that we may understand as the Summerlands. All beings that have lived harmoniously and consequently with a high degree of receptivity to energies will make this journey easily and without resistance. Although they inevitably make this journey such highly aware souls do not necessarily have to remain in this Summerland region in their entirety. A part of their eternal spirit may elect to return the place they lived in for the purpose of guardianship whilst the other part of their essential self remains in the 'after life'. Such was their level of esoteric understanding in incarnate Earth-life that these beings can control this and choose to do so for the good of the place they loved, as well as for the benefit of those from generations to come who have respect and love for the old ways. They divide their

energies between two levels of existence with full cognisance and eloquence.'

These awesome presences, aspects of the eternal essence of our wise ancestors, are consequently called the *Watchers*.

The Watchers maintain the energies of their special places and pass on the great insights of their time/race/creed to those who seek their council. These beings were so in tune with the land and the natural cycles of death and re-birth in their last life that they are more than able and certainly willing to act as unseen go-betweens twixt the apparent past and present. Again we refer to the *apparent* past and present as it is ever assumed here that time is not a linear progression but rather cyclical or even concurrent. The Watchers are such go-betweens in order for us to have a real experience of their culture and beliefs so that we may share in their respect for the land. We could witness them as both guardians and gatekeepers, those with one foot in spirit but one deeply rooted in their native soil, forming a bridge for the lost knowledge of their era to be remembered in the world again.

Here is an example of how a Watcher may work. I used to live in an area surrounded by hills on which there were many ancient earthworks and around which many legends had sprung up. Several of the hills had been 'UFO hotspots' in the Nineteen Seventies and had seen the original crop circles made nearby in the Nineteen Eighties. It was an area that was definitely considered to be spititually important. As well as the human evidence of sacred activity in the land there was an active population of barn owls there whose ghostly forms could often be seen flitting eerily across the roads at dusk. When wandering around the round barrows on the hills at night I came into in contact with an ancestral force there who I came to know as 'Owl Woman' as I saw her with obsidian black eyes, wild white hair and an air of inscrutability so reminiscent of that local raptor. I knew her as a formidable Watcher of her tribal lands.

I had always been very respectful of Owl Woman's benign watchfulness but a friend of mine was not so cautious when approaching the area at night to perform his own magical rite there. In short, he did not acknowledge her presence let alone ask for permission. Moreover when he did feel her near he overrode the feeling of being watched and the unease that gripped him as he stood in the field beneath one of the aforementioned hills. Consequently about half way through what he was doing he was treated to an apparition…not of Owl Woman but rather of his own deepest fear. This happened to be being caught in his magical act by thuggish locals intent on violence. So it was that he saw two drunken and yobbish males jumping over the hedge that boundaries the field and the adjacent road and coming up the field towards him menacingly. So realistic was this manifestation of his fear that he actually heard them talking as they approached him. Breaking out of his paralysed fearful state he ran and hid. And hid. Only to realise there had been no men and no threat. The land's Watcher had simply taught him a lesson in respect. I am certain of this as Owl Woman herself independently appeared to me on the night of this event, passing on her message so that I may alert my friend to his mistake and discuss its meaning afterwards.

Obviously from this tale it is always wise to approach any human-influenced sacred place with an awareness of the presence of possible ancestral Watchers, as well as any human-created site guardians (more on these in Chapter Thirteen on intentionally created energetic beings, often known as 'servitors'). The Watchers themselves are doing a vital job in these hectic and often destructive times, giving us the opportunity to liase with them when we so desperately need to reconnect with the more green-spirited values of our forbearers. We should certainly venerate their generosity of spirit for wishing to have communication with us modern humans at all as we must sometimes seem to them to be destroying all that they hold dear.

I have always aimed to make contact with the Watchers of where I live or visit to show my respect for their ways and to give thanks for their willingness to establish a relationship with us. I have asked that they pass on any insight, via thought or feeling, about their beautiful place of residence. We can all actively do this, by protecting ourselves and then tuning in to any higher presences as we walk in ancient sacred places or on tracts of land that have a long history of occupation. We would be doing ourselves a great service if we can open ourselves to the vital truths about living well that they can effortlessly expound to us as we walk with them in spirit. They can teach us about what the land needs and how to behave respectfully on it, putting the onus on what we can offer. They can tell us about the wildlife as well as the flowers or insects of their place, perhaps instructing us on what we may plant there. The Watchers will also enlighten us about how life was in their time, filling in any gaps in our knowledge in our local history with their real experiences. In this they are an invaluable source of hidden wisdom, the likes of which we could find nowhere else.

Beyond such an exchange of information and energy we can also gain inspiration from their strength of will, a will that allows them to remain, at least in part, with the land they love to guard it beyond death. Their dedication to their beloved region is only matched by the self-less dedication our companions show towards us as they constantly walk beside us. We can add our own dedication to the health and well-being of their particular area and become co-guardians, stewards of the land, dealing with any physical detritus (such as non-biodegradable litter) that affects the area while the Watchers will deal with the energetic detritus. Such co-operation between seen and unseen beings is crucial for the land, and for the planet, if we are to move away from destruction and towards a healthier world.

Now we have looked at the three main types of being we may encounter by chance on our astral, or physical, travels we can move on to looking at the unseen beings that we can actively meet with and work with regularly, forging a mutually beneficial relationship. The first of these are the avatars.

Avatars

Avatars are independent beings whose relationship to us isn't deeply personal and constant (like the companions) but nor is it wholly impersonal and indirect (like the angels). Whereas angels are the seemingly unreachable but awesomely beautiful forces that oversee, and companions are spirits who work closely with the details of our lives, avatars lie somewhere in between – both overseeing *and* getting involved, to a degree. In this they neither get tied up long term in the 'stuff' of a human life nor do they find it impossible to relate to it. They are beings of balance, drawing close to us for a specific purpose but only for a finite period.

By this we can observe that the presence of the avatars is not continuous but given as needed. To explain this we are well served by using the analogy of an avatar as a peripatetic teacher. In the same way as we can hire a teacher to brush up on our French before a holiday so may we call on an avatar to step forward with their particular energetic forté when we require to learn more about a related issue or way of being. Avatars act as unseen representatives of certain universal principles and make such matters pertinent for the individual, just as any decent teacher would do with their specialist subject. And, like all the great teachers, they will not necessarily become our friends but they will give us the benefit of their expertise, keeping a professional distance whilst changing our outlook and experience by their presence.

Whilst companion spirits stick with us for the duration, avatars can be called upon to help, or tutor us, in a particular matter – and that is all.

So, we can state that avatars are specialists and we can call on them for help in their particular field of expertise. They are also role models for us, displaying and emitting their particular brand of energy in a way we can readily assimilate. This we can do by simply soaking up their presence as it emanates its own particular vibration or by following their example. Because of the fact that their resonance is perfectly attuned to what they represent they are both our teachers *and* they are our lessons. If we are receptive then they don't necessarily have to do anything for us to grasp their meaning.

But what is their purpose? Well, even though the avatars are resolutely non-physical they stand to reveal to us the purest aspects of physical being, expressing the enduring energies that make up the human incarnate experience. They are concerned with the collective consciousness, as opposed to the individual details of lives, and can relate to humanity's human-ness purely as *an energetic experience made up of essential interactions and cycles.* The core aspects that constitute these essential energetic phases are those that they represent for us. These include love and passion, weakness and strength, revenge and conflict, forgiveness and acceptance or dis-ease and well-being. We call these *archetypal energies* – those that can be related to collectively by all who have walked the Earth. Avatars can be said to be archetypal beings that express such universal qualities as courage, wrath or joy to us through their very nature.

Let's consider some examples of avatars as they can be found in myth and legend from around the world. Their presence is felt in all countries and in all times. For example, the mythic figure of Mercury (Ancient Rome), also known as Hermes (Ancient Greece), is an avatar of effective communication, one that links together thoughts, ideas and words. Ts'ai-Shen (Japan) is an avatar of abundance, bringing assistance in matters of wealth or success – this latter aspect he shares with the avatar Ganesha (India) who is also a representative of wisdom. Ganesha is just one example of avatars who have several qualities within themselves. As a further example, Brigit (British Isles and Ireland) who is also known as Bride or Brighid, is an avatar of healing as well as inspiration and powerful transformation.

Other avatars have one major aspect but share this key quality with other beings. For instance, the legendary figure of Robin-in-the-Hood (Britain) is an avatar of justice in its simplest, purest form – a role he shares with Maat (Ancient Egypt), who helps to bring truth and order out of chaos, Tyr or Tiw (Northern Europe), who is concerned with fair play and right action, as well as Ida-ten (Japan) who is experienced as a guardian of just laws. Yet avatars are not always so cut-and-dried and some have influences that are more lyrical. For example, the fabulous figure of Jack-in-the-Green, or the Green Man, (Britain and Europe) is an avatar of fecund wildness, encouraging us to be playful as a frisking fox cub and as free as the stag that roams the moors at midsummer. Artemis (Ancient Greece), also known as Diana (Ancient Rome), is an avatar of a different kind of fierce wildness – that experienced alone on a moonlit beach or when spending time in solitude with the untamed deep self.

Regardless of our locality or our ethnicity these model beings of power exist in the astral and we can work with their primal force, or archetypal resonance, as well as encountering their profound mysteries in our daily lives. I myself have worked with the avatars of Ana and Morgan Le Fey (Britain) for stretches of time when I have needed inner strength and a more profound link to the land. But are such avatars at our beck and call, having been created specifically for our benefit? Yes, we could say that avatars have been created in accordance with human experience, to give assistance. Yet, paradoxically they also just *are*, standing alone as eternal aspects of being beyond our own little lives, existing with or without humanity's need. It is an endless chicken and egg scenario that we may enter into when we address the issue of what came first, the energy itself or the ability to experience that energy?

Here is an example of such an energetic dichotomy. When I was an angst-filled teenage artist I created (on paper and canvas) a flame-haired rebel character named Lian (pronounced as Lie-Ann, as in lion). Lian did all the things I could not do myself at the time and looked, in my opinion, far better than me with her wild hair and wonderfully outrageous clothing. As an illustrator I drew Lian over and over and wrote stories about her daily doings which were far more fascinating than mine. Years later two different psychic people (on separate occasions) saw the sketches of Lian I had worked into paintings and framed and said 'oh, her name's Lian, I met her when I was trance journeying!'. The question is, did I make Lian so vivid, such a living force in the ether that she took on my energies and a life of her own independent of me? Or did I simply chance upon her astral presence in my daydreaming youth and channel her through me onto paper? The whole area of 'creator' and 'created' is an interesting but inconclusive one. For those who are interested in this dichotomy the author Stephen King explores it eloquently within his 'Dark Tower' series of books.

Maybe we are better served in this instance to practice the acceptance of something that simply *is* rather than questing in an endless circle. All we need to know is that avatars are independent, wise and gracious beings that deserve our deep respect. Not our overt supplication or our disregard, just a fine line of balance between. And they will always help us if we ask with a good intent. But they are also *mystery* and beyond us even as they stand before us for a time. And this is as it is.

Another issue that comes up as regards the nature of avatars is their connection, if any, to deity. We will of course have noticed from the names we gave, such as Diana or Ganesha, that avatars are often regarded as deity figures. Let us for a moment consider the riddle of deity more closely. As we know, within spiritwalking it is helpful to approach the idea of deity as the Creator, or Source, a blend of male and female or positive/negative energy that is certainly in no way human-centred and so cannot truly be anthropomorphised. As we have previously suggested this is a mystery – the Great Mystery that cannot be unravelled.

How can we turn the ultimate Source energy into a humanised form when it created all universes, not just one small blue-green planet that contains humanity as but one species of hundreds of thousands. It is easy to understand how we need to have an expression of the divine that they can relate to directly, especially of the divine feminine as a response to unbalanced patriarchy. Yet the unfeasibility of having a supreme human figure as overseer of a predominantly non-human universe (or, more likely, universes) is but one of the deeply ingrained issues that we as spiritwalkers must tackle. Freeing ourselves of an illusion, especially one held onto by our families, schools and society as a whole, can be painful but it is essential if we are to relate to energies in an authentic way.

The need for an anthropomorphised expression of the divine is healthy and beneficial when it remains symbolic, an emblematic way of understanding energy, and does not come to be considered as an actual fact that there is a giant all-powerful woman, or man, 'out there'. The problem with this very concrete form of deification, the factual *person*-ification, of divine, or Source, energies, is that it limits us and gets us stuck…*and when we are stuck we are not open to energies.* As spiritwalkers it is vital that we remain open and allow ourselves to flow with *what is* as opposed to *what we have been told is* by another human being. All such literal deity figures have been, after all, brought to us by another person, we rarely encounter and make up our own! But is the whole notion of deity redundant? Perhaps it is only truly viable for a spiritwalker if it is a purely symbolic way of gaining deeper insights. And avatars are certainly equipped to give us such insights without us relating to them as gods.

So now we have an overview of their nature and purpose we will naturally wish to know where to find the avatars. As we would expect, the avatars dwell in the ambient level of existence that we know as the local astral but instead of them being in the regions closest to us, like the companions, they inhabit the regions that segue seamlessly into the *greater* astral. This is close enough for their being able to relate to us adequately but far away enough for them to have the distance to remain basically pure. We could say, perhaps, that whereas companion spirits are once-removed from our humdrum level of human being in the local astral, the avatars are twice-removed from the limiting and stultifying minutiae of any given life. They are able to remain pristine and untroubled by the daily grind of humanity. Yet saying this their archetypal and impersonal energies are everywhere, even in the most mundane of personal situations, so once again they are paradox and impossible to pigeon-hole neatly with a phrase.

Rather like astrology, to which certain avatars lend their resonance, they work in our daily lives whilst expressing energies and forces that are global, not provincial. For example, we may call upon Mars, also known as Ares, or to Thor, when we require passion and drive for a personal project, as these avatars are known for their courageous, vigorous and ardent energies that are 'larger than life'. Or we may turn to an avatar of universal healing and powerful purification, such as the compassionate Kwan Yin or her counterpart Kannon Bosaisu, when we need help with our very localised addiction or phobia. Perhaps if we were pregnant we would want to work with an avatar that has the encompassing energy of 'great cosmic mother', such as Anu, Kishimo-Hin, Frigg or Gaia. On the other hand, if we were to become a father, or needed help with issues relating to fertility, nurture and protection, we could convene with such avatars as the Dadga, or T'ai-Yueh-Ta-Ti, who are powerful representatives of the All-Father.

Similarly if we needed help in matters long-term partners we could turn to Isis or Juno/Hera, whose energies are, amongst other things, those of the archetypal devoted wife. If we needed help with growing things at home then we would be advised to seek avatars such as Ceres, Itzpzpalotl or Chicomecoatl who are all concerned with agriculture and the wider fertile land. The lesser always relates directly to the greater, the microcosm to the macrocosm. This is one more way of saying *as within, so without* for our small individual needs are always found in the greater whole and so what we need as people can always be related to by the avatars.

We have begun to look at the many names of the avatars here but some avatars do not have such culture-specific names, nor do they feel the need for one. Indeed, we may not feel that it is appropriate to use a name at all but instead wish to ask for specific help by referring to another sort of archetype. A wonderful example of this would be to call upon an avatar using the symbols of the tarot. For example, we could ask for an avatar representing the Fool to help us when we have a leap of faith to make. Or we could ask for an avatar who represents the Hierophant energy when we need to focus on our own innate spiritual wisdom. Likewise we may want to work with beings whose energy is close to the passionate King of Cups or the clarifying Ace of Swords.

Depending on our own cultural orientation we may also want to call on the animal representitive of a particular energy. In this way we may connect, for example, with Coyote the Trickster or the Salmon of Knowledge. These non-humanistic avatars are certainly just as valid as their counterparts.

We do not always need a name as a focus, rather a particular energy refined into a universal symbol that an avatar can interpret as their own 'calling card'. We are dealing with representatives of certain resonances here and all we need is a means of connection. Avatars are not concerned with ego and so as long as we are aiming for their energy with all due respect they won't mind what we do, or do not, call them.

Clearly, as we have already alluded to, we can meet these archetypal beings indirectly through reading or hearing myth and legend or by engaging in astrological study. We can surround our-selves in their symbology and immerse ourselves in their stories. Whatever we call them, or whatever our own particular cultural approach, we will be able to encounter their eternal energies in this legendary way. But such connection isn't all about reading the fables or looking at star signs. We can be actively involved by painting images of them, sculpting representations, creating music, poetry or songs inspired by them or simply by writing our own interpretation of their tale. By this we earth their particular power in our hands-on experience and feel their influence flowing through us as we become a conduit for it.

We can also meditate, or silently and prayerfully focus, on the mythic stories and symbols and so draw them deeply into our own being like life-giving air. By praying to the avatars we purposefully open a channel for contact to be established. We are putting out an astral call for the avatar of our choice to be present in our lives and to reveal certain truths to us through our experience. We may not actually encounter them 'in person', as we would through a trance journey, but we will get to know them as they reveal themselves in our seemingly mundane comings and goings. Such a prayer might be something like:

' *I call upon my companion spirits to support and protect me as*

I call to (name avatar) *to help me with* (name issue). *Spirits who come for my highest good, may* (name avatar) *draw close to me and be revealed to me in my personal and professional life. This I ask for my individual good and so for the good of all beings by reflection. So may this contact be made, in truth, love and wisdom and eternally with my gratitude for your care.'*

It is well to study, create and meditate or pray with an avatar as our central focus as their energies will indeed permeate into our experiences, giving us a meaningful link with their resonance. But we can also meet the avatars *directly and personally*, just as we meet with any other beings, by following a pathworking specifically designed to facilitate such an encounter. For this we need only the type of energy we wish to work with, or to understand better (such as the energy of healing, of regeneration or of peace) or the name of an avatar that represents the aspect of existence that we need to incorporate more fully into our lives (for example, Minerva/Pallas Athene for a sharp intellect and clear thoughts, the Merlin for intuitive wisdom or Lakshmi for increasing abundance)

What follows is an example of such a directed journey to meet an avatar although I am sure that with experience, and through close consultation with our companions, we can create our own versions.

It is taken as read that we will record this journey or have to read to us. It is also assumed that we will protect ourselves before, and ground ourselves after, this encounter.

A Pathworking to Meet an Avatar

1. We should close our eyes and hold the energy that we wish to contact and connect with uppermost in our awareness – be that

associated with a particular avatar in our minds or not. We should offer a small prayer that reveals our intention, something like:

'*I now journey to make a link with the authentic energy of* (name energy) *that is connected with the avatar/s* (name avatar/s). *I do this under the care of my companion spirits and with deep respect for all genuine beings that I may encounter. Let my quest be successful, for the good of my own development, and consequently for that of the All.*'

2. We now need to make the journey to our astral safe place and to meet there with our companion/s in the usual secure fashion. When we are in our astral office with them we should clarify our needs and ascertain with them whether this process is valid or not at this time. The companions can help us with all such decisions and give us any insights necessary for us to re-vision our intent.

3. If it is deemed appropriate then we now need to travel to a region of the local astral far outside of our usual office area. This is where the avatar we seek can be reached. For this we will need to attract the attention of a being that can act as a courier, transporting us into the fringes of the greater astral from the place where we currently are.

4. To attract the attention of such a being we need to fire an *arrow of desire* into the ether. This arrow is not harmful, rather it is made of the same cold-fire of our will and wish as is the protective flame we use in the astral safe place. Let us see it in our hands – it is aflame and so brilliant yet it can never hurt us! We will also need to envision a bow and arrow made of brightest, purest blue-white light. See the energy take form in our hands as we act as the creator, fashioning the ether into these shapes. Feel the cold-fire as it tingles in our palm. Feel the

subtle weight of it as it rests there, ready for action. Witness the glow of its power.

5. Now we should get ready to fire our arrow. We should not worry if we do not know how to do this act in 'ordinary' reality, the companion/s will show us how to do it here in our own astral reality. However we chose to do it will be effective here. In our minds we should hold our intention to meet a particular avatar or representative of a particular energy. Then, when we are absolutely sure that the intent within us can be translated directly into this burning arrow of desire we should lift the bow to the sky and let the arrow fly free, letting go and not trying to control where it lands.

6. After a time we will become aware of an approaching being – our avatar's messenger. This being could come from the air, or through any water that is present, or it could rise up from the ground. Similarly it could appear in a puff of smoke or arrive in a cloud of mist. It is, as we shall see, a kind of mythic messenger between worlds, perhaps half-human, perhaps a recognisable creature from folk or fairytale, perhaps a strange hybrid of beasts that we could not have conceived of ourselves. Its appearance will be as unique as the mode of transport it will offer to us. Whoever this messenger shows itself to be we should immediately circle it with cold blue-white fire and ascertain its authenticity, using the usual techniques.

7. Once it has been proved that the messenger is genuine, no matter how many attempts this takes to find a genuine being to help transport us, then we should ask them to take us to the place where we need to be. We may find that they invite us onto their back, or pick us up in their claws, or carry us in their arms.

Perhaps they are pulling a chariot or cart of some kind and ask us to get in. Or maybe they produce a separate mode of transport for us to use along with them, such as a hot air balloon, boat or some kind of tunnelling device. The way that this messenger appears, as well as the way that they transport us, is going to be totally particular to them. We need to be open to their approach.

8. When we begin to travel we should use our senses to make the experience as real as possible. See the sights, feel the sensations, scent the environment and hear its ambient sounds. If we are flying then take care to really feel the wind on our faces and the change in temperature as we rise. If we are going over land or water feel the motion or vibration. If we are being lifted then feel the being's body next to ours and smell their own particular scent. The more vivid the experience is the more we will get out of our encounter with the avatar.

9. When we arrive at our destination it is also very valuable to take in the new environs in the same way. We should thank the messenger and ask that they wait to return us to our astral safe place. If they do not wish to do this then we can call another one at the end of our meeting.

10. The messenger will then bring us into proximity with the avatar that we need to meet at this time. We must then immediately begin our checking out technique, encircling the being who approaches us, or who we approach, with our usual cold-fire. This may seem rude but it is what a wise being would expect from a genuine spiritwalker. They will not be offended.

11. When we have ascertained that the avatar, or avatars, are truly who they purport to be then the meeting or exchange can take place. Obviously this is totally unique and cannot be

described here. As the encounter is very much about particular energies we can expect to have to use all our sense and not just rely on being spoken to. This meeting will, no doubt, be a very intense experience for us, perhaps more so that we are used to, and so it is well to keep it relatively brief. Our desire to take in as much as possible when with such an incredible being may be overwhelming but we have to remember our own capacity to retain information and to assimilate external energy and we should know our limits at this time.

12. When we have given thanks and, if appropriate, asked to keep the connection open with the avatar, we will need to ask the messenger who brought us to take us back to our astral office. If we need to get a new messenger then we can ask the avatar to do this for us as this is their realm, not ours, and they know who to call. We can think of this as a kind of taxi service where the locals know the best people to call for the job. This messenger, if new, should be duly tested out using the cold-fire technique before we travel with them. Then after the return journey they should be thanked for their time.

13. We may then make our return journey via the astral office to 'ordinary' reality. We should be sure to thank our companions before returning to the manifest world.

14. We should then make our notes and ground ourselves fully.

Now we have the ability to discern these powerful, instructive avatars and to work with them we can look more closely at the next category of inspiring beings, the faeries. As these spirits are so deeply fascinating and their realm so close to our own they have the whole of the next chapter dedicated to them.

CHAPTER TWELVE

SPINNING ROUND

'Faeries are utterly monstrous and altogether charming, divine and devilish both. They have to be both ends of the spectrum to hold the rainbow between – the one that could colour our lives if only we would let it. To opt to acknowledge and work with the faeries is a step towards living a technicolour life of enchantment instead of a drab existence in shades of concrete and steel. Wouldn't we like to hear the passionate poetry of the rushing river or the sonorous sonnet of the sky as it wraps itself sensuously around the land? The Fey are the soul singers can give us access to these deep mysteries, bringing the rhyme to our reason in the most glorious, outrageous or subtle of ways. Our lives can be love songs, paeans of pleasure instead of pain and loss, even in the midst of modernity. Interaction with the transfomative Fey is like wearing rich velvet after a lifetime of hessian – and why would anyone choose the latter when they know that they can have opulence?'

From Guidance

What do we think of when we hear the word faery? Most likely what immediately springs to mind is the standard image of a dainty, gauzy-winged female, culled from the folklore, or fairytales, of our childhood. Perhaps, as people with an enhanced level of psychic sensitivity, we have even seen them in this way. Yet this is but one version of the flexible energetic reality of the faeries. The faery races, collectively termed as *the Fey* (the adjective fey meaning mysterious or strange), are not human even though they may have manifested themselves though time in a conveniently humanoid fashion. Such an image is never the absolute reality, rather the effect of the observer (ourselves) upon the innate mutable energy of the observed (the faery).

With faeries what we see is, to some degree, what we are. Or, for others of us, *what we see is what we expect to see.* What we see is also the result of the faery's own particular brand of wit and guile, psychically projected in response to our need. Whereas our dense human forms are basically the same, day after day, the faery beings we encounter have an energetic speed which can fashion itself into just about anything, depending on a subtle equation that includes the nature of the occasion, the type of observer and the innate resonance of the faery involved.

Faeries are composed of energy that is so fast and light compared to ours that they are like sunlight dancing on water. We can interpret them, or they can interpret themselves, depending on the prevailing factors of the encounter – these being:

- Their current environment
- Their innate nature and that of the spectator
- Their desires and those of the spectator
- The presence of any deep emotional charge such as rage

This ability to shape-shift is completely natural and usual for faeries but is enhanced by their equally inherent naughtiness and desire to fool us slower, denser humans. They usually have little or no time for us, depending on their mood, experiences or innate personality, and so a good measure of patience (as well as a hearty measure of good will and respect) is needed if we are to draw close to them at all.

The faery folk may see fit to present us with something reassuringly familiar or something beguiling, like a seductive nymph or handsome elf, but they can just as likely use their energy to manifest a shape that will confuse or revolt us, depending on their whim. This could indeed be humanoid but also any variation on a theme of animal, vegetable or mineral. Their essential energetic nature, capricious and brilliant, is such that they cannot help but do this – mischief is always their middle name.

If we do manage to make contact it is always on the terms of the Fey and it is well to be prepared for a display as they run through their gamut of inventive disguises. Our own brain, unaccustomed as it is to witnessing the unseen, then strives to make sense of what it is experiencing and this it does within the boundaries of our own imaginations as well as with reference to our own particular preferences and feelings. I myself have seen all sorts of faery guises from childlike, apple-cheeked beings that charmed me to strange scuttling salamander type creatures with human faces that alarmed me. The playful childlike manifestations have only ever occurred in beautiful, natural places that filled me with open admiration whilst any more disagreeable faery displays have occurred in areas where I felt as if I were trespassing.

One of my most enduring and rewarding contacts with a faery being was with Kefli, who first appeared to me as a spindly, spiky creation of twisted bark, mud and twigs. He was drawn to me, and I to him, when I was visiting a stone circle in the county of Cornwall, UK. Both he and I were brought together by our outrage at the other humans visiting the site. These people had left the remains of their picnic, including bottles of cider, left strewn about as dubious 'offerings' to the ancient sacred space and were engaged in a loud celebration that seemed to have no relevance to the place at all. Kefli's appearance in my psychic vision completely reflected his righteous indignation at the insensitivity of some humans, as well as his allegiance to the wild land on which we both stood. He was, to my eyes at least, the epitome of our spikey emotional response as well as being clad in the very fabric of the local area.

As a further example of this faery ability to energetically adapt and respond, two people I knew spontaneously encountered the same faery being in the same place. One has a very vivid imagination and an open-minded fearless outlook and so the faery appeared to him as a quirky hybrid figure with long froggy legs, a skinny man's upper body wearing a waistcoat of jay feathers, all topped off with a hedgehog's smiling countenance. The other person observing the faery energy is far more fearful and rather unimaginative and so consequently only saw a small, grumpy, gnome-like figure in dressed in a coat of dry fallen leaves. Because of this variation it may be impossible for any of us to categorically state what a faery truly looks like beyond the glamour and guile. Perhaps it would be wise for us to assume that the do not really look like anything other than how they feel, or how we feel, at a particular time. In this they are fluid, always in motion and ethereal in the truest sense – that is to say, *ether*-real...of the ether and very real!

Despite this vital flexibility of form, the Fey have been designated particular tribes or collectives in the familiar folklore that we no doubt grew up with. This labelling may have been given in reference to their place of residence or as regards any associated personality traits which resulted from their living in this particular location. For example, a dark and mysterious cave may have given its faery inhabitants a generally sinister or furtive aspect. Indeed it is accurate to observe that the faery folk have such a close identity to a land or region, or to a way of being, that they are indivisible from it and simply *are it* a way that modern humans have almost forgotten. The Fey are, without a doubt, energetic expressions based on their place on, and, indeed, *in* the land.

But can they really be labelled in the way that the folklorists of old, our ancestors, determined? The ethnic or cultural names that we know today, such as pixies, dwarves, elves and sprites, or kobolds, brownies, spriggans and kelpies, were obviously given by local people as an attempt to control and contain an energetic manifestation in their midst that was effectively inexplicable and resolutely unclassifiable. Such names as the Twyleth Teg (Wales) the Seelie Court (Scotland) or the Tuatha de Danann (Ireland) were given to what were perceived as various Fey races. However, if we choose to continue to identify them in such a way it matters not one jot to them as the Fey are perfectly happy to operate without human classification or jurisdiction. Human names given for the ease of human identification are not their priority, nor will they bow to them. In fact, like most things about us stolid, staid humans, they make the Fey react with (mostly) good-humoured derision and a desire to turn such silly orderly things upside down. As long as we give them, and that which they belong to our sincere and respectful consideration then they will respond to us accordingly with a measure of interest.

What we can say emphatically is that the Fey are always pure, vital and of the land – any land, for they are recorded across the world from South Africa (the Abtawa) to Japan (the Yosei). They are the *Earth-aliens* – of the land yet *unearthly* – as unknown and unknowable to the majority of modern humankind as a space dweller is or, indeed, the mysterious world of bacteria within our own bodies. Yet saying this they are always as near and as tangible as the Earth's inherent magic and mystery. They hold their wholesome earthiness and their unsettling strangeness in balance, creating an intoxicating (and of course paradoxical) blend. They are as old as the hills, as deep as the ocean and as awesome and inspiring as clouds that cast their fleeting shadows across meadow and plain. Like moonlight on a river they cannot be caught and kept, only witnessed as something beautiful and powerfully fragile. But they are clearly not a part of our daily experience in the way that birds or plants are. So where are they?

The Fey dwell in the strictly non-human version of the world that borders and overlays our own. We will know this parallel layer of existence to our Earth as the *Otherworld*. We call the faery's realm the Otherworld as it is shares the psychic space of our home planet yet it is resolutely *other* to ours, their reality being in quite a different dimensional plane to ours.

If we once again think of the Earth as an onion we will now be able to accept that the whole onion is in fact built up of many energetic layers – layers of vibration – of which the human's material world is but one. Our dense world has, as we know, neighbouring energetic layers such as the human astral which, being non-physical, vibrate at a slightly quicker rate to ours. Yet other *parallel* layers run *simultaneously* to ours, occupying the same space only at a different vibrational speed so that they remain, in the most part, undetectable to us. To return to our radio analogy if we sit at home at listen to our favourite local station on an analogue radio at

98.7 FM and then travel to the other end of the country and tune into 98.7 FM we will find a different transmission being broadcast altogether. Our original local transmission is still out there *in the same space* only we are now out of its range and not equipped to experience it. The frequency of the world of Faery is different to ours but the airspace in which they exist are the same. It just depends what our transmitter is set up to receive.

Saying this, the frequency of our world and of the Otherworld used to be far more similar than they are today. Even though the layers were still vibrating at different rates, given one is matter and the other pure energy, there was less of a gap between them and greater harmony of resonance. This meant that our world was more numinous and less prosaic whilst the world of Faery was less nebulous and more tangible. There was a cautious concord and cordiality between the two races and a deeper sense of connection and interaction despite the obvious 'racial' differences. At this time some humans and faeries even interbred and those with some faery blood in their veins still exist today. Even those with faery souls who have chosen to experience life inside human bodies can sometimes be found. Yet now the Fey have deliberately raised their vibration to make the gap between our lower frequency and their shimmering high one so wide that consequently the similarities between our realm and theirs are less distinct. This vibrational elevation, or escalation, is a response to our version of the Earth, as these energetic beings simply cannot bear what we are doing to our level of the planet, or how we choose to live upon it. The time when faeries and humans could easily walk between realms is now over although thankfully for us it is a vibrational gulf that is at present still bridgeable, if we know how.

Although the Otherworld is now operating at a far finer frequency than our Earthly version of reality both our experience of our manifest world and the Otherworld will still contain the same sort of natural features such as flowers, trees, hills and streams. Both the faeries and humanity may still even experience these natural features in the same corresponding places on their land. However, the Otherworldly experience of them would be far more sparkling, luminous and elegant than our human one, being as it is resonating at a much more refined and rapid rate. The otherworldly experience of such features would also be more magical – seemingly miraculous and deeply thrilling to behold. For instance, in our world it would be possible to admire the pleasant sound of a running brook whilst in the Otherworlds it may be possible to vividly hear the extraordinary living music of the water as it flows and the harmonious accompaniment of all the insects, fish and plants that live there. There would be a sense of blessed interconnectedness and synchronisation that we simply do not have access to here. There we could understand the living language of nature.

Similarly in this Otherworld of wonders a blossom in a hedgerow may produce a dazzling flower that is twice its normal 'human earthly' size, just for the sheer joy of blooming. This bloom may then give out an intoxicating perfume that is far headier and more beguiling than anything an earthly blossom in a country lane could emit, attracting a miscellany of unfeasibly brilliant butterflies each whose wings leave intricate, shimmering trails in the air as they flit about. Meanwhile its earthly counterpart produces a graceful blossom of standard size, delicate tint and faint perfume – beautiful indeed but without that essential *joie de vivre* of its Faery double, a bloom which is full of the passion of creation and a vigorous lust for life that persists in asking '*what if?*'

This sharing of natural features still continues despite the further energetic separation of the faeries realm from our realm. This sharing can, if the energetic circumstances are favourable, still create a portal or crossing place into the Otherworld from our own. A classic example of this is the 'faery mound', or 'hollow hill' that appears in both realms simultaneously. In the human world this would look, to all intents and purposes, like an ordinary green hill or mound yet in the Otherworld it would be a place of great beauty and wild enchantment, a place that would grant access to many different levels of awareness – a pivotal point. Glastonbury Tor in Southern England, said to be the domain of the Faery King Gwyn Ap Nudd and haunt of Morgan Le Fey herself, is such a place. In our world it looks like a solid hill with its man-made terraces and Christian tower planted on the top yet in the level of the Fey it is known as a hollow hill that holds a crystal cave in its heart and which has the power to be in several dimensional spaces at once. Marion Zimmer Bradley explores this concept brilliantly in her best-selling novel *The Mists of Avalon* (Penguin, 1993).

The relevance of such supposedly hollow portals is that the Fey live *inside* the land and that their energetic realm is somehow accessed *within* our own Earth, beyond its 'ordinary' reality or surface level. This is more of a symbolic way of understanding the location of Faery than it is literal. In symbolic terms this going within reveals to us how we must go beyond the human artifice and triviality of the mundane 'middle way' and dig deep down into our subconscious for the real treasure we have buried. When we go within as spiritwalkers we know that we quest for powerful hidden truth and so this within direction, alluded to in many Faery myths as the *Under* or *Lower* world, tells us where we must *psychically* journey.

So, the Otherworldly dimension of our Earth-space shares some of our features (such as the aforementioned hills or earthworks) but is still full of magic and mystery, with overwhelming colours, breathtaking scents and uplifting melodies prevailing over anything lack lustre or average. The Otherworld is a *sensual* world.

To the Fey the world is fundamentally exquisite and beguiling, vital and essentially elegant, and they are determined to remain that way. They are proud to be instinctively attuned to each ripple and subtle nuance of their glorious Earth as co-creators. Their counter-parts, the elemental spirits of nature, share this enchanted unseen world of the Fey and their deep love of the wild. Nature spirits are, like the faeries, independent beings that are fiercely protective of the land; land we ourselves live upon but experience in a totally different way. Likewise nature spirits are inseparable from the untamed land herself and are inextricably linked to the plants, rivers, mountains etc that are within the Earth's jurisdiction. The difference between the Fey and these spirits is that the nature beings and elementals are, as their names suggest, specifically linked in with one particular element or place. We can experience a fire or water elemental or the nature spirit of a river or rock whilst the Fey are connected to the land but not necessarily linked to one individual part of it.

It may be well to add in at this juncture that there are also *land wraiths* that may well be confused for a faery or nature spirit. These ethereal beings are quite literally the ghosts of the wild land. In our tame and cultivated countryside their essence laments that which once was – an unfettered growing and blooming of the native species there. These land wraiths are seldom mentioned and as I have encountered their mournful presence on many occasions in once wild areas regulated into rectangular fields and given over to intensive farming methods, it seems pertinent to include them here. Their sadness is all-pervaiding and an encounter with a land wraith has an almost unbearable poignancy for a sensitive human.

The Fey, although very much champions of the wild themselves, are more concerned with the poetry and mystery of existence and the wonder of life than either the land wraiths or their nurturing, protective counterparts the nature spirits. In this they are also divisible from the *genius loci*, or spirit of a particular place, although they may work very closely with such an energy for prolonged periods. They are harmoniously engaged with all who seek to love and honour the land but especially with those of us who seek beauty and lyricism in it. We humans can meaningfully engage with them if we have the right intent – an intent that can be accurately assessed as worthy or phoney by a faery or nature spirit in a blink of an eye.

Even if we have a noble objective, fey contact is not an undertaking to be entered into lightly. Many fairytales, such as that of Thomas the Rhymer or Oisin in Tir-Na-Nog, remind us of the fact that time is not experienced in the same way in the worlds of Faery. Once a human steps into such a highly refined, ethereal realm it may be very difficult to return to the dense reality of this mortal level of existence. It is even said that when a human tastes of faery food or drink (which is often only very mundane things like leaves with a faery glamour, or spell, cast upon them) that such a journey 'out of time' and into the seductive ethereal realms may await them.

Obviously such tales of humans being taken into the Otherworld by fey trickery are not 'gospel' but rather allegorical, containing vital information and holding a deep meaning that is disguised by the seemingly fanciful story. Our ancestors, being far more in touch with the living land and the energies of the wild places, would have been far more attuned to the land's unearthly aspects and would have most likely encountered the Fey themselves, or known those who had. Such seemingly strange tales of those who end up 'out of time' were actually encrypted lessons for future generations, giving us the benefit of our ancestor's direct experience with the Otherworldly. Such encryption within fiction may have been necessary during times when dabbling with faery energy was thought of as nothing less than evil and was discouraged in the strongest terms.

Saying what we have about the possible risks of contact with the Fey we may wonder why we would want to bother. The answer to this is threefold in the best fairytale tradition. These three interconnected things they can share with us are:

- *Working with energy for the purpose of positive trans-formation*, especially as regards re-greening the land. This re-greening includes natural magic worked with the tides of life for altruistic purposes such as effective environmental activism, dynamic organic gardening or becoming more at one with the seasonal cycles/the land of which we live

- *Bringing wild enchantment, lyricism and inspiration to everyday life* for a renewal of purpose and meaning, as well as for enhancing artistic endeavours. This includes writing poems or prayers for the purpose of personal or natural regeneration, seeing the extraordinary in the ordinary and celebrating it, finding our muse in the natural world and making others aware of

the beauty of creation through our own creativity
- *The gift of healing*, working with green allies (herbs and plants) and their nature spirits as well as with pure energy. This includes growing green allies with assistance from their protective spirits and making living tinctures and teas from their leaves and flowers, as well as weaving with Source energy and connecting with the life-force for the sake of bringing well-being back to others

The Fey are all active creators who are in constant interaction with their energetic environs. They continuously weave their own particular vision of the world, as it should be – healed, whole and full of joyous beauty – casting their glamour over all things and dancing the dream of life as they so eloquently envision it. This ability to confidently and creatively change things for the better is something that they can, and will, share with us if we approach them in the right way. Once we have established a good connection with them they see reawakening our own dormant skills as an irresistable challenge, finding it utterly incomprehensible that we do not already knowingly use our ability to co-create with the Source. Even in their innate distrust (and even contempt) of humanity they understand the benefits of a cooperative partnership where both they and we work for a better world – for what we do here affects their parallel world, all things being connected energetically. If our energetic 'layer of the onion' is damaged theirs will experience the contamination. The Fey will always act upon the truth that what we do positively on one level will affect the whole of Creation, putting this above any distaste about our species.

So, how do we go about meeting them and forming a relationship with a particular faery being? Well this we can do in two related ways, just as we approached the creation of a safe place for us to do our spiritwalking. We can do it in the physical world and on the appropriate astral level.

The physical side of our meeting a faery contact is growing increasingly more difficult for us today, yet it is certainly not impossible. As we have previously stated, our ancestors had more contact with the Fey than we currently do, before the Fey withdrew energetically from our level. This was partly due to there being more similarities between our world and theirs in a time pre-industrial revolution – our world was clearly much greener, cleaner, wilder and less populated then than it is today. Likewise people were closer to the land and to the natural cycles than they are now. Also our ancient ancestors had far less on their minds than their modern descendants and had a much greater openness to subtle energies and spirit presences. The worsening condition with our land, combined with our increasingly blinkered human notion of reality, is mirrored in the way that the Fey are increasingly energetically retreating from our dense level of existence. Indeed, the motivation for them to draw close to our level must be strong for the Fey to wish to do so. Yet there are still places in the physical world where actual crossing over and contact is possible.

These are usually wild places which are not so dragged down by human influence and therefore easier for the Fey to slip into. If we can imagine their coming into our space as if they are donning an heavy overcoat of energy, compared to their usual lightweight garments, then we can understand that they would not wish that metaphorical overcoat to become even heavier as it gets sodden with human needs, expectations etc. Therefore they have no desire to frequent built up, tamed regions but always opt for places where there is an abundance of green energy. As we have previously stated they also favour areas where a natural feature serves as a reference point, or portal, between our realm and theirs.

Examples of such places would be:

• Particularly striking/singular hawthorn bushes. The hawthorn is considered a faery tree in tradition. I would imagine this may be in part due to the way it so eloquently sums up the faery nature with the delicate creamy blossoms of spring and the seductive red fruits of autumn contrasting so absolutely with the vicious spikes of its thorns which are often hidden beneath. It is a wilful, beautiful plant which itself favours wild un-peopled places

• Places where two trees, especially hawthorn, join to form an archway that acts as a gateway between Earth's psychic levels of existence

• Trees that appear to have a hollow beneath the roots, a earth-tunnel suggesting an Otherworldly/Underworld portal.

• Places where there is a natural 'fairy ring' of grass or toadstools

• Secluded glades that can be entered into, leaving behind 'mundane reality' as we do so. Likewise any densely wooded grove that can be penetrated with difficulty, entering a place less accessed by humanity

• Places with fresh running water, such as naturally occurring springs where the energy is vibrant and unsullied

• Moor land or high, rocky places that humanity cannot build upon or even visited easily – places cleansed of any residual human activity by the buffeting wind

•   Untended ground left to return to a wild state that is distinct from the surrounding area, thus allowing us to access the primal aspect of the land

•   *Liminal space,* which could be said to be either a 'place of no place' or a 'place of all places' – somewhere which is neither one thing or the other, or both together at once. It could be said to be place where worlds meet, or worlds end. This could be found where two elements or aspects meet creating a boundary place, a literal borderland between one area and the next or a symbolic margin between worlds. The strand between the sea and the land is such a place, as is a crossroads which creates a central point which is all of those roads and yet none of them.

Also, as we have already mentioned, a grassy knoll or 'hollow hill' (thus named because they are portals to the Otherworld and so less energetically solid than our dense reality) can be an excellent place to make fey contact. These are usually natural but sometimes manmade, such as the mounds found over Neolithic burial sites. As an example, I have had strong Faery contact on the overgrown remains of a Norman 'motte and bailey' castle, now a hill guarded by two 'doorkeeper' ash trees and covered in a thicket of almost impenetrable hawthorns and brambles. The general rule (although faery nature goes against all human rules) is that the Fey love that which is inhospitable to human habitation or even visitation – places with lots of intense green energy, wildflowers, feral creatures and insects.

However, even if we spend time in such places there is no guarantee we will make a link with the unseen world of Faery. Faery nature is truly contrary and the Fey can be fickle to say the least. Quiet perseverance, as well as the sincere offering of friendship gifts, is recommended. Our companions can advise on suitable offerings to the faery denizens of a place and once we have made contact, either through sensing a presence or actually hearing or seeing them, then we will find that the faeries will gleefully ask us for particular things themselves. I myself have been asked (by various Fey spirits speaking to me *in situ*) for white chocolate, milk and honey, local ale and cheese and sparkly silver jewellery. Such gifts can then be offered by literally giving them to the earth or to the water. This works as the faeries consider themselves to be the essence of a place personified and so what we give to the land we give to them by osmosis.

These gifts are not bribes so that the Fey give us what we need, be that inspiration, healing or creative impetus. Our seemingly physical gesture is not a token one but actually a transference of energy. It says that we are here to form a relationship, not just to take. And it will be a relationship, for the faeries ask for an exchange that is beyond these simple opening gifts. What they require is that we take a little faery magic back to our jaded world and enliven the human realm through our own endeavours. They are prepared to share their enchantment and their muse with us if we then go back and spread the energy of their gift in as many green-spirited, Earth-friendly ways that we are able. The Fey really appreciate our pledging our own creativity to environmental commitments even though the idea of 'the environment' as being something apart from us is an alien one to them – their being of the land they see no difference between themselves and their Otherworldly Earth. As we have already pointed out the Fey have a vested interest in us behaving ethically at out own level – what we do will always affect their parallel layer of existence. They do have selfish motives for accepting our gifts and helping us, and who can blame them.

Along with any gifts it is recommended that we need to take a quiet mind to any fey haunt. The last thing the faeries want is yet more human clutter, be that energetic thought-clutter or litter. Also a willingness to leave if we outstay our welcome is advisable as no matter how much the Fey find us sincere and respectful they still won't want us hanging around them too much. It is rather as if we will pollute them, and consequently their psychic space, with our world's hectic and brutal energy, and perhaps our own mundanity, if we remain in their province for too long. Yet while we are with them there will be an intensity of contact that we will not find anywhere else and we will be uplifted beyond measure.

Now we have an idea of the physical regions that translate easily from our world into that of the Fey we can make it our quest, in the best fairytale tradition of our ancestors, to seek such places out for the purpose of forming a beneficial alliance. When we have found a suitable location we can then enhance our chances of making contact psychically there by undertaking a specific trance journey. We can do this to make a contact at the particular place of our choice or, if we haven't access to such a faery place, then we can do it to meet a Fey contact that does not necessarily have links to our area but rather is the right one for us to meet at this time.

A Pathworking to Meet a Faery Contact

1. We should close our eyes and focus on the reason we want to make a Fey contact. We should hold the particular reason we

wish to connect uppermost in our awareness. We should offer a small prayer that reveals our intention, something like:

> '*I now journey to make a faery link for the authentic purpose of* (name reason). *I do this under the care of my companion spirits and with deep respect for all genuine beings that I may encounter. Let my quest be successful, for the good of my own development, and so for that of the All by direct reflection. May the connection between the human realm and that of Faery be strengthened because of it and may the magic be brought back to this Earth through it.*'

2. We now need to make the journey to our astral safe place and to meet there with our companion/s in the usual secure fashion. When we are in our astral office with them we should clarify our needs and ascertain with them whether this process is valid or not at this time. At this time we can fine-tune any of our intentions and change our plans if necessary. The companions can help us with all such decisions and give us any insights necessary for us to re-vision our intent.

3. We now need to travel to the appropriate astral place, the Otherworldly regions outside of our usual office area, where the faery/s we seek are present. For this we will need to create a labyrinth on the ground, which we can walk. Here are some of the means by which we may do this:

i) We can 'grow' a maze on the land, using hedges to delineate the boundaries,

ii) We can cut the pattern into the turf, revealing the chalk soil below the grass in the manner of the white horses carved into the hills of Southern England

iii) We can carve the labyrinth directly into rock

iv) We can mark out our labyrinthine path with large pebbles or small boulders, either singularly or built up like a dry stone wall.

Our method is as unique as we are and in this place we are the creator. We now need to envision this wonderful serpentine maze/labyrinth appearing on the land before us.

4. When we have done this we should take the time to admire what we have fashioned from the ether, witnessing this new development as a living reality in our realm, admiring its contours and layout as we walk admiringly around its perimeter.

5. Now we should get ready to walk the labyrinth. We should not fear getting lost as we have created this and we shall instinctively know which way to go at any particular time. Our companion spirit/s can come with us as we walk but we must go first, stepping into the spiralling path with renewed intent. We should take care to watch our own feet as we move round and in and out, knowing that as we travel we are moving closer to Faery.

6. After a time we will come to the centre of the maze. We may feel a little dizzy or disorientated from all the twists and turns of our walk to the middle of the mystery we have laid down. Even though we created this passage to the centre it still seems like a riddle and as we stand at its heart we know that we must become dizzier still. If we wish our companions to make this final stage of the journey with us we should hold their hands and begin to spin. If we wish to travel on alone they will wait for us here. We now start to turn, either alone or as a couple, spinning round and around.

7. We are now rotating so fast that the world around us is a blur. All of our thoughts are on flying through the worlds into Faery. We say *'turn and turn about, the world is inside out, and I am in the Otherworld!'* as we go faster and faster still. Now, when we think we can go no more rapidly and we will surely fall, we count *'one, two, three'* and then, without thinking or fearing for our stability, we leap.

8. And when we land we are no longer in the maze of our own making. We are in a different, but similar, place – the changes are subtle but discernible. This place cannot be described here as it is particular to our own experience, and *very* beautiful. It may be almost the same as the physical place we have visited in our world to make a Fey contact only much more vibrant and luminous. Or it could be a totally different place to any we have ever seen on our version of the Earth. Wherever we are as we stand we use all our senses to appreciate where we are and the new sensations that the place brings to us. The more we can do this now, the stronger and clearer our experience of the faery being we are to meet will be. We should now invest our efforts in making the whole experience of this Otherworldly region as vivid as it can be, engaging with the sounds, sights, smells and sensations as they arise.

9. As we continue to get our bearings we begin to feel as if we are being watched. We draw a circle of protective blue-white cold-fire around our own feet and another before us on the ground and call out *'who will answer my call to the Fey? Who will step into my circle to speak with me in this place?'* Sure enough a being will, in its own time, appear inside our circle.

10. Using the usual checking our procedures we should then

prove that the faery being is genuine. No matter how many attempts this takes to find a genuine being to speak with us we should persevere – this is a far trickier land than we are used to and it may take more effort than usual. The appearance of the faery being may be startling or confusing for us, an exotic or bizarre form, or it may be deeply familiar and attractive. We should remember at this stage that a faery being is pure energy and that this guise is for our benefit, or theirs, only. Their display belies the shimmering light-being they really are, much as our human bodies are not who we really are 'in spirit' as souls.

11. When this is satisfactorily done then we should ask this being where we may go to communicate and form a link. We may find that they invite us into their home, or take us to a particularly wonderful spot where there may or not be others of their kind. If there are then we should ensure that we are under the protection of this true faery (and our companion, if they too are present). This faery will be supportive of our need to be safe in their realm as they have, after all, offered to confer, and possibly work, with us.

12. We should now begin to share with them the reasons we have for wanting an active link with Faery. While we are doing this we should use our senses to make the experience as real as possible. This meeting will, no doubt, be a very intense experience for us, perhaps more so that we are used to, and so it is well to keep it relatively brief. Our desire to take in as much as possible when with such an incredible being may be overwhelming but we have to remember our own capacity to retain information and to assimilate external energy and we should know our limits at this time. Our companions can, and should, advise us on this if we ask

them to, gently reminding us when we should leave if necessary. 13. We should ask the faery being if they can give us a token, or symbol, of the connection that has been forged. This will be something like a special stone or crystal, a silvered branch or maybe a shiny talisman. Whatever it is it will appeal to the faery sense of aesthetic beauty as well as having a sparkling or burnished quality to it. In return we may offer them a token from our world that we can leave for them wherever they wish. They may ask for whiskey to be poured on a special hill, for homemade wholemeal bread to be left under a rock or for a piece of polished sea glass to be placed under a bush. It may require some considerable effort by us to find the offering – faeries love quests! This exchange is important to the Fey, acting as a bond of trust.

14. Once this is decided upon we should bow, in a way that feels right, and give our thanks. Then we may take our leave, making sure it is right and proper to return to this particular faery being again. We can ask that if it is permissible that we appear in the same region of Faery once we have crossed over by spinning in our labyrinth. This will give us a sense of orientation and security. 15. Now we have to get back from the Otherworlds to our usual astral office. We may do this in much the same way that we came in, by returning to the spot that we first appeared in this faery realm and spinning rapidly, either alone or with our companion spirit. As we spin faster and faster, going at such a pace we feel we will fly off we should say '*turn and turn about, the world is inside out, and I am in my maze, amazed!*' then we may count '*one, two, three*' before leaping.

16. We land, with the companion if they are with us, back at the

centre of our labyrinth. In order to get our bearings we can walk slowly out again, taking note of all details and feelings as we do so, becoming used to this level of psychic reality.

17. We should then take our faery token and place it somewhere within the astral office that is special to us, where we will remember to interact with it. It should also be somewhere where the faery concerned will feel it is treasured. Perhaps we can envision a special box for it to lie in as we bury it under a tree or within a hollow part of its trunk. Perhaps, if the token is small, we could hide it within a shell or wrap it up and place it under a stone.

18. We may then make our return journey via the astral office to 'ordinary' reality. We should be sure to thank our companions before returning to the manifest world.

19. We should then make our notes and ground ourselves fully.

We could say that in the pathworking we have just completed we travelled to the Middle level of the Otherworld, the one that is closest, or parallel, to ours. The Upper and the Underworld of the faeries and their kin can also be visited when our companion spirits consider us to be ready – and when we have a good reason to do so. These Upper and Lower realms will lead us to places that are much less like our experience of the human world. The Upperworld of Faery is, as its symbolism suggests, a place of lofty ideas and ideals where the wisdom of the stars lies. By direct contrast the Underworld has symbolic connections with deep dark tree roots that probe soil enriched with the bodies of the generations that have passed before us. Consequently we may journey there to seek knowledge about the bones of the matter, subjects pertaining to health and profound ancestral wisdom. It was for good reason that the Christian faith chose to label this Underworld region as evil or hellish because it is indeed a place of intense experience and initiation that is only suitable for visits with a specific purpose.

So, for the experienced and intrepid spiritwalker there is much unchartered astral territory still to discover and such advanced journeys into deepest or highest Faeryland can be anticipated as truly groundbreaking. We are perhaps among the first people in many generations who are travelling *beyond* into that which was long ago considered lost. Like the Prince who came across the overgrown forest that hid the Sleeping Beauty we are having to make our own paths through the uncultivated perimeters of human knowing. Sometimes it may seem like lonely arduous work, bereft of any progression or meaning, but our reward in the end can only be worth it. It is the forging of partnerships with those who ride the backs of the stars and hide within ancient amber – the beginning of a romance beyond our wildest dreams. Our trusted companions will always advise us on when we are ready to progress to this level.

So, now we are conversant with the main types of unseen being we are likely to meet, apart from our companion spirits. These categories are, of course, not all encompassing but give us a better idea of who we can encounter either actively or passively. There are other types of benevolent being, such as animal helpers or star-born 'alien' beings, that we may want to invite in our astral office at sometime in the future for the sake of our learning. This we may do when, and if, the companion spirits deem that it is wise. The companions are, as ever, our point of reference.

But what about the beings that we don't want to meet? Who are they and what shall we do when we encounter them?

CHAPTER THIRTEEN

THINKING IN CIRCLES

'Do you believe thought to be an abstract, insubstantial and
inconsequential process, something that apparently only takes
place in the solitary cavern of your mind and doesn't affect
anyone else, let alone yourself? Spiritwalker, you know that
directed energy cannot behave so! Instead witness thoughts as
tangible, energy whittled and honed to sharpness by repetition
and emotion – focussed ideas with the keenness to cut through
and the momentum to fly free. Yes, these are *arrows* you are
fashioning and firing, not bubbles that pop as soon as they
reach the air! Some may land in the bushes, it is true, as you
did not fire them with enough conviction – but others? Others
will fly a long way from home and hit targets we have no
knowledge of. What chain reaction will we start from such a
careless release of such potent energy?
When will we take responsibility for our unseen actions as well
as our manifest gestures? We must witness our thoughts,
and those of all others, as real or live blind in a forest of
unintentional arrows.'
From Guidance

By now we will have encountered many pleasant and helpful unseen
beings. However, now it is time for us to consider those who are not
so agreeable yet who we will inevitably come across, both in our
astral work and in our daily lives as spiritwalkers. To do this we need
to look at the human astral.

Our Unpleasant Next-door Neighbours

We will need to pay special attention to this human astral level of existence as it is home to the majority of troublesome entities, disturbed spirits and unsettling energies we will encounter. As we previously stated in Chapter Six, this layer of the proverbial astral onion acts as a mirror, as well as a breeding ground, for all of our earthly foibles and worries and therefore it is only logical that it will be the spawning ground of the things that 'haunt' us the most.

If this prognosis of our astral mirror still sounds inordinately gloomy then it is it is only this way because of the present fearful, negative state of humanity. Of course humanity isn't all bad right now, far from it, but, as we know it seems to be our species' way to currently dwell on things that are less than uplifting or, indeed, agreeable. Hence the poor state of what has been etherically fashioned as our astral mirror image. Yet it is vitally important for us to emphasis that this negative condition is its *present* state, not its permanent one, and thus it can be changed at any time by our individual, and collective, positive will and wishes.

The present, and altogether temporary, state of the human astral is so dire because we humans have given shape to it via our own despondent, disempowered and often terrified musings over the millennia. The current outcome simply reflects our individual and collective sense of disturbance, disconnection and general dis-ease with ourselves over many years. Consequently this layer presently reflects our human fear and isolation above our spiritual security and serenity.

If we look at our own lives thus far we may find that instead of sending our compassion, security and satisfaction into the ether in a conscious way the majority of us have unconsciously, but very effectively, focussed on our dissatisfaction, dislike, distrust and disgruntlement with one person or thing or situation We may have drawn the line at actively cursing but we may have easily allowed our jealous, insecure thoughts to dance out of control, easily slipping into a disparaging or unconstructive reverie. This uncontrolled thinking may be about how we wish someone would get his or her come-uppance or go away, how much we would like to own X or Y (and how unhappy we are that we don't) or how it is so unfair that such and such a person is wealthy/talented/slim etc. when we are not. Up to now we may have considered such thoughts harmless, private musings contained only in the annals of our own skull, but we now know that it is everything is energy and that directed, emotive thought has an energetic existence beyond us, its creator.

Here is a working example of how we cloud the human astral regularly with our supposedly innocuous energetic creations. Let's think of our taking a simple car journey at rush hour every day. Now let's think of all the other people doing the same. The road we travel is filled with people wanting to overtake and get home quickly, all sending out their frustrations and annoyance. We effortlessly join in with this, adding our frustrated energy into the mix without even really being conscious of what we do. It's a negative habit we are in and it is currently easier to think these thoughts, and to get caught up in the collective rage and anxiety, than it is to be relaxed and easy about the unfolding events. Now let's multiply this road scenario by the number of other routes in our town, city, country etc. From this we can get an idea of just how much collective building with anxiety and irritation we do on a daily basis.

It may be quite an eye-opener to think that such seemingly trivial everyday anger and discontent should cause a 'colouring' of the ether that surrounds us all but when we open our eyes and minds to the unseen concepts we are discussing then *how could these things not affect us on a wider scale?* We all need to wake up to the extent of our personal, as well as our collective, thought-power and just what it's being allowed to shape itself into 'out there' in the unseen. For one who works with unseen energies the etheric imprint of frustration hangs above a traffic queue as surely as a fug of carbon monoxide does. It is very real. And as it is repeated day in, day out, it does not disperse; rather it grows and takes on form. Before we know it we have all unwittingly created an energetic monster in the human astral.

Here is another example of how we regularly participate in an escalation of fear along with others that we don't know. The daily news that we watch is a 'collective nightmare', geared to pressing all our buttons and activating disempowerment and fear. So many of us focus on this daily display of all the things that are wrong in our world which we can, on a personal level, do very little about. This we do with mounting horror, sadness and, of course, yet more frustration, as we believe more and more that we can't change things and that we live in a corrupt world. Every day we reinforce this sense of helplessness and mistrust, along with all our neighbours near and far who are doing exactly the same. It is this unified negative feeling that has maximum raw power to affect the ether. We cannot help but adversely influence the malleable astral level that surrounds us when we are all focussing on such disturbing fare as war or famine, displayed so graphically – so *realistically* – in our own homes. The token 'feel good' story often tagged on to a series of horrific news reports does little to make us refocus into the positive aspects of existence.

Perhaps if we are still unconvinced of our current preoccupation with negative states of being then let's now consider the centuries of terror that the human astral has stored up before we even got here in this incarnation. Here we are not discussing the fear generated by a nightly news bulletin, which is always once-removed and 'life through a lens', but by the actual *active* terror of being tortured, raped, starved or murdered which was par for the course in the Europe of other centuries. For example, the Catholic Inquisition made a lasting detrimental imprint on the unseen. Living the joyless life of a peasant was hard enough at this time without also being victim to a cruel interrogation. Even if one did not fall foul of the authorities and their insane random accusations then living under the omnipresent threat of a hellish afterlife was enough to generate vast clouds of fear. With all its attendant terrors of suffering or damnation this era alone has left a very unpleasant stain on the human astral.

As we have established we have the opportunity to begin changing the human astral *right now*, such is our personal power, but it is well to acknowledge that up to now we too have been responsible for its present state. What each individual dwells upon counts and the effect is cumulative, resulting in a collective dream of fear instead of love. This need not be the permanent way of things for the more we become aware of our thoughts the better our chances of changing the way we mould the astral levels that surround us. We have to become *response*-able – able to respond positively and not react defensively and self-ishly as we have always done. We need to consider if we are inadvertently creating things that we do not want and turn our thoughts around so that what we make in the ether is desirable and beneficial to us.

We can consider this unseen work of observing and changing our thoughts as they arise to be life changing and groundbreaking – a major part of what we as spiritwalkers. To address our negative habits and become fully responsible for our emissions into the psychic atmosphere we simply need to focus away from the transient human experience and back into the eternal *Now* where fear and isolation have no place. When we are centred in our interconnected eternalness as 'spiritual beings having a human experience' then we cannot help but feel that all is well, rejecting any habitual feelings of anxiety or insecurity. Although it will require much determined effort to re-programme ourselves into positive thoughts it is still eminently achievable. When we apply ourselves wholeheartedly to the process of moving towards what we want, rather than dwelling on what we don't want, then we can re-address the energetic balance incredibly quickly – at the speed of thought in fact. As we read these words we can decide to give credence to the amazing transfomative, creative power of our thought and to never again allow our potent imaginings to run riot like an untrained dog let off the leash in a field of rabbits. This surely is a move in the direction we want.

We may have another more personal motivation for such a cleaning up of our thoughts as what we dwell on must affect the *within* aspect of our existence just as surely as it colours the *without*. What we put out externally *always* has internal repercussions – the microcosm always reflects the macrocosm, all things being connected. Therefore our projected hatred, anger, fear etc. will certainly impact somehow on our own physical health. I had a very graphic illustration of this process recently when my own overwhelming (apparently mental) anxiety about certain issues began to have an effect on my body in the most extraordinary ways. I actually started to manifest what I feared, both in my physical being and in my personal environment. If we need any more convincing of the benefits of watching our thoughts then let us take on board that we create our own dis-ease as surely as we fashion our own perceived external reality! In acknowledging this we also own that we are powerful and *that we can change at any time.*

We will cover this application of our thought-power again in Chapter Seventeen, the chapter that focuses on how we can regularly clean up our psychic act. For now we need lead this movement towards real, sustainable change by positive example in our own lives. We can show that negative thought is undesirable by being unfailingly appreciative and admiring in our own contemplations – having an attitude of gratitude – whilst also pronouncing optimistically and anticipating confidently. By this we fulfil our desire to only create loving, generous forms from our thoughts.

To cement this new ethos within us, and in the world, we can actively affirm our intent by saying something like:

'Let there be peace and let it begin with me,
Let there be hope, and let it begin with me,
Let there be compassion, and let it begin with me,
I am the creator, let change begin with me'

As Mahatma Ghandi is famously quoted as saying 'we have to be the change we want to see in the world'.

We need not be discouraged if the world does not immediately change as soon as we decide to make a positive difference. However, it is possible for us to be realistic about the current state of the energies we humans have emitted/created *and* be optimistic about our individual part in changing the collective energy. Even as we acknowledge where humanity is currently at we can be moving in the right direction and not unintentionally bolstering the undesirable status quo. As with so many areas of spiritwalking it is an energetic balancing act.

This balanced blend of optimism and realism is centred on a very different notion of what reality actually is, and an acknowledgment that we all create it and can change it. It means that even as we think and act with loving care we need to be aware of *what is*. As spiritwalkers we have to understand the imprinted energies, or entities, that have been created as a result of all the long-term negativity in the human astral that we previously mentioned, including those thoughts that are ongoing from other sources. These very real entities we may know *thought-forms*, manifestations that in future our positive thoughts can help counteract and, ultimately, prevent.

Unintentional Thought-Forms

The *unintentional thought-form* is, as the name suggests, an energetic entity made unconsciously by persistent emotionally charged thoughts. By the continual negative dwelling we have discussed we imprint the ether of the human astral and fashion it into the shape of our dominant thought.

For instance, if we repeatedly think of getting our own back on a rival we will colour the ether and mould it accordingly, thus creating a vengeful entity. We could then 'feed' this entity with energy by having further vicious little daydreams on how the object of our rivalry could be brought low. Similarly if we were to consistently gaze at a successful colleague and wish that we had what they have then we may consequently be responsible for fashioning an avaricious, or 'vampiric', entity that would be intent on taking our colleague's energy. We could also quite easily create a thought-form out of our constant worry, which would manifest itself as a 'little black cloud' that would bring depressing, anxious energy with it.

There are so many instances in modern life where we may find ourselves repeatedly doing something tedious, a regular bus journey through a dull part of town for instance, which gives us ample occasion to dwell on our more negative feelings. It is so easy for us to slip into a dismal, disapproving or dissatisfied reverie that becomes a habit, thus unwittingly creating entities from the pliable energy all around us every day. Here is an example. I witnessed a woman's single-minded obsessing over a man at work. She didn't really even want him but she was bored in her job and he made a distracting focus for all the things she felt were lacking in her life. The woman had no idea that her 'harmless dwelling on him' could have such a startling, affecting outcome as it did. When he turned up looking dazed and somewhat resentful on her doorstep, with the glorious bunch of flowers she had imagined him bringing her, then the reality of her 'harmless imaginings' became clear. She had manufactured a potent predatory thought-form that had influenced this man against his natural inclination. The situation then had to be rectified using psychic methods that we will discuss later in Chapter Sixteen.

Like the woman in the example above we all may, at sometime in our lives, unconsciously worked up enough thought-energy to create an energetic being to represent our will. We must now accept, once and for all, that we are all creators and whatever we channel our energies into will create *something*. This something is always the embodiment of the emotional energy we put out. It is, then, obvious that if we concentrate on our anger we will manifest a raging, resentful thought-form and if we focus on our fear we will fashion a restless, nervous one. And if we now concentrate our musings on pleasurable matters and our desires on being kind and calm we will create an atmosphere of great joy, serenity and benevolence. Such a form would not need to prey on others for sustenance. Its primary energy is one of contentment, there is not the avarice or desparation of feeling that constitutes a negative thought-form.

The negative form, or embodiment, we are discussing here will need more of the same energy to sustain it once it has been *man*-ufactured. Just like a physical being it needs food, which equates to fuel (or energy) to maintain its manifestation. For example, if we cease to provide a thought-form with our own anger then it will soon become attracted, like to like, by any other person who can feed or re-fuel it with something equally potent. Our creation of it is only part of the problem as its demand to be sustained, or made even bigger, is the next phase which makes the situation ongoing – the need to be fed goes on, out of our control. It is not a loyal being, or one with ethics; rather it is entirely motivated by its selfish need and has no morality, preference or care. It just takes and only gives out its own emissions for the sake of attracting yet more of the same to itself. It is just driven to continue existing above all else.

In this the thought-form is an astral parasite, not an en-souled being, and without the individual fate, or *karma*, that we associated with soul. It relies solely on our external input for its continued survival and has no motivation but to *be*. It is rather like a baby bird that never grows up, always with an open beak, yet it has not the individual spark of spirit that gives that bird its own presence and being. Indeed, I have witnessed a thought-form with a huge gaping beak, a rather hideous image that haunted me around the time that I was dealing with someone who desired something that I had.

Thought-forms are less like people and rather more like the eerie phenomena of ball lightening. They are not beings of free will but are instead programmed to do a certain thing, seemingly of their own volition. And, like ball lightening, the thought-entity will carry on their destructive path seemingly possessed of an intelligence thus giving us the impression when we encounter them that they have a persona or consciousness. The thought-form has neither; it is just an entity moulded from the 'plastic' ether that needs to survive and which can adapt itself in order to manipulate. It has the most primitive instinct to continue to and is a good mimic of human energy, *but that is all*. If we fashioned a human effigy of plastic here in the manifest world we would not expect it to be en-souled just because it had a recognisable shape, ditto our creating a form of the ether.

Let's consider a thought-form as a balloon – a balloon that we have inflated, filled with our own breath or life-force energy. A balloon that we hold by a thread that we tied to it. If we let go of the thread the wind will carry our balloon and thus it will have the appearance of travelling on its own. The wind allows the balloon to seem alive, en-spirited. Perhaps as the wind carries it along someone else will now catch hold of our balloon's string and hold onto it. Perhaps the balloon will need re-inflating so that person will fill it with their breath. Perhaps then the person who holds it will be distracted by a new event and so they too will let go of the string, allowing it to travel to its next 'host'. And so on. Here our comparison ends as being made of perishable material the balloon will eventually burst if over-filled, or it will snag on a thorn or simply become worn out, whilst a thought-form can go on growing whilst there is a host to feed it.

Another analogy that will help us further grasp this process is that the thought-form is like a tiny snowball that keeps on getting rolled, even absent mindedly, until it becomes so big and unwieldy it has a life of its own and rolls off without us, seeking more snow to make it bigger and continue its existence. This is when thought-forms become truly pesky, like a monster of Frankenstein, for we cannot hope to contain them once they reach a certain point. Even if we were aware of them, which most often we are not, we cannot necessarily stop them before they go off seeking someone else to prey on for raw thought-energy.

Here is a diagram that expresses this process.

Diag.9 *The Creating and Sustaining of a Thought-Form*

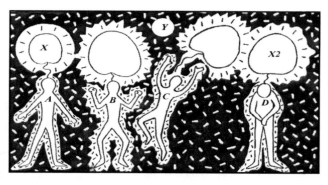

Y expresses the ether/spirit energy all around us. The figure **A** is having negative thoughts (**X**). In figure **B** these thoughts have coalesced and grown as the person has given them much more time and energy. In figure **C** we see the person has had a positive change of circumstance and is no longer thinking the negative thoughts/having negative feelings therefore the thought-form (**X**) is no longer being fed. It detaches from the originator of the thoughts and looks for another negative person to feed from. At figure **D**, a new person, the thought-form attaches itself and begins to get bigger again. If figure **D** had not been available then the thought-form, now **X2**, would hopefully have 'melted away' again into the ether, unsustained.

Here is another example of how a thought-form can be manufactured and sustained. I was told by a student that his shared house was being terrorised by an unseen presence. On investigation this presence turned out to be a thought-form that had originated when another man had been dwelling, in a predatory sexual fashion, on the student who had approached me. The student himself had been having lustful thoughts about a different man and rejected the first man's advances. Being rejected, the first man ceased to have his intense thoughts and the thought-form needed a new source of sustenance. The student, bristling with his own pent-up sexual energy, had provided this sustenance and had brought the thought-form back home with him.

Obviously being in a student house full of vibrant and sexually active young people was a meal ticket for such a thought-form and it had grown fat and unwieldy on their unchecked energy. Thus it appeared to have a life of its own when in fact it was just feeding off their output. Its squalid, invasive presence in their home reflected what it was – a collection of sleazy thoughts looking for more of the same. The girls in the house described it as 'a dirty old man'.

If we were all well versed in such matters then the students would have identified the problem and could have rid themselves of the thought-form purely by retracting their own energies for a while – effectively starving it into extinction. However instead of this the students panicked at the invasive unseen presence in their midst and the offending thought-form grew so bloated on the resultant fear energy that it was no longer going to be identifiable as what it originally was. They perceived it as an evil ghost haunting them. Only I, as an observant outsider, could get to grips with what it truly was and 'diffuse it' safely.

As we can probably now appreciate such forms can be responsible, despite their lack of soul, for causing the unsettled atmospheres that we give interpret as 'ghostly'. Indeed a great deal of the 'poltergeist' type activity people experience is just the result of a thought-form trying to provoke us into giving it some etheric food – most notably fear. Poltergeist simply means noisy, or troubled, spirit and although thought-forms are not en-spirited they certainly are entirely troublesome. Like tiresome children or naughty animals these unwelcome guests will energetically bug us in the most niggly ways as they are patently not capable of much else. They are just 'cosmic debris' that we didn't even realise we had left lying around and therefore are responsible for the most irritating and pathetic displays of 'power' (which patently show how little energy they have if they are willing to engage in the tactics of trying to make us feed them). Like lightening they strike wherever they find the most likely point to 'discharge', or attract, energy and this obviously causes discomfiture if not outright havoc.

So, an unintentional thought-form has not the awareness or individuality we associate with soul. But what about thought forms that have been deliberately fashioned?

Intentional Thought-Forms

Intentional thought-forms are nowhere near as common as those created unintentionally every day. This is because we need a heightened understanding of the unseen to go about fashioning such an entity consciously, which is (sadly) more than the average person currently has in our society. Indeed, the conscious creation of thought-forms is generally the domain of those with an interest in the magical arts. It is well for us as spiritwalkers to understand this process, as we will undoubtedly come across an intentionally created thought-form at some time in our work.

When we create an intentional thought-form to do our will, or to represent our desire, we may see it as a servant to our role of master. For this reason some people know them as *servitors*. This name gives us a sense that they are not real beings, rather etheric 'robots' that we may programme to act for us. When we use our mind's eye to create a being in such a way we are literally conjuring something up from nothing, enchanting the ether by charging it with our intense will and wish. The resultant creation will be, to all intents and purposes, like a programmable computer or even a microwave, two man-made items that definitely are not en-souled beings but servants of humanity, dependant on us. We can put in our instructions and achieve a set result but the being will not have its own status, drive and persona.

Protective intentional thought-forms are, thankfully, the most commonly created kind and although they may seem intimidating their core role is to look after something, most usually a place of power on the land. The ancients, who (as we have previously discussed) were more pure and focussed in their intent, were adept at fashioning such positive servitors to act as site guardians for their most sacred places – places such as Stonehenge in the South West of England. I have encountered the guardian of a series of burial barrows at the Stonehenge site, as well as having a close encounter with one guardian of the Henge itself, and a more formidable energetic duo I have yet to encounter elsewhere. Their obvious power and stature were enough to physically push me to the ground on one occasion. They were doing their 'installed' task of protecting their site with great aplomb and although they were entirely intimidating and awesome they were not negative in any malevolent sense, just doing their (pre-programmed) job.

There are some formidable protectors still around today such as those within the old entrance to a prominent Abbey here in South West England, revealing to those who have the eyes to see them that our Christian forebears, as well as our pagan ancestors, knew how to psychically shield their sacred places. The ancients of whatever religious persuasion knew how to build things to last, just like their monuments, and were clearly willing to spend huge amounts of time and energy in their ongoing protection. Consequently their thought-form guardians are still discernible even now and are certainly formidable as the day they were fashioned by our spiritwalking predecessors.

In comparison to these enduring energetic creations a more recently fashioned intentional thought-form may only have a limited life, owing to the fact that our level of commitment to such magical acts, along with our ability to have such intense focus, has waned dramatically in recent times. Our modern mind, full of phone numbers, pin codes and song lyrics, is highly cluttered and unfocussed compared to the brain of a Neolithic or Iron Age person – or even a Medieval one. Add into this that our ancestors were part of extended families and tribal groups which had much more of a collective sense than we do in our fragmented society and we can also see how their collective power would add to the potency of their astral creations. We are blighted by our own trivia, as well as our sense of personal one-upmanship and isolation, and so our more contemporary thought-forms will finish any programmed job and then simply melt away. They will fade, like a thumbprint on a condensated window, leaving an energetic residue that only a discerning spiritwalker may spot. This is why the spiritwalker needs to be disciplined and trained, so that such acts of deliberate creation, if performed for positive purposes like protection, can be as effective as possible and have considerable longevity.

However, there may be another reason for the longevity of an intentional thought form that is unconnected to our skill. This may be because an independent spirit has hitched a ride within the spiritless form and inhabited it, giving it a 'lease of life' that is not desirable.

Rogue Spirits

Rogues are those disembodied spirits who drift around the human astral level like highwaymen, waiting for the chance to hijack a source of energy that we have kindly manufactured for them. In this they are rather like joyriding car thieves, jumping into a vehicle that does not belong to them and careering around the area in an alarming fashion until the vehicle is empty of fuel – or it is crashed. Rogues are non-human en-souled wild cards and should *never* be trusted.

Sadly many of us do end up trusting them. Often when we begin our spiritual quest we end up taking part in unwise pursuits, like the Ouija board or a séance, as we desperately try to make contact with the unseen by the only 'horror movie means' that we know. The meaning of Ouija is clearly 'yes, yes' in both French and German and so we can see that using it is the equivalent of giving the affirmative to whoever (or whatever) comes to answer our call – just like opening our front door, shouting for company and allowing strangers to come in. Perhaps we will be lucky and only those who are respectful and honest will appear, or maybe we will be crushingly unlucky. Obviously once they are so openly invited then the more devious or the destructive guests may not care to leave of their own volition. It is a gamble that is not worth taking as, in the vast majority of cases, we will be opening our psychic door on the astral equivalent of a bad neighbourhood – this being the human, or 'low', astral. Thus we will inevitably achieve contact with a rogue that will persistently pester us until it can get energetic sustenance from us in terms of fear, anger or confusion.

If we have ever tried this hazardous means of unseen contact in the past we will know that when we ask for a spirit-being to appear, for example asking to speak with the spirit of a genuine African wonderworker or South American healer (or the Emperor Napoleon, our deceased Uncle Robert or just someone out there that can help us get a girlfriend) we are often rewarded with a less than scrupulous response. There is no security whatsoever in a liaison made on the low astral and what we get is never the truth. Sadly I myself was drawn to the Ouija as a teenager because at the time it was the only way I knew how to make (supposed) spirit contact. Initially the Ouija told me that I was communicating with my dead Grandmother although once the session progressed the contact entity then decided it was a powerful alien called Jehophret. This soon lost its effect when the rogue ran out of things to say about alien life and so it ended up trying to convince me and my friends that it was the Devil by tricks such as making a nearby candle flame grow to an alarming size or turning the letters on the board backwards. It then went on to implode the glass we were using and to 'haunt' me effectively for many years. This it did until I eventually found a teacher who could instruct me in the art of spiritwalking proper. I was then able to rid myself of this pest in the manner I describe in our penultimate chapter.

These charlatan spirits are more than willing to read our thoughts during a Ouija or séance – thoughts which are very plain to them as they are, of course, being emitted on their level. Consequently they will begin by offering us whatever we want to hear in response to our secret musings, thus gaining our trust. Once we willingly let them in to our psychic space they then fill us with all sorts of false hope and outlandish predictions, gleefully provoking us into negative emotive responses. We may then stop the séance and try to forget about what has happened but things rarely end there as the rogue cannot help but want to push things further and further. We have opened ourselves up to them and they will 'haunt' us afterwards unless we can learn how to cleanse ourselves of their influence, or have them removed.

The rogue's technique is usually based on the most tacky horror film scare tactics – the classic bumps in the night, bad smells, oppressive atmospheres etc. Another possibility is that they may push us to worship them in some way. When still misguidedly consulting the Ouija I once found myself communicating with the (apparent) spirit of Henry the Eighth, who of course demanded I utterly surrender myself to his power. The rogue's weak point is definitely seeking our foolish admiration and they can easily be detected for what they are by their desire for a god-like status. No honourable being would ask for our worship or total submission, *ever*. The more advanced we are the more we grasp our innate connection with all life and we know that we are not above anyone or any thing.

With this in mind I am always horrified to hear how undisciplined and unprotected people roam the power spots of the British Isles invoking some apparent god, goddess or mythic figure without a hint of discernment, let alone an understanding of the astral levels. I can imagine that when a 'god' is asked to appear any number of rogues and thought-forms jump at the chance to show up rather like the epic film *Spartacus*. When the crowd is asked for Spartacus (the condemned rebel slave) to acknowledge himself, and thus to be saved, and a dozen voices amongst the condemned men pipe up '*I'm Spartacus!*' This classic scene is brilliantly parodied in Monty Python's *Life of Brian* when Brian is pardoned and suddenly there are scores of Brians claiming to be he. In the same fashion a rogue will yell out psychically '*I'm Jesus!*' or '*I'm Hecate!*' or even '*I'm the spirit of The Great Pharaoh Ramesses XI, venerate me!*' if they think it'll be the best way of getting us to respect them. Which low entity of energy would refuse the chance of a free energetic meal and a chance to wheedle into someone's psyche for the purpose of feeding there?

As an example of this, I have always found it impossible to sit quietly on Glastonbury Tor, a veritable hotspot for seekers somewhat haphazardly invoking all sorts of deities and spirits, without suitable astral safeguards in place. Whenever I have done so I have encountered rogue spirits dressed up as important religious or cultural figures, from John the Baptist and the Archangel Michael to Sir Ian Mc Kellern dressed as Gandalf from the film *Lord of the Rings*. The rogues delight in pulling imagery from our psyche and approaching us with what they think we will respect or be in awe of. We give them the identity because they haven't got one of their own. *In this we should remember they are weak.*

To get the behaviour of rogues further into perspective here's a different analogy for us to consider – what hungry shark would refuse a human leg dangled in front of them by an incautious swimmer? The wandering jokers in the astral pack cannot help themselves, it is their nature. It is our job, as discerning spiritwalkers, to avoid dangling our limbs in their stagnant water and to rise above their level. By aiming higher than their level we avoid their tawdry trickery and give them no grist for their mill. If we are diligent and aware then such tricksters will not be able to hoodwink us, no matter how plausible, powerful or pleasant they seem. We should *never* take anything unseen at face value without applying our protective measures.

As spiritwalkers we now know categorically to avoid the human astral when we aim to make a productive contact. Yet we can still bump into unwanted beings from the *beyond* on our travels through both the seen and the unseen worlds. Although rogues are fundamentally anonymous these unwanted beings are truly unknowable and will never assume an identity for us as they have nothing about them that a human may grasp. These beings are so unknowable that they may remain nameless.

Nameless Beings

Here I speak of unseen primordial creatures, those which we may experience as being *demonic* simply because they lack any human attribute we could consider cordial or approachable – or even identifiable. As demons are just human constructs they really have nothing to do with these extraordinary, unsettling beings – beings that are quite literally 'out of this world' and therefore exempt of our judgemental categorisation. What we are discussing here is really a *rude* being in the sense of its rudimentary quality and essential rawness. A nameless being is not civilised, it is primitive with all the power of an unrefined energy.

Even though nameless beings are not of our world they are, for some inexplicable reason, of our energy matrix. Perhaps this is due to such beings once having physically inhabited this Earth in deep pre-history. Their ilk certainly appears in our myths and legends as dragons, worms or monsters, each complete with their obligatory slaying by humanity. By this we may perhaps speculate that we made them physically extinct long ago but their spirits continue to haunt their own stomping grounds. Such unnameable beings also pop up in stories as unwieldy sea serpents – beasts that dwell within the fathomless watery places, such as the famous Loch Ness Monster in Scotland. Such shadowy presences almost certainly had a legitimate part of this planet once upon a time but have long since retreated into an astral layer of it – hiding rather like large spiders in the furthest darkest undisturbed corner of a shed. Their ongoing, if sporadic, presence and their raison d'être remains a mystery even as they continue, albeit rarely, to surface in the awareness of spiritwalkers.

Such presences have the ability to influence us just as a thought-form can influence us, although unlike thought-forms nameless beings very definitely have their own spirit and purposeful presence. Let me give an example.

I know of a very active nameless being which 'lives' in an area of an English city once known as 'standing stone hill', a region reputed to be haunted by hobgoblins. Although it may once have dwelled in this ancient hill's landscape its astral space is now not rural but, incongruously, part of a rambling Victorian house on a busy urban crossroads. It dwells in the same psychic space as the human inhabitants of the house whilst having its own unseen habitat that is something far more elemental. It has what can only be described as an unseen lair in a corner of a disused upstairs room as well as influencing a network of cellars. Needless to say these areas are highly unpleasant for a human being to enter – and not a little dangerous.

This nameless being of our example does not lend itself to usual human descriptions but rather comprises of impressions. It has, perhaps, a long rippling throat with suggestions of many rows of jagged teeth and a bottomless stomach – none of which fit together in any tangible way but simply are part of its essence. At any rate, from our human perspective it is decidedly disgusting to witness, being as repulsive and disturbing as a writing octopus may be to us if it were suddenly put in our bedroom. Its very incongruity and unfamiliarity render it repellent.

I first encountered this being when I was meant to be staying in the Victorian house one evening. I had long since been told of the presence in the uninhabited area of the house and was aware of the affect it had on the family who dwelled there. Although the family were close and loving, and with no little measure of psychic skill between them, this nameless being still somehow managed to make them fight with each other for no discernible reason. When it became active it would promote violent feelings among them, and even on occasion uncharacteristically violent acts, and it cause rifts that it seemed to relish. It also gave people the feeling they were going insane and indeed one family member had died in that room speaking of the horrors coming out of its walls. On top of this it sometimes entered their physical layer of the house and had, amongst other tricks, tried to slam the lid of the piano on a child's fingers. Fortunately the family's own indomitable companion spirits had stepped in to protect her.

Despite all this the nameless being did stay dormant for periods of time and so the family somehow co-existed in its psychic space and it in theirs – a set up I found quite extraordinary. I was usually aware of its possible 'appearance', energetically speaking, and was (usually) psychically defended against it. However, one evening during a relatively dormant time for the being we were simply sitting around talking about films, quite forgetting any possibility of this creature's presence. Suddenly my awareness was forcefully pulled from me. It was instantaneous and quite terrifying and I lost all sense of the room, finding myself being thrust along what can only be described as a ridged tube, rather like a length of industrial hose…the thing's 'throat' I presume. I was being inexorably sucked down towards what I knew would be complete and utter madness.

Somehow I called for help and immediately connected with my friend, the eldest son, who held on to me, bringing my awareness back. As soon as I 'came to' again I bolted for the door but he stopped me, saying that my fear would only make it worse. Instead he called on psychic protection from his family's powerful companion spirits who were long in the habit of dealing with such things. As he did so we heard a neighbouring door open, a loud rushing noise like a raging wind coming through, followed by a huge slam as the thing hit hard against the door of the room we occupied. I knew the psychic protection of these impressive companion spirits had stopped its presence entering the room and I was very grateful. We were kept apart from the full force of the energy of this being and everything calmed down again as its presence retreated back to its 'lair'.

I was very shaken by this event. I should have been more psychically observant and strong but I went from being so relaxed into such a completely unexpected and terrifying event that I was completely off guard. I have now had to take on board that as a natural spiritwalker I am a bright flame to astral 'moths' and so have learned how to be much more vigilant since this time. It was an excellent wake up call for me and I hope it will help the reader acknowledge their own innate ability to attract beings, entities and energies that others do not.

Even now I still have no idea how a family can co-exist with this unseen presence. It is clearly a thing out of time and place for this has not been the realm of such 'monsters' for millennia, if ever. Again we could liken it to living with a brilliant predatory creature like a spider, a spider that sits quietly in its astral web most of the time and then strikes with a cold and deadly speed, sucking our energy and leaving us a husk. Due to its profound sense of place I believe that this form, whatever it may be, came where long before humanity did and has made this area its home. We simply stray into its astral vicinity, like flies into a web, and occasionally get caught. That the family in question could live along side this dreadful unfamiliar being without fear or too much trouble is a great indictment of how we can adapt if we have the spiritual maturity, a strong connection to Source and correct protection procedures. It should also give us the faith that, with awareness of the existence of such beings, we too can hope to deal with them with such strength and certainty if the need should arise.

Now we have covered some of the inhuman unwanted beings we may encounter as spiritwalkers let's return to our study of the lower etheric levels. Here we shall look at the fascinating subject of those wandering human spirits who have become trapped in the realm of the low astral – those we know as *ghosts*.

CHAPTER FOURTEEN

WANDERING IN CIRCLES

'Identification with our bodies can be as non-sensical as identifying ourselves as our car or our house whilst on this earth. We are not this *thing*, this generous collection of cells that holds together for the duration of our experience – instead we are rather like a hand inside a glove puppet. Once a puppeteer's hand withdraws from within a puppet body the audience does not mourn, rather they accept that the thrilling show is over and so they go on their way filled with gratitude for enjoying a good performance. Identification with the body after death, and denial of the supreme animating life-force that wore it but has left it, is as futile as lamenting the limpness of the puppet after the show is over. Nothing beneficial can be gained by our forgetting our essential nature or mistaking the temporary show we witness as the full reality.'

From Guidance

Before reading this book we have probably always referred to any spirit activity as being caused by either poltergeists or ghosts, perhaps without really knowing the distinction between the two. The former, as we now know, can be considered to be the result of non-human thought-forms or rogues who are looking for attention, or energetic 'food', by means of employing the basest scare tactics. The latter, ghosts, are certainly human in origin and the consequence of the spirits of the dead remaining *in situ* in our astral atmosphere, for one reason or another. These human spirits we will know from here on in as *lost souls* as it moves us away from the idea of ghosts as scary spectres and links us in with their tragic, vulnerable humanity.

As we have previously discussed, when we die our soul leaves the single physical point of perception it has whilst in our body and moves to a broader point of non-physical perception in the etheric region we have previously classed as the Summerlands. We undertake this process of changing dimensions by travelling through a portal of some kind, usually a tunnel, into the light of unity, wisdom, peace and love – returning to the Source. It is such a blissful journey that the majority of us undertake it gladly. It is like suddenly waking up sighted after an eternity of blindness or taking off a blindfold to discover we are in a room filled with people when we thought we were alone. Yet there are souls who do not naturally find themselves moving towards the light – those who wilfully resist it – and instead of flying free into a new way of being they become snared by their old way of being. In hanging on to what they know they become trapped in the nearest level to our human one, the human astral.

There these souls can be found wandering in confusion – confused because the place that they are now in *seems* so much like our own manifest realm but clearly isn't the solid, workaday world of the 'living'. They are, in effect, now stuck in the world's energetic reflection – its etheric imprint – along with all the other detritus such as thought-forms. Although these are *bona fide* human souls their overriding thoughts have kept them in the realm of thought and thus they are now in a disturbing place where the chaos and pathos of humanity's musings is fully apparent. Whereas physical human life is often said to be a beautiful illusion, the half-life of a lost soul in this astral limbo is more like an unpleasant delusion, created by the deliberations of a turbulent and unsettled collective human consciousness.

If we have already accepted that compelling human thoughts can create independent forms then we would also be well served to give credence to the idea that our practised, potent thoughts can tie us to a particular reality after death. All repetitive, dominant and emotionally charged thoughts are incredibly powerful and if we can take no more from this book than realise this then we will have done ourselves a great service. Our prevailing thoughts can tether us to this plane as effectively as any rope or chain, making our spirits earth-bound prisoners of the nearest unseen layer to our own.

What follows here is a list of how just some of our powerful emotional thoughts can keep us in a self-inflicted bondage even after the physical death of the body that created the thoughts in the first place:

• Guilt – *Feeling as if we lead a life that was filled with sin, as defined by religion. Not wishing to move on lest we be judged. Feeling we must somehow stay and make amends for our supposed sins. Feeling overwhelming remorse that ties us to the people/creatures/land we have harmed*

• Fear – *Terror of what lies beyond life. Being afraid of a void in which we will cease to exist. Being scared of a hellish afterlife of condemnation and torment. Having an abject fear of being without the familiarity of the body and bodily things. Experiencing a blind panic that we cannot cope without those we have left behind. Wanting to go back to safety, security and 'reality'*

- Anger – *Not wanting to be dead at all, feeling it was unfair and as if we had more things to achieve, unfinished business, on the manifest Earth. Feeling furious at one who killed us or at someone who did not do enough to save us. Experiencing frustration that we lived a life where we wanted to express ourselves but did not. Wanting to return to our life to sort these feelings and situations out*

- Pain – *Our own overwhelming physical anguish tying us to the body, as we are so frightened of the pain we feel that we cannot imagine freedom from such torment*

- Loss – *Dying in grief for the loss of a loved one or from a sad life. Such grieving can be addictive and shut us down to the possibility of a reprieve. All seems hopeless and we just want to keep on with the 'safety' of our mourning state*

- Bitterness – *Dying with a sense of not having done anything, having lived an empty meaningless life and of being thwarted by people or situations. Wanting to go and change what held us in such hollow misery and not being able to accept that this life is over, that was all that we got and our opportunities to change things have now run out*

- Mental Illness – *Dying with the confusion of chemical imbalance or under the influence of tormented thoughts. Not knowing reality for fantasy and so not realising death had occurred instead of another hallucinatory episode. Having had delusions and unpleasant voices in life and fearing to meet the 'real thing', which may be demons or monsters, in death*

- Jealousy – *Dying in a state of resentment towards someone who took what we wanted and couldn't have. Feeling passionate about wanting to be with someone who is still alive and hating those who get to remain with them instead*

- Overwhelming Love – *Not wishing to leave a spouse/child/parent/friend etc. Being bound to the body by our deep affection for a living person and our overwhelming concern for their well-being. Needing to look after someone/thing and fearing no one else can do it like we could*

- Regret – *On dying perhaps wishing we had shown more love in life and needing to show it now, therefore experiencing a need to stay and prove our love to the living*

- Control – *Not wanting to leave someone behind for fear they will do something we don't want them to. Wanting them to know we are still watching them and won't let them do something against our will*

- Revenge – *Wanting justice to be carried out on the perpetrator of our murder or injury. A need to 'haunt' the place of our death for want of telling what happened. There may be a need to pursue the murderer and a desire to hurt them back*

- Addiction – *'Just one more drink/bet/pill/erotic encounter...'*

- Shock – *Dying so unexpectedly that we are unaware of death and so carry on as if the body is still alive, even when confronted by the sight of our own dead body. An example of such a death would be being in an explosion or being hit by a truck. This sudden death response also applies to murder*

It may be well to note here that although we have mentioned the possible effects of chronic mental illness on our soul after death this does not apply to those who have learning difficulties or have sustained brain damage. Those who have chosen bodies with learning difficulties have souls which are untouched by the limits of their physical selves and may suffer much less from such confusion after death, being as pure in their responses as young children. Likewise the brain may be damaged in some dying people but the awareness of the soul is intact and glad to be released from a body that no longer works. Such people, especially those who have been in a coma and have been very close to the Otherworldly (unseen) dimensions for a time, would be far more wiling to give up their damaged body and fly on than someone who is in the grip of a tormented set of thoughts.

To back up this distinction between the brain and the soul it has been revealed by several well-documented cases that the brain itself is not so vital to a productive life as we once assumed. For example, an honours graduate in mathematics was found by the late Dr John Lorber to have less than 1 millimetre of cerebral tissue covering the top of his spinal column, yet he could still function successfully in the world. Had the Doctor not been required to CAT scan his cranium the discovery would never even have been made, posing the question of how many of us actually have the all-controlling brain we think we have? Dr Lorber himself subsequently found several hundred perfectly well-adjusted and functioning individuals with 'no detectable brain'. This reinforces that if the brain is damaged it does not mean the eternal awareness within is – that which we consider to be our 'mind' is much more 'non-local' than this.

So, if we are physically damaged or mentally impaired yet emotionally open and fearless we still have a far better chance to pass over into spirit smoothly than if our body was sound but our thoughts and feelings were ruled by anxiety, greed or hate.

That which tethers us are our *overwhelming* feelings upon death; certainly not the simple, transient human regrets most of us would have if we passed away from physical life today. Such thoughts are passionate beyond what is normal and healthy and, as we have observed from our previous list, quite obsessive. Some of them cannot necessarily be helped, like an unexpected or painful end, but we can control some, like jealousy, much more if we are aware of such negative responses and habitual thoughts right here and now. Yet some of our thoughts are so programmed in as to beyond emotion. They have been given to us as solid belief or irrefutable fact and therefore it is harder to weed them out. Such thoughts would be those given to us by church, state and family who were (and in many places still are) in control of what we received as worldly truth.

If we recall our point about centuries of religious subjugation having the power to create fearful thought-forms in the human astral then we can appreciate that this same fear has been such a problem for spirits attempting to leave their bodies. It is hard to go into the light whilst dreading the possibility of what may come next. Terrible doom-laden thoughts pertaining to versions of the 'afterlife' have been drummed into our psyche through the ages, most usually to keep us in submissive fear so that we would behave in an orderly fashion. This fear can hold true even after our body gives out and we effectively become a free spirit again – it can keep us in slavery beyond the grave. Who would want to leave the Earth no matter how grim our physical life had been if the after-life meant fire, brimstone and pitchforks? Or the damnation of an endless lonely night of rejection? It would seem far easier perhaps to stick with what we knew, i.e. the physical world, than for us to move on to the next terrifying level of existence.

The irony of a soul trying to avoid a supposed Hell is that when we remain stuck in the human astral we *are* in a sort of hell, the likes of which we would not find had we gone into the light. Our sudden inability to affect change on Earth and having our loved ones fail to see us would certainly seem hellish. Along with our invisibility we will have also put ourselves in a realm in which bizarre and uncontrollable things haunt us – the thought-forms and collated psychic debris of the human astral.

Before I was drawn to this area of spiritwalking I used to believe that there were few lost souls, trusting that the prospect of going into the loving light with our trusted companions as our guides would override any residual apprehension. I found it hard to take on board that there could be anyone that reluctant to leave Earth and to move to the wonderful, welcoming place in the universe where they should be. However, I promptly received guidance, and accompanying illustrative experiences, which proved me sadly wrong. I have now seen for myself the heart-breakingly long 'queues' of lost souls who need help in their transition, stuck as they are in the twilight world of the human astral with only the occasional guiding light (like ours) to show them that there may be a way out of the mess that they have placed themselves in. Some of these lost ones may not be coherent or aware of anything much except that they are drawn to our soul shining in their darkness.

Here is a cross-section of those waiting in a 'queue' that I once experienced when working with another spiritwalker at his home:

- An abused and murdered child trapped by their need for their body to be found where a corrupt Priest had buried it with several others in a tiny English hamlet
- An American victim of the Vietnam war who was still

screaming as his guts were apparently blown out from him in an endless replay

- A Eighteenth Century peasant man who was suddenly, and fatally, struck by lightening as he worked in the fields and who wouldn't accept that he was dead even though people could no longer see or hear him

- A wealthy Victorian young woman whose illegitimate child was taken from her and bricked up elsewhere in the house whilst she was kept prisoner in her room and sent mad on laudanum

- A small dog that had become separated from its human companion during a fire and couldn't stop searching for her. The lost souls of animals are not common, as they live their lives in full connection to Source and therefore have little difficulty moving from physical to non-physical being, yet strong emotions like loyalty, or a sudden traumatic death, can sometimes make a creature remain *in situ*

- A soldier from the English Civil War still standing with his flag whilst bloodied and broken, surrounded by an unbearable stench of cordite

- A 'cry for help' suicide victim who had wanted to be found before it was too late...yet wasn't

Before we move let's consider this latter point, suicide, in more detail, as it is a very painful and controversial area that will sadly no doubt affect us as spiritwalkers sooner or later.

Suicide is Painless?

Obviously suicide creates lost souls although not as many as we may think. This is because the person involved usually intends to die and welcomes death, therefore making the journey into the light willingly, passing into spirit with ease. The companion spirits will be there at the transition to take them through the portal into the next dimensional plane and those who had wished for this release will go with them gladly. There is no panel of judges waiting to condemn them on their arrival in this new state of being. We ourselves are our only judges! In the case of such a willing suicide it is only the fact that they have given up on their life's opportunity that makes them feel regret when they reach 'the other side' – this and the fact that they have caused unnecessary suffering to those that they have left behind. Our own assessment of such a disappointing attempt at our incarnation is the only condemnation we receive.

So, there is certainly no external punishment waiting for these souls, only a kind of reflection and rehabilitation undertaken with wise and compassionate facilitators – a sort of 'twelve-step recovery programme' for spirits. This recovery process may mean that suicides are 'out of circulation' for a while as they get a chance to meditate on what went wrong and how they could have better responded to their problems. This is why those who have passed over into spirit by their own hand can seem very far away from us – a situation which is often interpreted as the suicide having gone somewhere 'bad.' I myself was very frustrated not to be able to speak with two men who I knew had deliberately killed themselves (in the same reliable way, using a pipe on the exhaust of their car) until I understood this rehabilitation process. Such spirits are *never* in a castigating prison situation and are only ever on a temporary healing retreat with professional spirit-helpers, the duration of which cannot be quantified in human time.

However, when a person *inadvertently* kills themselves, whilst just wanting help or to draw attention to their suffering, then things are clearly intentionally, or energetically, different. Once a person who was only making a cry for help actually succeeds in terminating their physical life, and thus permanently leaves their body, then there will be huge remorse – perhaps enough to keep them *in situ* when they leave the physical and enter the unseen level of existence.

If the 'cry for help' suicide feels panic, fear, or overwhelming regret at the point when they (inadvertently) pass over into spiritual being then they may well hang on to the relative familiarity of the human astral levels. This they will do, wandering lost and ashamed as they desperately try to make amends or to change things some-how. This is when they enter a level of blind torment, oblivious to everything but their own suffering, and, for a time at least are, quite beyond help. All they want is to go back and do things differently but quite clearly they cannot. Although they could get immediate help and strength from their companions spirits, and be granted safe passage to the next level of existence with them, they are instead completely overcome with longing to return to Earth and so it is that they just stay tethered to it, floating in an etheric no-man's land of guilt, shame, pain and 'if only'.

As we have established, there is no external retribution for a suicide – *absolutely not* – but there certainly can be this ongoing self-inflicted hell of penance and a stubborn reluctance to move on through pain, guilt and loss. The sensitive, beautiful film 'What Dreams May Come', starring Robin Williams, expresses this tragic state of limbo perfectly. The plot of the film is that a female artist loses her two children and then her husband (played by Williams) and thus kills herself from a seemingly unbearable grief whilst filled with regrets and recriminations. Instead of entering the joyous technicolour dreamworld of her husband and children (who went on easily into the light of the Summerlands) she instead enters a dimension which mirrors our own human realm but which is nothing but a lonely prison for her. There she gets stuck in a grotesque parody of life until her husband (in spirit) bravely comes to her hellish state of energetic existence to find her.

This film has a tendency to strike a chord with many people, as sadly we all seem to know someone who has taken their own life – perhaps willingly, perhaps mistakenly. I myself am aware of at least seven adults I have known who no longer wanted to carry on with the 'school of life' and wanted to 'go home early' to the perfect peace of spirit, thus opting out of valuable lessons and precious experiences on Earth. I know how hard it is for those they leave behind, how these people torture themselves with what they could have done to save the souls involved, and I have no doubt of the pain the particular people had when they ended their human incarnation by their own hand.

Of course such tragedies are avoidable. If we all understood the ways of spirit, indeed if we were all taught to *walk with spirit* and to feel our own connection to Source and to each other, then such travesties would never need to happen. We would all be far more *au fait* with the ways of the eternal compared with the transient tests of the corporeal. Then perhaps we would be more supportive, less competitive and genuinely able to see the folly of 'bailing out', no matter how hard things get for us in the mortal world. In our re-membering of who we are we would never forget that these tests of life are not external exams with an adjudicator but rather tests we chose to set for ourselves, with joyful experience and soul-development as the only aim. And, of course, we would do this with the full knowledge that we only ever take on an experience that we can handle, even if it does stretch us to our (perceived) limits.

As spirits aware of our own equality, and deep connection to All, perhaps we can now more readily step forward to support people who think themselves failing some divinely appointed and unattainable grade. It is part of our role as spiritwalkers to encourage a gentle, wholesome re-membering of why we are really here – and that it has nothing to do with winners and losers. It is vital that we can communicate our understanding of incarnation as a co-operative experience for mutual growth, creative expression and enjoyment, not a humourless competition with delineations of success and failure.

Yet even as we strive to make this supportive scenario a reality we must still accept that there are still many lost souls caused as a result of suicides, along with all the other reasons, such as unexpected death, that we have previously listed. Because of this it is well for us to understand how and why lost souls haunt us as they wander through the human astral on their various relentless missions.

The Last Hangers-On at an Endless Party

When we die and go back to being 'in spirit' we have chance to reflect on the difference between our previous temporary human existence/s and our eternal spiritual presence. However, lost souls have no such period of calm speculative separation, continuing to experience a ravenous attachment for all things connecting them to their human identity, including a deep and unhealthy attachment to people places and emotive events. Thus they linger in the etheric region that surrounds us, occasionally breaking through into our dimension by wilfully pushing at the ether with their presence but most often simply being felt as ripples and undercurrents in the human astral fabric around us. This 'haunting' process works in several ways, depending on the reason behind it.

Stakers and Claimers

Some lost souls acknowledge they are dead but refuse to let go of what was theirs, instead letting greed, jealousy, desire or a simple fear of loss root them. They wilfully cling to their property and previous personality and make their presence felt strongly, usually 'wearing' an astral version of their previous body in full regalia. In this the lost soul evokes its previous self, creating an energetic facsimile in order to attempt to reinstate itself somehow – even if that must be by intimidation. The result is an oppressive atmosphere which may be accompanied by the issuing forth of strong personal scents and loud footsteps. Astral activity may well focus around a previous bedroom with the spirit looming over the current occupier of 'their' bed or even sitting down on it. Some particularly disgruntled souls have tried to tip people out of 'their' bed or rip off their bedclothes whilst others may throw things at us. This variety of lost soul will certainly 'act out' in some way if we challenge its idea of personal space, witnessing us as strange interlopers in their construct of reality. So convinced do they become of their claim to that area/house etc that they consider *us* to be haunting *them* rather than vice versa. With our current experience of time as a linear progression this is clearly not the case although with the acceptance of the eternal *Now* the issue becomes more complicated. Perhaps we can discuss this with our companion spirits as an advanced subject.

Reiteraters

Some souls have no idea they are now discarnate and continue to experience their most emotional life-scenes or their last moments *in situ* whilst manifest earthly life goes on around them for a year, a decade, a century or more after their physical demise. They are totally lost in the experience of being that they were, perhaps because their death was sudden or perhaps because they were not ready to pass over and therefore the reality of this has been denied on some level. All they know is that same pattern being repeated, time has no meaning and neither do we, the physical beings in their perceived space. If by chance they do somehow become aware of us outside of their eternal replay loop they become frightened and disturbed. They emit the frequency of their practised emotion, causing us to feel the sorrow, anger, pain or fear of whatever event keeps them trapped in the local ether. We may also witness them going about their business in the way that they had at a crucial moment before they passed over, perhaps clutching their throat dramatically, furiously pacing up and down or being hung from a beam or thrown from a window. They will give this display before promptly disappearing, having used up the burst of energy that this re-enactment took. They do what they do and then leave our atmosphere again to wander the astral before building up the energy, or stealing it, to replay the scene again. This kind of astral interference, or performance, can also be confused with activated *residual* or *imprinted* energy – a mere etheric replay without soul – but more of this in Chapter Fifteen.

Disorienteers

Due to exceptional trauma on passing, such as being in a sudden road traffic accident that resulted in instantaneous death, some have lost all conception of who they were or what they are, let alone where they now exist, and are just roaming around our nearest unseen level in the utmost confusion and distress. This can also happen if the soul has been lost for a long time and has gradually become more and more disorientated and forgetful of its own nature. They can no longer see anyone, nor can they feel their guiding spirits close by.

Overseers

Some lost souls have learned to walk the balance, knowing they are dead and being at ease with this but still not wishing to leave their role and position to go 'into the light'. They are benign presences that are simply out of time and place, perhaps wishing to gently enjoy or watch over an ex-home or garden. This is not a desirable state of affairs but much less troublesome and distressing than the previous types of lost soul scenario. Of course, individual souls do have a choice to opt out of moving on and if it isn't disrupting anyone else then we cannot order them to move on. Their companion spirits will remain at a respectful distance for the time when they do wish to make the journey onwards.

Whatever their *modus operandi* or reasoning, these vagrants between worlds need kindness and care from spiritwalkers such as ourselves. After all, they *are* spirits such as ourselves; only without the fleshy 'suit of clothes' we are currently wearing. Therefore we need to behave with the utmost respect and compassion, no matter how exasperating, incomprehensible or frankly disturbing the spirit's current state is. The term generally given to working gently with lost souls is called *spirit rescue*. Spirit rescue is only ever undertaken for the purpose of *moving lost souls to the place in the universe where they should be to best receive healing* and this release of our fellow spirits from their 'nowhere existence' to a purposeful and loving space is an exceedingly valuable job. However rewarding it can also be terribly difficult, draining and often distressing. Such advanced work is only suitable for an experienced spiritwalker and therefore it would be running before we can walk to discuss it in depth here. If we are still interested then we can discuss this valuable work with our companion spirits when we have achieved a good working relationship with them.

Yet before we move on to learning how to send such lost souls onwards we will need to consider other forms of disturbance that we will inevitably come across. So common are these disturbances that they may lead us to be convinced that we have a lost soul when we do not and therefore it is vital that we understand their nature now so that such confusion cannot occur.

CHAPTER FIFTEEN

GETTING OUT OF THE LOOP

'You pass through the material world like comets, each with
your own uniquely glorious trail to blaze. You are heavenly
bodies and you each have the potential to shake heavens as you
pass through this time and space with such fabulous intensity.
And in your wake you will always leave an impression of the
journey – the joy, the sorrow, the overwhelming desire – no less
real than the dust and gas that follows an actual comet. Yet on
and on you travel, hanging on for dear life to this apparent
reality, oblivious to the impact that your fleeting manifestation
has any energetic impact upon your surroundings...let alone
one that will remain as a testament to your passing.
Your life, *all* life, is like every star that has ever shone – it
lingers on in the fabric of existence, burned into the retina of
universal memory. Why not take the chance to shine now
and make your particular afterimage a dazzling, not a
dismal, one?'
From Guidance

In this chapter we will look at two other forms of energy that can
cause disturbance that may be considered ghostly. These are *residual
energy* and *earth energy*.

1. Residual Energy

When we speak of residual energy we talk about the lingering life-
force of a being that remains in the atmosphere after their death.

When someone dies they leave an energetic trace of themselves and their unique life behind, rather like a charred scent remaining after a fire. This scent will, over time, naturally disperse as the person that created it moves on away from our dimensional reality. However, given the right circumstances this psychic impression of what has gone before can get caught in the ether and becomes recorded there, embossed into the energy of that place or level of being. This is when the residual energy of a person, or even of an event, becomes an *imprint*.

Embossing the Ether - Imprints

The reason why residual energy becomes imprinted is partly due to location and partly due to the emotional emanation of the original person or action that took place there.

Firstly, with the location, the prevailing materials and conditions affect how much energy is likely to be stored. Stone seems to be a particularly successful storing device for energy, as was amply demonstrated by the Neolithic builders of ancient monuments, such as chambered cairns and long barrows. The Neolithic builders knew that stone is an excellent accumulator and amplifier and that certain stone, like granite, is more effective than other types. If we think of stone as able to soak up the sun's rays during the day and gradually release this heat at night – the same principle that is used within a night storage heater – then we can appreciate how stone also soaks up other ambient energies. It then releases, or radiates them, when meteorological, geological or other triggering conditions, such as the presence of a sensitive person, are favourable. This means that the essential energy of any event can be captured in stone, the original essence being released over and over from the operational storage rock. This effect is then enhanced by the inherent dampness of most old places, water of course acting as an excellent conductor for energy – in this case the residual energy of someone's intense emotional output or their ambient vibration.

The natural energy accumulation in stone, along with the dampness inherent in old buildings, explains why so many old pre-brick halls, barns and castles are considered haunted – they have just become the equivalent of a recording device for a particularly potent energetic impression. Many supposed hauntings result from this imprinting in stone and are, in fact, nothing more than a replay.

Secondly, we find residual energy gaining such longevity in the ether because the original events were heavily charged up with high emotions of one kind or another. The scenes from the past are enlivened with passion or tragedy and have effectively burned themselves into the atmosphere of the place with their emotion, just as we would burn music onto a CD via a laser. As human lives clearly hold all sorts of emotive events and history is full of collective expressions of emotion then it can come as no surprise to us that imprinted energies are by far the largest cause of all perceived hauntings or disturbances – especially in places of great human drama and historical import such as fortresses, palaces or old public houses.

Examples of typical energetic imprints would be:

- The same scene from a battle seen frequently in a castle grounds
- An army endlessly marching up an old road, oblivious of the level of any new road or wall there
- Someone falling out of a stone second storey window with

stone mullions, over and over
- Someone walking up and down a room in a manor house as if searching for something

These are examples of repetitive re-enactments of important and emotive events. No matter how distressing they may seem to us they are only reruns of old energetic programmes – there is no soul present there, no more than in a projection of a film onto a screen. Indeed, if we tried to interact with the imprinted replay we would be ignored, as there is really no one there. We may experience the burst of emotion associated with the imprinted manifestation but again that is only residual energy being released, rather like gas bubbling up from a swamp, and is not a cause for concern. No matter how the atmosphere may feel it is the lack of reaction to external stimuli, or a spiritwalker's attention, combined with the repetition of the exact performance, that shows us we have an energetic imprint before us and not a lost soul.

Yet another reason for energetic imprinting that pertains to the construction of the location is the unnatural *layout* of old buildings and settlements. When I say unnatural I mean that nature does not, as a rule, go in for the angular structures with box-like dead ends that we humans do. Energy likes openness, flow and roundness and does not take well to the human penchant for linear corridors, closed cubby-holes and enclosed stairwells. Energy that is 'heavy' with human emotion will not disperse well from such restrictive manufactured spaces and it can build up and stagnate, simply bound to keep on surging in a continuum of trapped power. If we add in this restrictive linear layout to constructive factor of damp stone then this why most old mansions with their labyrinthine rooms, dark passages, pantries and uninhabited areas are most often cited as 'spooky'. These rooms and passages are simply 'spooked' by stuck tainted energy that has become lodged in the unnatural crevices of a system of closed compartments.

Trapped Residual Energy

Whenever we hear of a haunted place it is (usually) an older property and has a corridor, stairwell, passageway or uninhabited room that is part of the disturbance. It may even have its own supposedly ghostly presence ambling up and down there, over and over. Yet there is usually no lost soul present, only repressed energy which has built up and over the ages and which cannot disperse due to the lifeless, boxy confines of the passageway or staircase. Indeed, most of the apparent ghosts of legend are often no more than hemmed in residual energy that is trapped as it collects in cut off corners, walkways and dark nooks. This lingering life-energy develops into the shadowy shapes and ethereal forms that are then witnessed as the 'grey ladies' and 'dark hooded monks' etc. of our hauntings.

Here we can think of the grey fluff that gathers under a bed or in the furthest corners behind furniture and then extend this concept to the unseen. What haunts a corridor is usually just an accumulation of energetic matter that becomes unsettling as it rolls around its enclosed space, gathering more energy to it. In this it is rather like a thought-form with its energetic snowball effect. This is not to say that actual lost souls of ladies or monks don't exist, it is just that in the majority of cases our limited human consciousness will perceive amorphous residual energy as the nearest thing that it can grasp – hence the transference of amorphous dirty energy into a shadowy female in grey or a man in a dark cowl in our perception.

Even if a building is of modern it can suffer the same problems of stuck energy if:

- It is particularly compartmentalised
- It has windowless corridors
- There are rooms that often remain shut or dark

I myself lived in a modern block of flats that centred on a corridor that ran the whole length of the building. This corridor was particularly narrow and dim in the basement, a place that was always 'spooky' to be in. The whole building was designed around long passages and boxy rooms and it was one of the most psychically disturbed places I have ever lived in. I experienced many dark figures walking around and regular bad atmospheres that could not be explained away. Nor could they be easily dispersed as they always came back, no matter what I did. I did some research at the time and discovered that this seemingly attractive flat (which was built in a very desirable area) had an inordinately high turn over of previous tenants, showing me that they too had found it uncomfortable for some reason. It was a design that favoured the accumulation of residual energy to the detriment of those who tried to dwell there and short of knocking it down to restructure there was nothing that could be done to change it. Sadly to add to this inherent problem it had also been built on the site of a battle and the resulting disturbed energy of that event inevitably had been released by the land into the 'trap' of the building, where it was then effectively imprisoned.

Ordinarily life-force energy, once released, will eventually dissipate and fade, being dispersed by light and movement – rather like milk being absorbed into hot coffee when we stir it. If we could all dwell in circular, airy spaces that allow for circulation we would not suffer from such energetic problems. This healthy flow is increased when there is a high percentage of inhabitation, and therefore movement, in a place. From the Neolithic through to the Iron Age people knew about such effects – and so chose to live in round dwellings with no limiting corners and corridors. Many contemporary tribal peoples still opt for this design. We modern Westerners persist in building our houses against the flow of nature and then wonder why things go wrong, energetically speaking!

Clearly if we face such an energetic problem then light and motion are the antidote to stagnation and stuck-ness. A simple process of visualisation, imagining bright clean light filling the place vigorously in a sweeping movement, rather like a clean cool breeze whisking around a room when the window is opened, can be effective. Or we may visualise clear sparkling energy like a tide, washing the space clean in a flowing motion, flooding into all those nooks and crannies and effectively 'washing them out'. We can also use sound, utilising the top range of our voice or a sustained high note of an instrument to a shift in the vibration, effectively stirring up the energy with a change of frequency. I myself was advised to make a silver branch – a collection of twigs painted silver strung with tiny silver bells – which I could shake in such spaces. Moving around vigorously in the space, chanting an uplifting mantra clapping or perhaps joyfully dancing to upbeat music would also be appropriate. This visualisation or sound process would need to be repeated by us (or others) if the old energy is particularly heavy and the space particularly sealed in. If we are to live in such places then we will have to include such energy cleansing acts as a matter of routine.

So, this is how we could approach residual energy trapped in a space. But what do we do when recorded information is being replayed when it is no longer needed; say in a home that is disturbed by past re-runs of old emotional events? Dealing with an imprint of residual energy is clearly not like dealing with an actual person or even an entity. It is like watching a film, a replay – something energetic stored in the surroundings just as information is stored on a DVD – and so we simply need to 'wipe the disc'. We need to deactivate the root recording by overlaying the original imprint with something stronger, cleaner and brighter – basically blanking it. Again we would do this by seeing, feeling, or hearing this new higher, brighter energy flood into the structural matrix of the place, overriding the original stored information with a pure, fresh vibration. Our companions can advise us of the appropriateness of this choice and can inspire us with creative ways to carry out a cleansing effectively.

Before we move on we need to stress a vital rule for an accomplished spiritwalker here. *This blanking, or interfering with 'programming', is definitely not advisable in the case of a stone circle or ancient monument of any kind*! It is only recommended when someone has to live in a house disturbed by residual recorded imagery and needs to have some peace. We should *never* tamper with monuments that we have no real idea of the meaning or purpose of, especially as they may lie on points or flows of power, such as ley-lines, and are more than likely to be precisely and gracefully aligned with them.

This leads us onto our next section.

2. Earth Energies

Ley-lines, the natural 'cables of power' in the land, are like ancient monuments in that they cannot be cleared, only worked *with* or *around*. They are pure bands of electro-magnetic energy that flow with the earth and are not to be meddled with by us, even if we think we know what we are doing. Many well-meaning folk have spoken of ley-lines being turned 'bad' and of their struggle to 'heal them'. Can any of us be sure and certain of the validity of such a statement? No matter how well meaning our intervention can we really take such a task on to ourselves?

The best, most responsible thing to would be to ask the companion spirits to pass our concerns about an apparently disrupted/corrupted line or sacred place on to the beings that oversee such matters. These may be the site guardians or ancestral Watchers, or Fey/elemental beings that live within the astral levels of the place. *These are the experts.* For me, to dabble with latent earth energies and their accompanying ancient monuments would be the equivalent of going into the main generating service station for electricity and claiming to know how to overhaul and supply power to the region. To try and 'heal' a ley-line is like claiming that if we can hold the electrical cables that supply our area in our hands that we can somehow make them work better. It is unthinkable to channel so much power through ourselves. We may help the beings who oversee such matters but we cannot rush in headlong alone, no matter how heartfelt our intent.

By the strength of the feeling I am projecting here I am stressing the awesome power of these natural serpentine lines of vital source-force that run in bands across the small blue-green planet on which we are lucky enough to live. If we consider this authentic power as real, just as the power points in our own bodies have been considered real by mystics and physicians down the ages, then we will acknowledge that anything built upon one, i.e. a home, would be subject to very powerful influences. We need to acknowledge what natural waves of concentrated energy in the land can do to things, or people, placed directly upon them. No doubt, yet again, the ancients knew this and only built their non-dwelling temples and sacred places upon such force-lines, *not their homes*. Perhaps, in direct relation to the electricity that we create ourselves, we are only just waking up to how ill advised it is to build homes near to pylons and sub-stations that supply power. It is the same principle. We are not meant to live at/on the source!

Saying this there are always those, like the extraordinary British healer Matthew Manning, who have claimed to live on a ley with marvellous results. However, he is indeed *extra-ordinary* and certainly more experienced and adept at channelling and transforming energy than the average spiritwalker. The usual effect would be far more than most of us would be willing or able to transmute or translate in our daily lives!

Indeed, we can predict that ley-lines would be responsible for more than a little 'poltergeist style' activity in a dwelling built upon, or even near, them. This is certainly the case in Avebury, in Wiltshire, UK, where an entire village was built in amongst the stone circle there...some walls even utilising broken up stones from the original ring! If the dwelling was unfortunate enough to be built where lines converge or cross, as in Avebury, then effects would be multiplied and 'haunted houses' full of apparent poltergeist activity would be the norm. Clearly this effect would be made worse again if the person dwelling in the house was an adept receiver of unseen energies, or a sensitive. Such sensitive people, like the stones themselves, are natural amplifiers. No doubt there are some that are the exact opposite of Matthew Manning and are so psychically closed down as to be utterly unaffected by such omnipresent force but those who are reading this book clearly do not fit into this category and would be well advised to avoid such a place of residence!

We can obviously accept that places of ancient significance, such as megaliths and burial sites, would have been chosen for their particularly potent earth-energy and so it is worth considering that if we experience a troubled atmosphere at such a location it is probably due to the underlying forces of the land, and our reaction to them, and not necessarily to the presence of a spirit or entity. Saying this any wandering unseen beings will naturally gravitate to any lines of force, witnessing them as vast luminous pathways in the relative confusion of their existence. It is possible that they will use ley-power to sustain their presence on this plane and perhaps even use this network of energy as a means of travelling across the land, visiting the 'powerhouses' of the ancient sacred sites on the way. Nothing is cut and dried within our craft and we should always take a holistic view with the help of our companions.

As a general rule of thumb, if we are witnessing balls, or orbs, of light then we can almost certainly attribute these to the inherent *geo-physical conditions*, such as fault lines or underground water systems, and to the electro-magnetic properties of the area – not to an individual 'ghost' or rogue. Balls of light are commonly sighted at places of concentrated earth-power and although they may have been attributed to spirits and U.F.O's they are almost certainly the result of a natural energetic interplay in the affected area. I myself know how tempting it can be to equate amazing anomalous balls of light to ghostly presences and strange craft. I myself encountered a huge orange ball hovering over Stonehenge in 1990 – a story I tell in my first book, 'Season of Sorcery' (Capall Bann, 1998) and which has also been recounted in works by both Albert Budden and Alan Richardson. The ball of light I witnessed did seem to have an intelligence, even to interact with me, and its potent energetic presence was enough to turn a piece of fruit black within minutes! Yet I understand that it was probably a result of the extraordinary geological/energetic power of the land there. I have also witnessed balls of light seemingly dancing independently on Glastonbury Tor, which made me feel, at least for the time I was mesmerised by their display, that I was dealing with *beings* rather than just light-forms. Yet again this is an area of outstanding geological and energetic activity. From this I have learned that unless we are aware of the *terrestrial* causes for such phenomena then we may easily allow our perception to be swayed by our prevailing belief system. Further information on witnessing and interpreting these light phenomena can be found in the excellent works of Paul Devereux, some of which are listed in the suggested reading section at the end of this book.

So, we cannot change, or banish, such light-forms, no matter how profound their affect is on us both physically and psychically. They are as natural as bubbles rising in a fizzy drink and we do not need to do anything with them but observe with awe. The spots where these phenomena occur show that they are places of pilgrimage only and they are not meant to be dwelled on, or even, perhaps, near. We cannot change what is inherent in the land and therefore cleaning, cleansing or altering the energy there in any way is not only ill advised but downright dangerous. If we take one piece of advice on board here it should be that *it is always wise to know when we can do nothing and when we can genuinely act for the good of the All.*

So, let's move on to the work we can actually do when a place, be that astral or physical, is haunted by a real person or entity.

CHAPTER SIXTEEN

CLEANING UP

'Energy can be moved and shifted just as matter can. For what
is matter but energy at a particular vibration that gives us an
illusion of solidity? We can always deal with an unseen
resonance by clearing it away, just as a responsible parent
would do with a child's scattered toys. However, as
spiritwalkers we acknowledge that those with *awareness* must
be given care and consideration and cannot simply be swept up
at our whim without dignity. The impetus, for us as empathic
beings, is to do what is best for the All and this can only be *to
will the energy concerned to occupy the space in the universe
where it is meant to be.* We are simply putting the round peg in
the round hole as opposed to allowing it to bang against the
square hole with unpleasant results. Life is a series of such
moves, be they physical or not. We are simply becoming active,
as conscious co-creators, in the harmonious distribution of
life-force as opposed to our previously powerless and
confused selves.'

From Guidance

We have already covered the main types of unwanted or misplaced
being, or energetic disturbance, that we may meet, both astrally and
physically, in the previous three chapters.

To recap, these are:

- Unintentional thought-forms

- Intentional thought-forms/servitors
- Rogue entities
- Nameless beings
- Lost/trapped human souls
- Residual Imprints
- Trapped Residual Energy
- Earth Energies

What we need to know now is how to deal with disturbances both seen and unseen, as they occur.

Firstly we shall consider the unseen aspect of our work as spiritwalkers and find out what to do if we meet a being we consider to be unfamiliar, unexpected and possibly unwanted while we are on a trance journey. For this we will need a method of containing and dismissing any spirit, entity or energy that enters our psychic space whilst we are in our astral office or beyond it in unknown unseen territory. What follows is such a strategy.

Removing Unwanted/Misplaced Beings on Astral Journeys
We have already been given, and are no doubt regularly using, techniques that enable us to safely and effectively 'check out' whether an invited spirit who visits us within our astral safe space is authentic. As we know we can draw a figure of eight upon the ground using either the active finger or a tool, such as a wand, to direct the white/blue cold-fire of protection. We then ask that the spirit that we wish to meet steps into the other half of the loop from where we are standing. Once they are within our protective loop we can then challenge them by pointing our fire-beam at them and asking them to show themselves, three times. In addition, if we feel

it is necessary, we can also hold up our 'truth mirror' so that their true form is shown to us.

If the form that is revealed is contrary to the form they have initially presented then they are an intrusive, uninvited force in our space. We then have *carte blanche* to banish them. This we do by evoking and using an inter-dimensional portal in the form of a beam or column of cold-blue-white light, the light-energy being transparent enough for us to still witness the being within. This column will both fix them in place and give them the ability to travel to wherever they need to be – it ascends up to a place beyond our knowing and extends down through the ground on which we are standing, beyond our sight. While the intrusive being is contained within this column we say something like:

> '*I ask that this being be returned to the place in the Universe where they should be at this time, the place where they may best receive what they need to heal and grow. May they be taken now for good and all as their place is not here!*'

To raise some energy for this and to show our intent then we can either stamp our foot or clap our hands three times whilst proclaiming:

> '*Be gone! Be gone! Be gone!*'

We can then see the spirit begin taken up, or down in the column of light, or simply vanishing from it. Where they go is really none of our business and we should not dwell on the outcome, being certain that it was the best thing for all concerned. Once our intruder has departed via this portal of light then we can then start again by invoking for the true spirits we seek to appear within the loop of the figure of eight.

This method is fine if we are routinely summoning a spirit, such as a companion, to us. But what if we are going about our astral business and an unfamiliar being appears in our territory unexpectedly?

In the case of an unwanted being just showing up in our astral space we need to be 'quick on the draw'. This time we use our fiery blue-white protective flame to draw a line of fire on the ground before us. This line is *alive*; it writhes like a serpent on the ground, ready to do our bidding. If we direct it with our intent it will then snake across the ground, lightning-fast, and loop itself around the intruder, keeping them safely within a circle of flame. If this imagery seems a bit aggressive to us then it is well to remember that although this cold-blue fire is powerful cannot hurt anyone. We are not behaving antagonistically by taking this approach; rather our action is a symbolic holding gesture that any being will understand. This sensible precautionary act effectively holds them within our boundaries so that we may then check them out without hurting anything but their pride.

We must then ask what their motive is for appearing. Using the pointing device of our extended intent, sending out a beam of blue-white fire from our finger or wand, we should point and then ask:

'I greet you stranger but must ask, do you come for my highest good? Answer truly as you are bound to do in this place!'

If the answer is a categorical *no* then we will be able to banish them immediately, using the column of light and accompanying words we have just mentioned. Even if we feel they are not outwardly malevolent but are making us uneasy we may still do this. After all, we are not harming them, simply sending them back to where they should be because *their place is not here with us*. However if we feel easy in their presence and they say *yes*, that they do come for our highest good, then we will still need to test their authenticity. For this we utilise the same principle of asking them to show themselves truly, three times, using the pointing beam of fire and, if necessary, applying the 'truth mirror' technique.

If the incomer turns out to be an authentic spirit who has come for our highest good then we can release them after this testing is accomplished, withdrawing the blue-white line of fire by allowing it to uncurl and snake back to us. We can then welcome this amenable being to our astral domain.

Our intention when we interact with other beings in astral space should be to walk the line between being a bully and being a wimp, using our psychic strength wisely and kindly and showing that we are in control yet not domineering. We always have the right to a trouble-free astral space with only authentic and well-meaning visitors in it. In this our astral space is like our earthly home – in both we have the authority to ask an unwanted, unruly, harmful guest to leave in a polite but firm way. Our banishing and checking out routine may at first appear discourteous or long-winded and fussy. Yet experience has shown me time and time again that with practice what seems like rudeness or rigmarole becomes something entirely natural and effortless. Firm-handed methodical diligence now always saves time and trouble in the long run.

So, it is easy to identify an unwanted or lost being when we are in the astral office as they are unfamiliar and out of place, like gatecrashers at a party. And, as we grow in confidence and experience, we will find it easy to check out unknown beings in the wider astral and will, no doubt, find ourselves being checked out ofor our authenticity and good intent in return. But how do we know we have an unwanted being in a *physical* place of work, or in an earthly residence or manifest local area? To answer this let's now move on to actively diagnosing, calling up and removing unwanted presences or energies in our daily physical lives.

Diagnosis – Identifying an Unwanted Unseen Presence in the Manifest World

Before dealing with any disturbances we clearly need to ascertain whether the supposed haunting is made by a discernible, and therefore *removable*, presence or whether it is simply an imprint, trapped residual energy or the result of the Earth's own forces. We can diagnose if the problem is residual or energetic through observing the contributing factors involved.

These are:

- The location, age or structure of the site
- The repetitive nature of the apparition/s
- Whether the apparent presence interacts with people or wants our attention or whether it is oblivious to us

If the factors seem to be pointing strongly at an imprint – for example if we have a damp old stone manor with a corridor seemingly haunted by a mute grey figure with no personality – then we can deal with the matter by responding to the problem of troublesome residual energy as we discussed in Chapter Fifteen, clearing the space with the techniques we now have at our disposal. However, if this does not cure the problem then we will probably need to apply a technique for dealing with a genuinely unwanted presence that is not residual or a poltergeist-type energy disturbance.

We have mentioned many of the signs of an unwanted presence or independent awareness elsewhere in this book. Here is a much more comprehensive checklist for us to consider when faced with any psychic problem in our manifest world.

1. Are there any 'unseen sightings' or actual manifestations?
These would include:

- The appearance of spectral human or animal forms, either nebulous and shadowy or more opaque and apparently solid
- The inexplicable presence of orbs, flashes or streaks of light which may be visible to the human eye or only to a camera (Note: care must be taken here to eliminate any other reason for the light anomaly's pressence, such as dust or moisture in the air)
- The animation of inanimate objects, such as a book seeming to be thrown, a door latch rattled or a table lifted
- Apports – the appearance of unfamiliar items, such as coins or jewellery, seemingly from out of thin air
- The manifestation of inappropriate fluids or odd substances
- Inexplicable electrical fluctuations which make appliances or lights behave in an erratic fashion
- The appearance of writing and/or imagery on a previously clear surface

- The disappearance of important items, such as keys or a diary, which then reappears sometime later in a different and incongruous place – a favourite shoe appearing in a kitchen drawer for example. (Note: Items can sometimes be taken by our companions for our own protection. For example, some prescribed medication was removed from several different locations in my room, never to appear again. I now realise that this was to save me from taking inappropriate drugs. If the disappearance of an object has meaning and isn't just a random 'theft' then it may well be for positive purposes. Dialogue with the companion/s can obviously clarify this.)

2. Are there any inexplicable or inappropriate sounds to be heard?

These include:

- Banging or crashing, particularly a noise like heavy furniture being thrown across a room or a wall being knocked down
- A strange metallic or electrical snapping or cracking sound without origin
- Inexplicable knocking or tapping of any kind
- The babble of indecipherable voices from an empty room
- Disembodied screams
- Disembodied laughter
- Disembodied footsteps
- The sound of unearthly music playing faery-like melodies
- Music with no apparent physical origin, such as a brass band

playing indoors or drumming seemingly coming from inside a wall
- The noise of squeaking wheels, like a rusty bicycle being ridden
- The sound of crying which has no manifest source
- The sound children playing when there are no children present
- The sound of one's name being called when no one is there

3. Inexplicable or inappropriate scents with no manifest source

These include:

- The sudden and inexplicable stench of human or animal faeces which vanishes without a trace as soon as it is noticed
- An odour like rotting meat which has no root cause
- A waft of floral perfume like roses, lavender or lilies which has no source and disappears completely, not lingering like an ordinary scent
- An electrical burning smell which has no origin in this world
- The inappropriate and overwhelming smell of damp or mildew which again vanishes without trace once noticed

4. Sensations

These include:

- A feeling of prickling or tingling on the skin which cannot be contributed to a manifest cause – a 'spine-chill' or goose bumps
- The hairs standing up on our body with no good reason

- Being physically touched when no one else is present
- An atmosphere of intense cold or sudden extreme heat for with no explanation as to why
- A sudden change in atmosphere that makes things seem as if they are in slow motion and every movement is an effort – a 'syrupy' feeling as if we are moving through soup. This can also make seeing what is in front of us difficult as if we are indeed peering through treacle.
- The sudden and unsettling impression that the world has become two-dimensional and flat, like a cartoon or card board cut out

Once we have determined through balanced diagnosis – including both practical deduction and spiritual consultation with the companion spirits – that we do have an actual spirit or entity problem then we can actively summon the unwanted being. We only ever do this summoning so that we may send them on, not so that we may commune with them. These beings are out of their right and intended place in the universe and therefore all we need to do is swiftly deal with their safe passage to their true place of being at this time. This we will need to do in both the troubled area in the physical world, and in the corresponding human astral level, at the same time.

Here's how we do it.

Banishing an Unwanted Being from the Manifest World

Wherever the activity or disturbance is centred in the building or place we should sit down and make ourselves as comfortable as possible. If the problem is person, not place, centred (meaning it follows them wherever they go rather than occurring only in a particular area) then we should sit with that person, face to face.

We should take a good look around us, or directly at the person, taking in all the environmental details that we can – including sounds, smells and sensations.

Then we should close our eyes, holding the overall impression we have of the room and or/the person involved, and go about the procedures for trance, that is grounding, centring, breathing slowly and deeply and then protecting ourselves fully. These steps should all be in place before we think about opening up to the ambient energies of the area we are in or to the person that we are with.

When we are adequately relaxed and confident in the level of protection we have achieved then we should state our intent, this being something along the lines of: '*I wish to identify that which troubles this place/person and, with the help of those genuine spirits who have an interest in this case, send them to the place in the universe where they should be at this time, for their place is not here.*'

Now behind our closed eyelids we should replicate the room we are in or the person we are with, seeing them vividly in our mind's eye. We should imagine/envision ourselves to be sat in the very same place that we are *physically* positioned only in its astral, unseen equivalent. This is the space we need to be in to look beyond the normal, 'ordinary reality' version of the area we are in/person we are with, concentrating on the layer behind what is usually known and seen for truth in the world. When we can experience it/them with convincing clarity behind our closed eyes then we are ready to proceed.

Now, on the floor of the astral version of the room we are in (next to any person we are dealing with) we need to envision a circle of cold blue-white fire. Let this apparition become a living reality as it licks and spits, the flames leaping and dancing just as a fire would in ordinary reality. Witness the flame growing up from the surface of the floor (be that stone, carpet or wood) without harming it and then imagine its energy sinking into and under the floor, beyond our inner vision, deep down – as above, so below.

Say, as an invocation, '*I have prepared a circle of fire for the being who troubles this place/person. Let them show themselves within the boundary-between-worlds that I have created for them, and may they show themselves truly! Now – show yourself, show yourself, show yourself!*'

With this we should use our index finger of our right (or active) hand to point at the empty space within the circle. Let a stream of will power, the intense blue-white light of our inner force, beam out to the place where we expect the being to appear. This is a strong yet compassionate gesture, firm but fair. We are doing this for the good of all concerned and so we need our will to be done.

Now a form will have appeared within the circle. Perhaps it is one of several or a singular being. It is not ours to discern who, or what, this being is. We do not need to peer at it curiously or analyse its shape or appearance. The shape before us may be obscene to our human eyes. It may be confusing, familiar, pitiful or beguiling. Or it may be nothing we can identify. We should not get involved with it, no matter what its appearance as we may start to feel fear, anger or sorrow if we dwell upon it, so weakening ourselves. Also we may start to feel a connection to them if we begin to empathise with them, thus risking them making a fresh link to this level of existence. Once we have identified that we have a form there we should immediately move on to the next part of the procedure without becoming distracted by the display that the being may have put on for us.

Now we should keep our beam of light trained upon the form and immediately ask for confirmation: '*May only those who cause an affray in this place/to this person remain within my circle. May those who truly cause this disturbance be held fast.*' This gives a final opportunity for the true culprit to show up and all others to vanish away.

Now we are truly left with the offending being/s who have caused the haunting and who are out of time and place. We now need to extend our circle of flame upwards so that it becomes a column of pure blue-white light that stretches up as far as we can see. We should also imagine it stretching down, below the floor level, off into the *beyond*. This column of light will hold them gently but securely until we call upon those beings that care for them to be present.

This we now do by saying '*May those who stand for this being/these beings be here now with us. Come now all guardians or caretakers and stand in this column of light with your charge, stand in the light that you may take them away in the light. This I ask for the good of all concerned.*'

We can now pause for the presence of these guardian beings to become apparent. As we have asked for assistance, so we shall receive it from the unseen realms – our astral call will be heard and responded to. In the case of a lost soul the beings assigned to this task may be their companions or their lost friends and relatives. If we are dealing with an entity that has no specific guardians there will always be less identifiable, but no less strong and compassionate, forces that will appear for the role of escorting them. Yet it matters not who comes or what they show themselves to be as again our role is not to get involved with any appearance or display, no matter how transfixing. We should maintain our focus only on the cold-fire of our column of protection and our fiery will projecting from our finger.

When we are aware of the presence of the appropriate guiding forces or beings appearing in the column of light we can say something like: '*welcome to all who come to take this being/these beings back to the place in the universe where they currently belong. I ask that they will now be escorted to their rightful space where they may they receive the healing they need. Let them return now to their proper level of existence, in harmony with all Creation. With thanks and in peace, love and light so may it be!*'

Again, as we have asked and intended so it will be. Our approach was respectful and caring and so will the response to it be. The being or soul will be taken up, or down, or simply removed from the column of light and sent off to the place where they can receive healing and be at peace.

Here we need to thank those spirits and beings that have given their help in this procedure, including our ever-faithful companions.

Then we can return to 'ordinary' reality and ground ourselves in the normal way. This will, of course, include reassuring the people involved that the process was a success. However, after this banishing ritual has been engaged in then it is vital to observe a vital spiritwalking rule: *no dwelling on what has happened*. This means no matter how tempting it is there should be limited speculation on those that we sent off. We should let them go, fully, being careful not draw them back into our reality with our focus. They have been in our atmosphere for so long that their energy is very used to being at our level and so we should not enable it to be drawn back again. To ensure this is so we should ask that the astral portal that they left by be permanently closed and we can visualise the column of light retracting and disappearing to back this request up.

We should then be sure to do a follow up visit, or session, if it is necessary. Spiritwalkers engaging in such work should always keep in contact with the persons or places we have cleared to ensure we have removed all the unseen problems. Our companion spirits can also help with keeping us alert to our ongoing responsibilities.

So, now we are able to safely meet with spirits beyond our companions and we are also equipped to deal with any being, energy or entity that we do not wish to engage with. We are well versed in protection and connection, knowing how to be energised and empowered. To finish we will consider how we can live pro-actively, enabling ourselves to be psychically strong and active just by changing the way we live our daily lives. A word of warning even at this late stage in the proceedings – the last phase of becoming a full time spiritwalker involves the 'dirty word' of all spiritual practice – discipline!

CHAPTER SEVENTEEN

KEEPING IT CLEAN

'You are happy to read many books a year on spiritual theory and to join different organisations that purport to help your psychic growth. Marvellous, we applaud this and welcome it. Yet you do this and still walk around coated in astral dirt as if, like a naughty dog, you have taken a roll in the mud after a bath. You cannot walk fully in this world any more, my sensitive friend! You must learn to be *in it* but not *of it*. This is an old wisdom, yet a perfect one. See the human world for what it is, love it none the less, but never again embrace it fully. Like a loving mother with teenager *do the right thing* and stand back from it, caring from a distance, offering your love and wisdom to it when needed but never being overwhelmed by it. Some call this way detachment, we call it holding balance. '

From Guidance

I describe my own disciplined way of spiritual living as *keeping it clean.*

This I aim to achieve in three ways:

- By making a conscious effort not to attract any negative/destructive/disturbing/unbeneficial energies into my daily life
- By making sure that I am not dulled or weakened by mind altering drugs or alcohol
- By removing any unwanted links and energies that do

become attached to me on a regular basis.

Let's look at not inviting negative energy into our world first.

Avoiding the Sordid Stuff

Firstly, I keep my psychic act clean by avoiding all the cruel, violent, morbid, disturbing, destructive and sleazy elements of modern human existence. This includes the actual physical aspects of all these things and that which is supposedly 'unreal' – anything experienced as 'life through a lens'. This latter category of reality includes all the versions of existence found in fiction, on the Internet and in the media in general.

This banning of all such unsettling aspects from my life may seem to be obvious to anyone who considers themselves to be even in the slightest bit sensitive or refined. And it may seem patently dull to someone who enjoys, quite innocently, the thrill of aggressive computer games or lurid scary films. Even those of us who enjoy the seemingly harmless everyday sensationalism and titillation of most (so-called) newspapers may find this level of self-imposed wholesomeness a little hard to take on board. For a self-confessed horror addict like myself, removing the sordid stuff from my own life *was* hard work at first, like giving up a particularly exhilarating drug. Yet the benefits I have experienced from this abstinence have outnumbered my cravings for creepy, disturbing stories that summoned an equally disturbing and intoxicating fear in me.

I first began to feel uneasy about my horror consumption when I found that I could get quite obsessed by squalid atmospheres, the 'lowlife' of society and the morbid details of other people's incomprehensible cruelty – which are all vividly depicted by the masters and mistresses of modern horror fiction. In my obsession I would then turn images and descriptions over and over in my mind, thrilling to the revulsion or terror they invoked in me. In this I am no different to thousands of others who have paid to see or read horror over the years. I revelled in it and dwelled upon it as harmless fantasy, the sort of sickening thing that could never happen to me in my ordinary existence so it was safe, wasn't it?

For two decades I believed that my desire to have the underbelly of humanity described or revealed in graphic detail was healthy enough because I would never dream of actually wanting to hurt anyone or see any harm done – quite the contrary! It was all in the mind, after all, and not in my reality. But then, as I considered the phrase *all in the mind* more closely I felt as if I had suddenly woken up from a long and deep dream, the danger of this passive consumption of aggression finally dawning on me. My mind is powerful! By engaging with the imagery and evocative vocabulary of horror I was evoking it, making it an astral reality through my applied thought. I was adding my own energy into the matrix that was established when the author wrote or the actor acted, joining forces with all the others who had avidly read and watched their creations. I was collaborating in the manufacturing of unpleasant thought-forms!

Horror books and films, and even depressing/disturbing music, such have a weight of thought-energy behind them when they are created and then consumed that a negative resonance, a disagreeable astral imprint, inevitably results. It matters not that what we are experiencing on the page or the screen didn't actually happen in three dimensions, *it still engages us as if it really is happening and our emotional response is still the same.* This emotional charge, combined with the established imagery we dwell on, is enough to create a etheric disturbance that is almost as potent as if we had actually witnessed, or even engaged in, a fearful scene.

The unseen process of creation we engage in with horror obviously begins with the author/screenwriter/musician who dreams up the unpleasantness, with his or her energy going into that imprint. It is then fed by the 'consumer' who reconstructs scenes and ideas in their own head as they watch, read or listen, becoming, in effect, the co-creator. This is a sign of effective writing as what author would not wish us to consider their creations as real and believe in them, allowing them to develop as we connect with them? By dwelling on these subjects we *feed* them, just as they were fed during their creation. We know now how thought-forms and the like work, all we have to do is imagine or focus enough, with a level of emotion, and the astral becomes imprinted, the thought-form becoming a reality. It's so easy to create a thought-form that we virtually do it, paradoxically enough, without thinking.

The intent of horror, be it a physical reality or not, is to shock and scare. Horror is not designed to uplift or to bring peace or equanimity, rather to emphasise and exploit the very base levels of being that we all seem to find so fascinating, albeit by proxy. The intent that we link to with that which is violent or horrific is not clearly wholesome or beneficial to the world in any positive sense. Horror stories dive to the depths so that we don't have to in 'reality', allowing us to witness the worst aspects of being without having to be physically involved. However, if we are spiritwalkers *then we know ourselves to be involved energetically*! We cannot separate things out when we know all things, seen and unseen, to be connected. It is only through the direct experience of our spiritwalking that we will come to grasp this connection as a truth in our daily lives. When we do this it becomes a joy, not a curse, to keep it psychically clean – for the good of *all* beings.

The same applies to things that are depressing or distressing. I have also learned that I have to remove myself from all forms of negative press and reportage. I do not watch, or listen to, or read about what passes for news. I do not dwell on things in the world that I can only look upon through a lens, or hear about second hand, with a feeling of hopeless distress – that is to say I do not render myself powerless by looking at a situation I cannot hope to change immediately. To most of us who pride ourselves on wanting to change things for the better this will seem a rather 'head in the sand' approach to reality, an unrealistic and 'fluffy' way of being. To me it is psychic self-defence and a way of ensuring that I stay strong and empowered so that I can tackle the things I really can do something about.

For example, as a passionate animal rights supporter I could get infinitely disheartened and deeply distressed right now by wading through the literature I have on the subject or by trawling the Internet for facts on the abuse of our fellow creatures. I tried this approach for many years and it made me so angry and so pessimistic about humanity that I was simply feeding more negativity back into the energy matrix. Now I choose to be aware of the injustices done to the voiceless ones in the way I live, minute by minute. I do all that I can within my power to cause no suffering myself, nor to support anything done by anyone else that causes suffering. As far as I am able I endeavour to choose a cruelty free life, following the broad principle of the Jain faith without being a strict adherent to its practices. I acknowledge my power and know that what I do makes a difference and adds to the positive energy for change that we all want to see happen. This way I am not blinkered to truth, nor am I mired in guilt and rage. I am doing what I can and am part of an energetic and practical solution that rejects cruelty of any kind. This is not giving up, rather it is giving out – I am being what I want to see in the world. This truth is inimitable: *it has to begin with me.* All other roads lead to both perpetuating the problem and weakening ourselves. Its always about knowing what you are *for* in life, rather than what you are *against*, and energetically feeding the desired reality. This is true personal empowerment for the good of the All – our interdependent individualism in action.

As a spiritwalker this may all seem like a hard road and no fun but we now have an awareness that brings endless responsibility. We cannot become unaware once we are aware of the true reality connectedness of existence. Witnessing existence in the multi-faceted way we now do it is virtually impossible for us to engage in anything that will introduce harm or hurt into the energetic web of life. Without wishing to sound overly moralistic or pious, for the sensitive spiritwalker indirectly indulging in any form of unpleasantness could be as damaging as continuously inhaling second-hand cigarette smoke...by passively partaking we are, perhaps, harmed.

It may be acceptable for a non-spiritwalker to release their pent up frustrations by playing violent computer games, or to follow their desire to understand the appeal of torture or murder through a book, but for us it is ill advised. It doesn't mean that we will become corrupt, evil, harmful etc. if we occasionally indulge in something sordid but rather that we will understand that in doing so we invite more of the same onto our earth-level. Our little indulgence adds up with all the other people's little indulgences, consequently making the positive work we need to do much harder. I had to ask myself *'does the world need more images of violence, degradation and abuse transmitted through my psyche from horror books and films?'* The answer to this could not possibly be in the affirmative!

In my life I have a hard enough time coping with the levels of human anxiety, anger, destruction etc. that are, sadly, commonplace at present without actively courting bad feelings, fear and their attendant entities. I have to *keep it clean* so that I can do the work and live effectively. If this means ensuing things that weigh me down then so be it. We will all have our weaknesses and in that we should guard ourselves, not feeling as if we are deprived but with a glad heart.

Meaningful Abstinence

I myself have to *keep it clean* in all sorts of other ways that the average person may consider deadly dull. For instance, experience has told me that I cannot drink or take recreational drugs. I find it impossible to leave myself vulnerable to the inevitable lost souls and astral detritus that flock to me when I am not in control of myself. I also find that I get ill very quickly if I partake in anything radically mind, or mood, altering. I am aiming to attune to the highest good and in order to do that I have to be alert, unencumbered and shielded.

In the case of drugs then unless we are particularly psychically disciplined, and can engage at a consciously higher level, then diversions such as cannabis can only open the doors of perception onto the human astral. For example, I have vivid memories of indulging in the supposedly harmless passing of a 'spliff' at a teenage party and almost immediately finding myself in a very different, yet no less vivid, reality – a version of Roman Britain in which I was powerless. Not a pleasant experience! I once also found myself possessed, albeit temporarily, by a low astral entity on partaking in a teenage binge. I have since seen, and removed, these black rogue spirits – black because they have no light of their own – that follow those sensitive souls who use cannabis, or indeed the more socially acceptable drug of alcohol, to any degree of excess. I personally know alcoholics that have seen these vampiric shadows clearly around themselves – *they are real*. The visionary Carlos Casteneda describes these rogue predators as *flyers* in his book 'The Active Side of Infinity' (Thorsons, 1998). If we acknowledge that we shine brightly, and we want to continue to do so, then we simply have to accept that we have to be careful – more careful than most – as we fully accept that the unseen, and the realm of subtle energy, is as valid as the seen.

This clean living really is nothing to do with being a highly evolved being who looks down their nose at a little good earthy fun, instead it has everything to do with owning and acknowledging how brightly we shine in this world and valuing that clarity for the good of the All. We are spiritwalkers, those who are already open and half way between this realm and all others, and so to make ourselves weak by the use of anything that makes me easy prey to dubious energetic influences is not advisable. This is not a hard and fast rule, only a suggestion for personal empowerment. I am not advocating the monastic life, rather offering common sense.

Freshening Up

The other way we can keep it clean is to learn how to remove unwanted energies that build up around our spiritual/psychic/subtle selves as the days go by. This I would recommend every evening before going to bed, just as if we were taking a wash to remove the day's grime.

The following procedure works well, especially if engaged in regularly:

1. With our eyes closed we should erect a psychic shield around ourselves. This could be a full space-style suit of white light, an electric blue rubbery bubble, a shimmering golden cloud or an egg with a mirrored surface. We can seal this with our favourite protective symbol, such as a glowing cross within a circle or a shining five-pointed star. Thus we invoke instant security.

2. We should then call on the presence and assistance of the spirits who come for our highest good, the companion spirits. They are always on hand to help but need to be asked to actively participate.

3. We can then ask the companions to remove any entity, energy or spirit that has become attracted or attached to us. The spirits can do this quickly without getting emotionally involved. We may witness this as a variety of sensations from a tingling to a pleasant localised heat.

4. We can then ask the spirits to send any entity, energy or spirit to the place where they should be in the universe; *the place where they will best receive healing for their place is not here with us.* Generally there is no need for us to know what we had attached unless we have a specific reason to understand what was affecting us and so we should just allow this removal process to unfold without undue curiosity.

5. Now we can ask that any psychic cords – draining or

damaging energetic links made to us by another person – be taken from us permanently and transformed in the appropriate way. To do this ourselves we can visualise any cords being buried in a strong earthy place that can absorb the energy, such as a sacred hill. Or we can see the cords being put into the flames for the purpose of regeneration.

6. We can then ask that we may then be shielded from any similar or repeat attacks. If we feel we are being 'got at' in a particular region – say our throat (affecting communication) or solar plexus (affecting our gut) – we can visualise ourselves wearing mirrored armour in the vulnerable place. If we do not know where this region lies then we can ask the companion spirits, but there will usually be some physical clue as to where we are being 'corded' by another. All we need do is reflect away any subsequent harm using our mirrored armour and leave the rest to the universe. Alternatively, if we know who is repeatedly getting at us and we feel that the situation is chronic then we can ask for our companion spirits to commune with the other person's companions and ask that this situation be changed.

7. We can then ask that we be bathed in the light of love, for the purpose of healing and renewal. We can visualise this ourselves as standing under a shower that gently washes us in brilliant warming light rather than water.

If we are prepared to follow the advice given in this chapter then we will have a heightened ability to live in a psychically open way whilst remaining immune to the more unpleasant aspects of manifest being. We will be truly ready to begin our journey as effective spiritwalkers in the modern world.

CONCLUSION

WALKING WITH SPIRIT

'*We never get there!* **Our destination is the tantalising bait but not the reason we are here. How can it be when it continually changes, becoming more enticing but endlessly, deliciously, further away? Instead of seeking validation from our imminent arrival at the perfect destination we should realise that once we reach this apparent station of completion we will only want to be passing through on our way elsewhere. We are, my friend, on travelling on the Circle Line! In this we should realise that our true reason for being in this fabulous material dimension, on this holiest earth, is to fashion our journey accordingly, lovingly. This is our craft and this is our purpose, our legitimate reason for being here in this space, at this time. We have come to get ourselves from A to B in the most considered, courageous, creative, compassionate and *joyous* way that we can. A and B are fundamentally irrelevant to this process. It is what happens between, and how we hold it, that matters more than anything.'**

From Guidance

This has been the hardest book that I have ever had the pleasure to write, as well as the most satisfying. Hard because there is always more that can be said and deeper that we can go and it is difficult to know where to stop. Indeed for the author of a book such as this there is never a real conclusion, only a pause in the journey where it is appropriate to take stock. I would feel very unqualified to write books such as these if I truly felt I had wrapped things up nicely and concluded all there was to say on the subject and so although this book is comprehensive it can never be completely definitive – how can it be when the universe, indeed universes, are unfolding even as we read these words? This book is simply a primer for the ongoing journey.

By wrapping up the book at this stage I feel I have left the reader with a snapshot of how to walk with spirit effectively, rather than a full and final statement. By writing *Spiritwalking* I have simply offered the basic equipment for an ongoing expedition into the unseen along with the encouragement needed to begin exploring in the first place. In this I hope to have enabled any seeker into the unexplained to make their onward journey with much more confidence and wisdom. For myself, as well as for the reader, the conclusion of this book marks a stable place from which we can plant a flag of achievement before inevitably moving on. Thus it acknowledges the inevitability that this work will, one day, be behind us in terms of our awareness.

I myself, even as I write, am discovering new and exciting aspects of the spiritwalking process and am consequently asking myself stimulating questions. For instance, I am now discovering that our companion spirits can be independent beings, just as we have described in this book so far, but that they can also be parts of our selves that have not incarnated into form. We give the spirits an independent identity as we often find it hard to take advice from ourselves, much in the same way as we prefer to see our companions as noble Native Americans as opposed to ordinary folk. In this we simply choose to dress bits of our own eternal energy up as evolved counsellors in order that we can give the information credence. It seems clear to me now that no one could be more qualified to guide us than a part of our selves and the ongoing challenge is for us to learn to accept our own wisdom. The mystery of their incarnation into form is certainly far more complex than I had originally thought and I hope that by my sharing my ongoing exploration I will inspire similar quests.

This development in awareness and endless forward motion is not only inevitable but it is *right*. We are as trees that keep growing towards the light even though our roots are now deep. By this our conclusion is an introduction to the next chapter – a chapter that is personal to us, unique as our fingerprints and as essential as a heart-beat. We must grow, reaching onwards into the ever-expanding unseen even as we feel our roots pushing further down, anchoring us in this reality. And this particular growing is something that we must do simultaneously alone and together, just like a tree that reaches selfishly for its own water and light yet is deeply connected to all the others in a forest. For one thing that we have learned, amongst the many insights shared in this book, is that *we are one another* – cells in an energetic body that is served by our questing, always for the good of the All. As we evolve and push the boundaries so do we bring all other beings along with us, like a wave.

Indeed, perhaps at this stage we may like to remember with gratitude just how far we have all come along the path to wisdom. Twenty-five years ago I found only sensationalist tomes about spontaneous human combustion and lurid accounts of witchery and devilry when I was searching in my local library for grounded advice on that which is considered unseen. Thank goodness things have changed in this last two decades and I am now able to share practical approaches and inspirational ideas with a wide audience in an accessible way. This is why this book has been so deeply satisfying to write, communicating as it does such essential wisdoms for living well. The suggested reading list that follows at the end of this work is full of the sensible advice and groundbreaking yet grounded material that is fortunately now available to us. No matter how far we take the concepts expounded in this book we can at least be sure that we move on with a mind that is ever more open into a world that is the better for our continued searching for truth.

Before we close let us address one final issue that will, no doubt, come up for us again and again as we continue the journey as spiritwalkers. What if spiritwalking is nothing but a load of fanciful speculation, the result of an over active imagination and a deep longing for meaning, and it is only coincidence that the things we have tried have worked out for us? What if it has no real relevance outside of the confines of this book and is seemingly worthless to the modern world?

To this question I will ultimately give the same answer as when people ask me about the validity or veracity of their memories from 'other lives'. This answer is, *does it matter if it works for us*? If it tells us something significant and compelling about who and what we are, and positively instructs us in the nature of existence, then surely it is worth pursuing no matter what the supposed reality of it? We can analyse something into the ground, as is the current penchant of humanity, mangling the mystery in an attempt to rationalise, but it seems self-defeating to try and dismantle a perfectly valid and vital approach to existence. Even if spiritwalking were nothing more than entertaining fantasy then we could all do with more use of our imaginations in our quest for meaning and a lot less mechanistic pulling apart, surely? If a way of experiencing life more fully isn't broken why try to fix it...or annihilate it with logic? We should always feel free to test out our spirituality, keeping faith in the process and ever holding the balance between dry skepticism and rigid belief.

Spiritwalking will always be beneficial as it gives us access to the apparent unknown without our being compelled to subscribe to any single doctrine. Its ethos is egalitarian and compassionate, its outcomes empowering and exciting. It openly offers a way of gaining insights through direct experience of the mysteries of life and death (and beyond) without hierarchy or dogma – a way that is proven and will enhance our daily existence. I myself have learned so much from its methods and have gained some incredible insights as well as much accurate and helpful information and it is my sincere hope that it can do the same for you, the reader. Yet even if we do not choose to pursue the craft of walking with spirit further then what we have read and experienced here can, at the very least, act a springboard to our opening our minds and using our senses more fully. To our being more alive in the eternal *Now*.

So, no matter what our path is to be, here's to the continued spreading of understanding, the development of all our psychic faculties and to the bridging of the chasm between this world and all others. Here's to an end to a fear of the unknown...and the unseen.

May we all have the courage, from this moment on, to *shine*.

GLOSSARY OF TERMS

The All/All-That-Is: The seen and the unseen realms, every aspect of Creation

Angel: Highly evolved discarnate being specialising in overseeing healing/peace

Animation: The vitality inside every part of Creation, that which makes it animate

The Astral: The unseen, layers and levels of existence beyond the physical

As Within, so Without: What is internal/personal is also external/universal

Avatar: A discarnate representative of a universal principle such as justice or peace

The Beyond: That which lies beyond our current manifest experience; the greater astral levels it may also be called the wild beyond as it is 'uncivilised' in human terms

Channel: A person acting as a conduit for unseen information

Channelling: The act of translating unseen information into manifest terms

Co-creator: One who realises his or her own Creator nature and so affects reality

Companion spirit: A discarnate being who walks with us as our unseen guide

Creation: All universes, be they seen or unseen, and all created beings who dwell there

The Creator: The One, the original essence of All from which all things proceed; the Essence we co-create with

Dazzling Darkness: The vast creative inner sea that is mirrored in the cosmos – as within, so without

Discarnate: A soul that is currently without a manifest guise or body

Displacement: The energetic interaction of all interconnected things

Dis-spirited: Having the soul or life-force denied or undermined

Earthbound: Remaining, wilfully or unintentionally, at the earthly level

Enchantment: Natural magic; the wild and beguiling power of the Fey

Energy: The unseen force that animates/creates all beings on all planes of existence

Enspirited/ensouled: Being possessed of a singular expression of life-force

Entering the Silence: Going *within* to reach the great *Without* by meditating, or being in quiet contemplation, using deep breathing

Entity: A collection of energy that has no human soul

Ether: The unseen energy that permeates all creation

(The) Ether/Etheric: The level of existence that we call unseen

The Forgetting: Our losing touch with our true essential energetic/spiritual nature

Greater Spirit/Mystery: The Creator; that which is beyond knowing yet omnipresent

Grounding: Becoming reconnected with the seen after working with the unseen

Guidance: Any positive instruction or information that comes from an unseen source

Guide: Our personally allotted companion spirit, who brings us spiritual guidance

Human-centric/centricity: A belief in the importance of humanity over other beings; an anthropomorphic speciesism

Imprint: Energy that has become impressed with an emotional resonance

Incarnate: To be in manifest form experiencing life in a body of any kind

Incarnation: The duration for which a soul wears a body in the manifest world/s

Individual interconnectedness/interdependent individuality: The one is One; we are one another yet separate

Intent: Our focussed will

Invocation: A prayer or declaration of our intent to a particular purpose

Journal: The diary of a spiritwalker where notes of unseen interactions are made

Knowing: A deep inner conviction of unseen truth based on spiritwalking experience

Leyline/Ley: A line of force or vein of power within the land

Life-force: The essential energy of creation that flows, also know as Chi or Prana

Looking Beyond: Turning our attention away from seen reality to the unseen realms

Lost Soul: A discarnate being who has become unintentionally or wilfully earthbound

Macrocosm: The *without* aspect of being, the greater All

Microcosm: The *within* aspect of being, the individualisation of the One

One/Oneness: Both the Creator and the unification of all singular aspects of creation

'Ordinary' reality: The manifest realm, everyday (seen) existence

Other: That which is not of everyday seen existence

Otherworld/Otherworldly: The Faery realm and that which is of the Fey

Pathworking: A pre-ordained trance journey for a particular end

Plastic: The malleable nature of the etheric levels, especially the human/local astral

Portal: A centre on the land/body where lines of power converge; a doorway

Prayer: A heartfelt statement of intent aimed at invoking (positive) change

The Re-membering: Our recollecting of our true spiritual/eternal nature; a return to the source before death

Residual Energy: The resonance left behind by a person or event

Rogue Spirit: A low astral dweller, an amoral psychic con-artist

Seeing: The ability to witness energies and beings beyond 'ordinary' reality

The Seen: The manifest, physical level of existence we experience in our daily life

Servitor: An intentionally created form made of energy designed for a purpose

Site Guardian: An intentionally created thought-form made to look after a special place

Soul: Life-force energy that has become individualised; our personal spirit-self

Soul Group/Soul Kin: The other cells in the spiritual body that we work well with; our *cell*

Soul-tied: A meaningful link forged between souls for a specific purpose

Source/Source energy: The Originator of Creation and its animating life-force

Spirit: The essence of creation; life-force or animating energy

Spiritwalker/Spiritwalking: One who *looks beyond* and works with the unseen

Summerlands: A Celtic term for the energetic realm of the dead where our souls go between incarnations

Thought-form: A coalescence of energy imprinted by our repeated thoughts

Trance: A calm and controlled state of *looking beyond*

Journey: A specific way of accessing the unseen realms whilst in trance

The Unseen: All that is beyond material form, the non-physical/spirit realms

Vibration: The unique resonance of an energy/spirit/being

Visualisation: A way of using the mind's eye to create a desired vision of reality

Watcher: A discarnate soul that has chosen to remain earthbound to guard a place

Will and Wish: Using our focussed intent to bring about a desire

Will-power: The force of our essential essence that may be positively directed

FURTHER SUGGESTED READING

Alternative Realities

'*The Dark Tower Series*' - Stephen King, *Hodder* 2003-2005

Astrology

'*The Astrology Bible*' - Judy Hall, *Godsfield* 2005

'*Understanding the Planetary Myths*'- Lisa Tenzin-Dolma, *Quantum* 2005

Beyond Religion

'*The Jesus Mysteries*'- Timothy Freke and Peter Gandy, *Thorsons/ Element* 1999

'*Jesus and the Goddess*' - Timothy Freke and Peter Gandy, *Thorsons* 2002

'*The Laughing Jesus*' - Timothy Freke and Peter Gandy, *O Books* 2006

'*Beyond Belief*' - Peter Spink, *Piatkus* 1996

Chakras/Energy Portals

'*Wheels of Life: User's Guide to the Chakra System*' - Anodea Judith *Llewellyn* 1987

Earth Mysteries/Energies

'*U.F.O's, the Electromagnetic Indictment*' - Albert Budden, *Blandford* 1995

'*Earth Lights*' - Paul Devereux, *Book Club Associates* 1982

'*Earth Lights Revelation*' - Paul Devereux, *Blandford 1989*

'*Places of Power*' - Paul Devereux, *Blandford* 1999

'*Fairy Paths and Spirit Roads*'- Paul Devereux, *Vega* 2003

'*The Sun and the Serpent*' - Paul Broadhurst and Hamish Miller, *Mythos* 1990

'*Needles of Stone*' - Tom Graves, *Turnstone Press* 1978

'*Spirits of the Stones*' - Alan Richardson, *Virgin* 2001

Faeries

'*Strands of Starlight*' - Gael Baudino, *Warner* 1993

'*The Travellers Guide to the Fairy Sites of Britain*' - Janet Bord, *Gothic Image* 2004

'*Fairy Lore*' - Anna Franklin and Paul Mason, *Capall Bann* 2000

'*Good Faeries/Bad Faeries*' - Brian Froud, *Pavilion* 2000

'*Faeries*'- Brian Froud, *Pavilion* 2002

'*The Greening*' - Poppy Palin, *Wild Spirit* 2005

'The Faery Faith' - Serena Roney-Dougal, *Green Magic* 2003

'The Fairy-Faith in Celtic Countries' - W.Y. Evans-Wentz, *New Page* 2004

General Spiritual Development

'The Inward Revolution' - Deborah Benstead and Storm Constantine, *Warner* 1998

'Lucid Living' - Timothy Freke, *Books for Burning* 2005

'Dancing the Dream' - Jamie Sams, *Harper Collins* 1998

Green Spirituality

'Earth Wisdom' - Glennie Kindred, *Hay House* 2004

'Timeless Simplicity' - John Lane, *Green Books* 2001

'The World is in My Garden' - Chris Maser, *Polair* 2003

'Green Spirituality' - Poppy Palin (writing as Rosa Romani), *Green Magic* 2004

'Craft of the Wild Witch' - Poppy Palin, *Llewellyn* 2004

'Living Druidry' - Emma Restall Orr, *Piatkus* 2004

'Easy-to-Use Shamanism' - Jan Morgan Wood, *Vega* 2002

'Behaving as if the God in All Things Mattered' - M. Small Wright, *Perelandra* 1997

Healing

'Anatomy of an Illness'- Norman Cousins, *Bantam* 1979

'You Can Heal Your Life' - Louise L.Hay, *Hay House* 1984

'Love Yourself, Heal Your Life Workbook' - Louise L.Hay, *Hay House* 2004

'The Healing Journey' - Matthew Manning, *Piatkus* 2001

Interconnectedness

'Illusions' - Richard Bach, *Pan* 1978

'One' - Richard Bach, *Pan* 1988

'You Are, Therefore I Am' - Satish Kumar, *Green Books* 2002

Inspiration and Upliftment

'The Secret Garden' - Frances Hodgson Burnett, *Children's Golden Library* 1911

'The Diary of Anne Frank' - Anne Frank, *Pan* 1954

'Man's Search for Meaning'- Viktor Frankl, *Rider* 2004

'No Destination: An Autobiography' - Satish Kumar, *Green Books*

'*Peace Pilgrim*' - Peace Pilgrim, *Ocean Tree Books* 1982

'*Pollyanna*' - Eleanor H. Porter, *Wordsworth Editions* 1994

Life Between Lives

'*Journey of Souls*' - Dr Michael Newton, *Llewellyn* 1998

'*Destiny of Souls*' - Dr Michael Newton, *Llewellyn* 2001

Near Death Experience/ Death and Dying/ Life After Death

'*The Truth in the Light*' - Peter and Elizabeth Fenwick, *Headline* 1995

'*In the Light of Death*' - Timothy Freke, *Godsfield* 2002

'*Life After Death*' - D. Scott Rogo, *Book Club Associates* 1986

'*Life After Life*' - Ian Wilson, *Macmillan* 1997

Meditation and Connection to Source

'*Getting into the Gap*' - Dr Wayne M.Dyer, *Hay House* 2003

Other Lives/Selves

'*Hands Across Time*' - Judy Hall, *Findhorn* 1997

'*More Lives Than One?*' - Jeffrey Iverson, *Souvenir Press* 1976

'*Soul Resurgence*' - Poppy Palin, *Capall Bann* 2000

Psychic Protection

'*The Psychic Protection Handbook*' - Caitlin Matthews, *Piatkus* 2005

'*The Art of Psychic Protection*' - Judy Hall, *Findhorn* 1996

Psychic Questing

'*The Seventh Sword*' - Andrew Collins, *Arrow* 1992

'*The Circle and the Square*' - Jack Gale, *Capall Bann* 1997

Science/Spirituality

'*The Tao of Physics*' - Fritjof Kapra, *Shambala* 2000

'*The Field: Quest for the Secret Force of the Universe*' - L. McTaggart, *Harper* 2003

'*The Holographic Universe*' - Michael Talbot, *Harper* 1996

'*Supernature*' - Lyall Watson, *Coronet* 1973

'*Earthworks*' - Lyall Watson, *Hodder* 1986

'*Dark Nature*' - Lyall Watson, *Sceptre* 1996

Self Empowerment

'Feel the Fear and Do It Anyway' - Susan Jeffers, *Hutchinson* 1987

'The Road Less Travelled' - M. Scott Peck, *Rider* 1985

Soul Retrieval

'Soul Retrieval' - Sandra Ingerman, *Harper* 2004

Spirit Contact

'The Gift'- Mia Dolan, *Harper Collins* 2004

'One Foot in the Stars' - Matthew Manning, *Piatkus* 2003

'Spirit Messenger' - Gordon Smith, *Hay House* 2004

Symbols

'Dictionary of Symbols'- J.E. Cirlot (Editor), *Routledge* 1983

'An Illustrated Encyclopaedia of Traditional Symbols' - J.C. Cooper (Editor), *Thames & Hudson* 1979

Tarot

'Tarot Therapy' - Steve Hounsome, *Capall Bann* 1999

'78 Degrees of Wisdom' - Rachel Pollack, *Harper Collins* 1997

'The Glastonbury Tarot'- Lisa Tenzin-Dolma, *Weiser* 1999

The Power of Thought

'Real Magic' - Dr Wayne W. Dyer, *Harper* 2003

'The Power of Intention' - Dr Wayne W. Dyer, *Hay House* 2004

'Ask and It is Given' - Esther and Jerry Hicks with Abraham, *Hay House* 2004

'The Amazing Power of Deliberate Intent' - Hicks/Abraham, *Hay House*

Unexplained Phenomena/Hauntings

'Haunted Homes: True Stories of Paranormal Investigations' - M.Dolan, *Harper* 2006

'Season of Sorcery' - Poppy Palin, *Capall Bann* 1998

'Poltergeist! A Study in Destructive Haunting'- Colin Wilson, *Caxton* 2002

Working with the Fey

'The Hedge Witch's Way' - Rae Beth, *Robert Hale* 2003

'Working with Fairies'- Anna Franklin, *New Page* 2005